Thanks for all
you do to make the
world more trustworthy!
Best Regards
Ron

navalent

powering your transformation journey

To Be
Honest

Lead with the Power of
Truth, Justice and Purpose

Ron A. Carucci

PRAISE FOR *TO BE HONEST*

Ron A. Carucci has put his finger on what our organizations and our world needs most right now—truth-telling in a way that people can hear, and closing the gap between who we say we are and what we do. In *To Be Honest*, Carucci recognizes that serving justice is not only a leader's and an organization's highest purpose, he has given us a well-lit path to meaningful work, joyful community, innovative organizations, and the society we want for our children and theirs.

Jay Coen Gilbert, Co-founder of B Lab and the B Corp movement, and CEO at Imperative 21

A powerful tour de force! *To Be Honest* is an exceptional compilation of stories, well-researched insights, and truth for leaders to keep the trust of their teams and lead through difficult situations. This is a must-read for every business professional if they want the keys to building trusting, foundational leadership.

Marshall Goldsmith, *New York Times* bestselling author of *Triggers*, *Mojo*, and *What Got You Here Won't Get You There*

The world is clamoring for leadership they can trust and emulate. As our experience of dishonesty has escalated in business, government, and all forms of media, we continue to raise the bar exponentially for honesty in our leaders. In *To Be Honest*, Carucci provides leaders a treasure trove of practical guidance and inspiring cases to shape their personal leadership, and their organizations, into examples of honesty others will be proud to follow.

Jennifer McCollum, CEO at Linkage

To Be Honest is a fresh look at a concept our world has too long taken for granted. Ron A. Carucci masterfully weaves together inspiring stories with groundbreaking research—you simply won't come away from this book unchanged.

Dr. Tasha Eurich, *New York Times* bestselling author of *Insight* and *Bankable Leadership*

Honesty with ourselves and in our day-to-day interactions is a force multiplier. But how do we achieve this? Ron A. Carucci brilliantly gives us the frameworks and stories to help us leverage honesty as a superpower to generate hope, trust, and a lasting legacy for ourselves and those around us.
Sanyin Siang, Professor at Duke University, Executive Director at Coach K Center on Leadership and Ethics at Duke University's Fuqua School of Business, and winner of Thinkers50 Marshall Goldsmith Coaching and Mentoring Award

Nations, corporations, universities, and communities of all kinds are hungry for greater honesty from their leaders and organizations. However, even the most well-intending among them fall short in delivering truth, justice, and purpose to those they serve. *To Be Honest* will dramatically change that story. Read this book with your entire team and—together—change the world around you. There is so much at stake.
Jim Clifton, Chairman and CEO at Gallup

Leaders, at every organizational level, are increasingly facing the challenges of our complex world where their leadership and character are put to the test. Great leadership today spans well beyond our corporate walls into society and the communities in which we operate. *To Be Honest* is a powerful guide for any leader who wants to lean into candid, messy conversations confident and prepared, bolster your courage to do the right thing, even when it's hard, and live fully in your purpose instead of being asleep at your own switch. You will emerge from your experience of this book more passionate about truth, justice, and purpose than you imagined possible.
Sandy Stelling, Vice President of Strategy, Analytics, and Transformation at Alaska Airlines

There are so many reasons to read Ron A. Carucci's new book, but if I were to name just one, I would say because it will help you see that voicing and enacting your values—effectively—is actually *possible* in so many more ways and contexts than we typically believe it to be. Through positive stories, through compelling research evidence, through inspiriting and accessible prose, Carucci shares hope, commitment, and, importantly, actionable strategies for values-driven leadership. Readers cannot help but come away both more inspired and more morally competent.
Mary C. Gentile, PhD, author of *Giving Voice to Values* and University of Virginia Darden School of Business professor

A practical, resourceful, and fascinating must-read for any organizational leader. *To Be Honest* is a thoughtful book rooted in years of psychology and behavioral science research. Supplemented by personal stories and journeys of those who have faced the challenge of what it truly means to be honest and how that principle fundamentally affects behaviors, Ron A. Carucci masterfully created an action-oriented resource to be used in the workplace and beyond. One would be remiss if *To Be Honest* did not reside in their personal library.

Tiffany A. Archer, JD, Ethics and Compliance Officer at Panasonic Avionics

Our world is starved to move past polarization and "we–they" behavior, and come together to embrace our differences, and have greater civic discourse on the most important issues of the day. What we need is a guide on how to do this effectively—with empathy, moral leadership, and the courage to be honest. *To Be Honest* is an inspirational, compelling compass to guide us on the path to become the best versions of ourselves and the most honest we can be.

Ananya Mukherjee, Provost at University of British Columbia

To Be Honest is an absolute gift of timeless (and timely) wisdom and persuasive empirical evidence. You can read this book to be a better person or to be a better leader. Either way, the world wins. Ron A. Carucci pulls off a wonderful trick—he invites us to get uncomfortable and reflect on the gaps between our aspirations and our behavior, but he does so with warmth and grace, through accessible and, at times, deeply moving stories. Better still, he offers practical guidance to help us build more vibrant organizations through honesty, integrity, justice, and empathy.

Miguel Padró, The Purpose College, The Aspen Institute

To Be Honest

*Lead with the Power of
Truth, Justice and Purpose*

Ron A. Carucci

KoganPage

First published in Great Britain and the United States in 2021 by Kogan Page Limited

2nd Floor, 45 Gee Street
London
EC1V 3RS
United Kingdom

122 W 27th St, 10th Floor
New York, NY 10001
USA

4737/23 Ansari Road
Daryaganj
New Delhi 110002
India

www.koganpage.com

Kogan Page books are printed on paper from sustainable forests.

ISBNs

Hardback   978 1 3986 0066 9
Ebook   978 1 3986 0067 6

British Library Cataloguing-in-Publication Data

A CIP record for this book is available from the British Library.

Library of Congress Cataloging-in-Publication Data

Names: Carucci, Ron A., author.
Title: To be honest: lead with the power of truth, justice, and purpose / Ron Carucci.
Description: London, United Kingdom; New York, NY : Kogan Page, [2021] | Includes bibliographical references and index.
Identifiers: LCCN 2021001346 (print) | LCCN 2021001347 (ebook) | ISBN 9781398600669 (hardback) | ISBN 9781398600676 (ebook)
Subjects: LCSH: Honesty in the workplace. | Leadership–Moral and ethical aspects.
Classification: LCC HF5549.5.H66 C356 2021 (print) | LCC HF5549.5.H66 (ebook) | DDC 174/.4–dc23
LC record available at https://lccn.loc.gov/2021001346
LC ebook record available at https://lccn.loc.gov/2021001347
Copyright registration number: TXu 2-228-601

Typeset by Integra Software Services Pondicherry
Print production managed by Jellyfish
Printed and bound by Sheridan, USA

For all those who fight every day for a world of greater truth, justice, and purpose. For your unsung heroism, your silent suffering and sacrifice, and your inspiring example, this book is dedicated to honoring your stories so that the rest of us might, in some small way, emulate them.

A portion of this book's proceeds will go to

The Equal Justice Initiative
(www.eji.org)

and

Ethical Systems
(www.ethicalsystems.org)

to support the extraordinary work they do in the world.

CONTENTS

FOREWORD

I am a social psychologist who moved from a psychology department (at the University of Virginia) to a business school (New York University's Stern School of Business) in 2011. The bridge I crossed was business ethics—my entire career has been spent studying moral psychology, and in 2011 the world was still digging out from the rubble of the global financial crisis, which was caused in large part by bad ethics at many financial institutions. I therefore thought this would be easy; all I had to do was apply my research, and the research of others, to corporate life. I thought, "Surely when business leaders see the research on how to promote ethics in their organizations, they'll want to apply it." I founded a non-profit collaboration of researchers at EthicalSystems.org to make the academic research accessible and applicable to anyone trying to improve their organization and its ethical culture.

If you are in the business world, you are probably now laughing at my naïveté. It is hard to understand what is really happening inside a company, and harder still to change its culture. Furthermore, everyone is busy, they don't have time to read research summaries; they want answers to the problems they are facing right now.

That is why this book is so important. *To Be Honest* is the best book I have read about corporate culture, and Ron Carucci is the best guide I can imagine for anyone who wants to set off on the arduous journey to strengthen their culture.

What makes this book so great?

- First, Ron is charming and disarming. His love for this work shines through on every page. You get to know him and trust him as you read the book.

- Second, Ron backs up his claims with hundreds of citations from the academic literature. He is building the bridge between behavioral science and business that we try to build at EthicalSystems.org.

- Third, the book distills the lessons gleaned from his own 15-year research study comprised of over 3,000 interviews Ron and his firm conducted with corporate executives and employees. To understand a company, you can't just gather quantitative data; you have to be something of an anthropologist—an expert listener and observer. That's Ron, and his firm, Navalent.

- Fourth, Ron gives you a simple yet powerful framework for thinking about ethics: honesty is the goal, but it's an expanded conception of honesty, incorporating truth, justice, and purpose. To be honest, you have to say the right thing (truth), do the right thing (justice), and say and do the right thing for the right reason (purpose).

- Fifth, unlike any book that an academic like me could write, Ron gives you hundreds of specific ideas for increasing honesty in your organization. Each chapter ends with suggestions for how to "get busy," followed by a recap of the most important ideas in the chapter. This is a book designed to be turned into practice, to help you address the problems that you face right now, as well as heading off the problems you'd otherwise face down the road.

In short, *To Be Honest* is a practical, fun-to-read and backed-by-research guidebook for improving your ethical culture. It would be an ideal common read for the leadership team at your company—or perhaps for all employees. If your team were to read one chapter each week and discuss it each Monday morning, I can almost guarantee that in 10 weeks, you'd have a more honest company, one better able to gain the trust of all stakeholders, and better able to attract and retain the most talented employees.

In our age of social media, anxiety, and political polarization, corporate cultures are changing. I can see this change in the MBA students I have taught since 2011. With each passing year, students care more about sustainability, ethics, and corporate social responsibility. They expect to have more "voice." So, change *is coming* to your company. It's going to involve some difficult conversations, and perhaps elevated levels of internal conflict. In the last few years, I have heard people in many organizations say they feel like they are "walking on eggshells," or "walking through a minefield." Anchoring your culture and your conversations in a rich and shared conception of honesty will help you to navigate these hazards, and guide your company or team to a healthier, more cooperative way of working together.

Jonathan Haidt
Thomas Cooley Professor of Ethical Leadership, NYU
and author of The Righteous Mind

ACKNOWLEDGMENTS
A great big giant thanks

The acknowledgments page is my favorite part of a book to write. Like looking out over an expansive mountain terrain after a long hike, it allows me to step back and realize how far I've traveled, and how many people accompanied me on the journey. No book comes to life without the efforts of many, and it's an honor for me to thank so many here, from the bottom of my heart. (Like every author, I'm terrified of leaving someone out, so if I did, please know I'm sorry!)

To the thousands of women and men whose stories I've had the honor to hear over the last 15 years, thank you for your courage to lead, and the vulnerability to be honest about where things could be better.

To the brilliant thought leaders and executives who shared their hard-won wisdom and invaluable experiences with me, this book is so much richer thanks to your generosity. Dr. Tiffany Jana, Ryan Honeyman, Vincent Stanley, Rob Bilott, Michael Sandel, Amy Edmondson, Sanyin Siang, Tiffany Archer, Kim Scott, Dan Ariely, Ed Townley, Kathleen Hogan, Chris Campbell, Riaz Patel, Daniel Kahneman, Bernard Banks, Richard Bistrong, James Detert, Hubert Joly, John Rosling, Roberto "News" Smith and Malachi "Spank" Jenkins, Nick Skinner, Marin Alsop, Floribert Kazingufu, Dr. Michael Gervais, Arthur Brooks, and the dozens of other leaders and inspiring individuals whose stories, research, and perspectives grace these pages, you'll never know the degree to which you've broadened my world, and with it, of all who read this book.

Jon Haidt, I'm ridiculously humbled that you lent your wisdom and voice to this project by penning the foreword (and for the conversations and interviews I've enjoyed over the years). I'm grateful for your generosity and sacrifice, and far more, for your undying commitment to creating a more whole and honest world through your work. Serving alongside you to change hearts and minds at Ethical Systems and Open Mind is a thrill and privilege.

To Be Honest had a world-class hands-on team helping to construct and launch it:

- To the team at Power Analytics, for your sharp expertise using IBM's Watson Artificial Intelligence technology to mine the thousands of interviews leading to the conclusions that formed this book, a huge thanks for your talents.

- Adam Rosen, your editorial prowess and surgical maneuvering that (sometimes painfully) sharpened the book's message, clarity, and structural integrity. Your insights are a gift (that sometimes required a glass or two of Pinot Noir to fully appreciate).

- Kristof Szabo, your video artistry is unparalleled. Thank you for your hard work, late hours, and creative genius that put the launch of *To Be Honest* and *Moments of Truth* into such wonderful video format. You make us all look so much better!

- I had the best research assistants I've ever worked with. Elizabeth Borcia and Kimiko Davis, your willingness to dive into the deep end of the pool, and scour the world to uncover supporting data, statistics, stories, annotations, and secondary research, was breathtaking. Your passion for the project, on-the-spot responsiveness to my barrage of queries, and your exquisite organization of all of that information to put it right at my fingertips when needed were nothing short of amazing (thank you Ludmila Praslova for introducing us!). Without you, I'd still be floundering.

- To the many readers who offered practical and thoughtful feedback to polish the message and stories, sacrificing your time with such kindness meant the world.

- Jarrod Shappell, for your friendship and care as I wrestled with my early ambivalence about taking on this project, for your ongoing creative ideas to shape how we brought the book to life, and especially for your co-hosting the series *Moments of Truth* that showcases the book's ideas, along with Kahlil Smith—thanks to you both for your abundant contributions to bring this book to the world with perspectives, insights, and stories I could have never offered. You both are gifts of truth, justice, and purpose in your own rights, and I'm grateful for the privilege of working alongside you.

- To the remarkable team at Kogan Page – Oscar Spigolon, your elegant cover design captured everything I'd hoped for, and beautifully honors the gravitas of the topic; Heather Wood, Arthur Thompson, and the production team, and Martin Hill, Courtney Dramis, and the rest of the marketing team—what a delight it was to join forces with you and find as many creative ways as possible to help the world discover *To Be Honest*.

- Kathe Sweeney, well, you had me at hello. From the moment we met, I knew I was in the hands of editorial royalty and that, as a true thought partner, you were a big "cut above." Your conviction about this book (sometimes even stronger than mine) was the fuel I needed to build it and proudly bring it to market. I'm grateful for your partnership, and now your friendship. You have restored my faith in the publishing industry!

I've had the gift of being surrounded by so many friends and colleagues whose love and support were pivotal to the years it took to build this book, which sometimes included some dark and murky seasons:

- To my Navalent colleagues, thanks for our shared convictions about what it means to help organizations be more honest and whole, and for doing world-class work with passion to enable remarkable transformations.
- To all my Recognized Expert Community (REXers!) friends, and my fellow MG100 Coaches, (there's just WAY too many of you to list), your undying support and inspiring energy have been a treasure. I feel so fortunate to be journeying together, stirred by your brilliance and tenacity. Thanks for all the virtual hugs, high-fives, and needed kicks-in-the-pants.
- And to Dorie Clark, I don't know what I did to deserve the gift of having our paths cross all those years ago, but I am one thankful man. You've become one of my most treasured friends, and along the way, an executive coach who helps me take my own medicine, a wise sage who helped reinvent my understanding of my career and my voice in the world, a caring mentor who got in my face when I threw whiny tantrums, and a caring friend who loved me through the heartache of the tumultuous journey to get here, celebrating every small and large victory I sometimes failed to see. Without you, this book would never exist. Your brilliance is imprinted between every line. So much love and gratitude to you.

To my siblings, still here and long gone, thank you for your fierce love and undying support, and for always kicking my ass to "get busy." And to the rest of my big, giant family across the miles, you know how much I love you. You all make my heart beat stronger.

To my beloved family, Barb, Matthew, and Becca, I wake up every day because of you. You are the greatest blessings in my life. Your enduring love, the life that we share in its beautiful and messy forms, and all our sidesplitting laughter, make me want to be a more honest man every day.

And to my God, a God of truth, justice, and purpose, your endless love, mercy, and grace invite me to more of what it means to be honest. All that I have, and all that I am.

Introduction

Here's how these things start.

You are in a business review meeting where people are presenting their goals for the coming 12 months, following a tough year. Everyone is presenting wildly optimistic strategies for growth that are totally disconnected from each other and supported by sketchy data. You're sure that if you went around the room and asked each person "What is our company's core strategy?" you'd get as many different answers as there are people. But you also know that the desperation behind these unrealistic commitments is being fueled by people not wanting to be seen as uncommitted or incompetent.

* * *

It's annual performance review season, and everyone is nervous about whether they'll get a raise. People are worried the boss will only give to his "favorites," so everyone is busy embellishing their accomplishments while diminishing everyone else's to make their case. There's a widespread feeling that the game is rigged.

* * *

You walk out of a meeting during which a major problem was discussed but no clear decision was made about how to address it—no one even talked about the real reasons for it. Despite this, everyone exchanged knowing glances about the obviously unspoken explanations. Now it's unclear what's supposed to happen—and the people who *should* be taking charge seem curiously relieved there was no resolution.

* * *

Two historically rivaling departments are facing a major customer problem and are forced to work together to resolve it. Each is blaming the other for the problem, arguing over whose budget should pay to fix it and exaggerating the other department's responsibility for the calamity.

Do any of these scenes sound familiar? These are more than just routine irritating experiences in organizational life. They are the conditions that set the stage for much bigger problems. Left unresolved, here are the crossroads that can follow.

In the mid-1980s, two manufacturing companies learned that their products were poisoning people, in some cases, fatally.

One of the companies, which had suspected this was the case for decades, mounted a colossal cover-up, continuing to poison and kill people for another 15 years. The other launched a comprehensive investigation into their entire manufacturing process, leading to a transformation of their supply chain that included using only organic raw materials that no longer poisoned people.

* * *

After emerging from the 2008 financial crisis, financial services corporations had to find new ways to compete. Exploiting the deregulation that had allowed their industry to issue questionably backed subprime mortgages to high-risk borrowers with poor credit was no longer an option. One financial services powerhouse doubled down on restoring trust with their customers and ramping up high levels of service across all their markets. Another firm, (once) one of the highest-regarded companies in the world, hatched one of the most corrupt schemes in corporate history, cross-selling hundreds of millions of dollars of unauthorized products to unknowing customers.

* * *

Two employees from two different companies are each sitting around a conference table in meetings with their respective boss and peers. In both meetings, people face a complex problem that presents a major threat to the company's future. In one meeting, amidst a spirited conversation about what could be done to solve the problem, the employee offers a wildly unorthodox idea that at first draws silence from her group, making her feel uncomfortable for having spoken up. But her boss sees something insightful in the idea, invites the team to build on it, and the conversation leads to a breakthrough. In the other meeting, after finishing a long tirade about how disappointed he is, the boss asks his team for their ideas on what needs to happen to solve their problem. The room grows more silent as the boss grows more impatient. The employee in that meeting knows how to solve the problem but concludes the risk of speaking up is just too great, so he chooses to remain silent.

* * *

In organizations all over the world, people stumble upon crossroads like these daily. Some appear inconsequential, like the earlier scenes. Others show up with world-changing implications, like the latter scenes. When the rubber hits the road, some companies and leaders make transformational choices of integrity and courage. Others, well, don't. We all want to believe we'd be the honest hero in the story if faced with the challenge.

But would we? What determines which way things turn out? What influences how we choose one option over another?

Those are the very questions this book seeks to answer.

Me, And How I Got Here

Several years ago, in my role as consultant and advisor at my firm, Navalent, a strategic organizational change and executive leadership consultancy, I was sitting across the conference table from the executive vice president of strategy for a $30 billion global food company. Let's call him Rick. His company had just been through a failed acquisition. What he told me that day stunned me: they'd suspected all along it would go bust:

> We spent nearly $3.5 billion and we all were afraid the whole time it would fail, but kept our mouths shut. It didn't fit our portfolio, and we knew we didn't actually have the capability to be successful together. But we did it anyway. Deal fever kicked in. We embellished data, we denied our concerns, and we exaggerated the upsides we doubted would ever materialize. In hindsight, we were too afraid to admit the risks. If I'm honest, we'd lost our core identity while the world of food had dramatically changed around us. And because we don't really know who we are anymore, we're grasping at straws and trying to make things up as we go.

The carnage in the wake of this failure was extensive—damaged careers and families, demoralized employees, cynical customers, distrusting and angry shareholders, and the loss of public trust.

Why did a group of reasonably smart, well-meaning people so willingly lie to themselves, their employees, and their shareholders? How was it possible that such destructive choices were made by leaders with so many punishing outcomes? Why couldn't they have just been honest with each other?

In the years since that meeting with Rick, my colleagues and I have had hundreds of similar conversations and conducted thousands of interviews that sounded just like his. Whether we are speaking with global powerhouse brands, promising start-ups, midcaps or non-profits, the patterns in the stories feel the same regardless of the size or type of organization. During these comprehensive conversations, employees prophesy about the impending doom they believe their company is ignoring. They lament about their boss's pathological behaviors. They opine with deep insight about the "unfair" dysfunctions surrounding them and offer practical wisdom about what they would do to correct them if they could. They even confess their own shortcomings and contributions to the madness.

They're willing to speak honestly to a stranger, but not to their colleagues, and not when it matters most. Sometimes the reason is a sin of omission, and not speaking up. Other times it's a more active form of duplicity—embellishing data, throwing a colleague under the bus, or making promises they know they can't keep. But either way, the consequences are devastating.

I left that meeting with Rick feeling particularly discouraged about my work as an organizational behavior expert, and with a sense of futility about my role in creating organizations that were more honest, just, and fulfilling. I'd devoted my entire career to helping organizations be honest with themselves because I believed that self-honesty was the only real path to transformation. But if they weren't willing to take action on what they'd learned about themselves and the advice I offered, what was the point?

I stewed over this. And then my problem got personal.

I realized I was no different than Rick. Scenes of my own dishonesty and injustice came streaming into my mind as I tried to imagine why Rick and his colleagues made the choices they did. I recalled the time I was interviewing for a job at a prestigious company where they kept telling me I didn't have "the right pedigree" for them, and feeling so inadequate and offended that I made sure I sounded like I had "pedigree"—which is really just code for pretentious and condescending. I was so determined to get them to hire me that I succeeded. I hated the company, and after two years, I left.

I also remembered a time when my boss was being pressured to accelerate a major change project and feeling so bad for him that the person leading it was failing, damaging the reputation of our team and credibility of the program before it even rolled out. Seeing the opportunity to be the hero—and win points with my boss despite the risk to my peer's image—I committed to stepping in and getting it done. I justified my critique of my colleague's failure as empathy for my boss and his frustration. Or the time when I took my five-year-old to a birthday party in a neighborhood of people far more successful and wealthier than I ever hoped to be and had to listen to other dads talk about their expensive cars and ritzy vacations. When one dad turned to me and asked about my summer vacation plans, suddenly I was going to Europe. Of course, in the back of my mind, I was already planning the lie I would later have to tell about why the trip was abruptly canceled due to "a work emergency."

I reflected on the significant pain Rick and his colleagues were in, and in turn had caused. They had feared extinction as a century-old company and were desperate to act because they couldn't admit they didn't know what to do. I thought about the astounding implications of how the story *could* have gone had they shared those truths *with each other* instead of just *about each other* after the fact and wondered what could have possibly prevented them from doing so.

Likewise, if I had decided to be honest and fair with that hiring manager, my boss, or my fellow dads, and not given into the dark emotions those situations made me feel, how else might my story have turned out?

Reflecting on these moments, the interplay between an individual's choices to be honest and do the right thing—or not—and the systemic factors surrounding those choices came sharply into view for me. Why, under certain conditions, would otherwise honest people choose to be dishonest? Why would otherwise kind-hearted people choose self-protection and to be unfair to others? And if we could understand what those conditions were, could we change them to make honesty and justice more likely?

I decided to find out. And what I discovered radically upended my understanding of honesty… in the best possible way.

I suspect it will do the same for you.

Charting a New Course

Many are also growing weary of organizations that say one thing but do another, driven by fear and self-interest. In August 2019, 181 Business Roundtable CEOs from some of America's top corporations signed a revised statement of purpose of the corporation. Business Roundtable is an association of chief executive officers of America's leading companies. To set sweeping change in motion, this is what they declared:

Statement on the Purpose of a Corporation
Americans deserve an economy that allows each person to succeed through hard work and creativity and to lead a life of meaning and dignity. We believe the free-market system is the best means of generating good jobs, a strong and sustainable economy, innovation, a healthy environment and economic opportunity for all.

Businesses play a vital role in the economy by creating jobs, fostering innovation and providing essential goods and services. Businesses make and sell consumer products; manufacture equipment and vehicles; support the national defense; grow and produce food; provide health care; generate and deliver energy; and offer financial, communications and other services that underpin economic growth.

While each of our individual companies serves its own corporate purpose, we share a fundamental commitment to all of our stakeholders. We commit to:

- Delivering value to our customers. We will further the tradition of American companies leading the way in meeting or exceeding customer expectations.

- Investing in our employees. This starts with compensating them fairly and providing important benefits. It also includes supporting them through training and education that help develop new skills for a rapidly changing world. We foster diversity and inclusion, dignity and respect.

- Dealing fairly and ethically with our suppliers. We are dedicated to serving as good partners to the other companies, large and small, that help us meet our missions.

- Supporting the communities in which we work. We respect the people in our communities and protect the environment by embracing sustainable practices across our businesses.

- Generating long-term value for shareholders, who provide the capital that allows companies to invest, grow and innovate. We are committed to transparency and effective engagement with shareholders.

Each of our stakeholders is essential. We commit to deliver value to all of them, for the future success of our companies, our communities and our country.[1]

This radical departure from shareholder primacy, the paradigm that has governed corporate priorities for decades, earned an understandably mixed reception. For many, it was a shining glimmer of hope that equality and opportunity could be within reach for all, and that honesty and justice could prevail, stemming the tide of growing inequality. But for others, cynicism abounded. Where was the tangible action behind the words? Would shareholders tolerate the possible implications for their investments? Who was going to enforce adherence to these new norms? Business Europe, a leading business advocacy group for growth and competitiveness at the European level representing 35 European nations, issued a similar declaration for their 2019–2024 agenda of "prosperity, people, and planet." Their ambition is one of unity and resolve, saying, "We will all have to join forces to deliver a European Union that will create prosperity for Europe and its people, while also managing the transition to a sustainable future to protect our planet."[2]

In the time since their release, several dramatic events seem to have accelerated growing commitment to the sentiments inferred within these statements. The Covid-19 global pandemic, at least thus far, has revealed the best of corporate humanity and compassion from many companies, which have stepped up to provide new levels of service, generosity, sacrifice, and care for their employees, customers, and communities. And on top of that, we're facing a global uprising of civil unrest in response to centuries of racial injustice set in motion by the brutal murder of George Floyd (both of these events were happening during the writing of this book). Here again, many corporations came up with unapologetic statements of intolerance for racial injustice and pledged unwavering commitment to anti-racism. And behind those statements, many await tangible action. The long-term implications of these events remain to be seen, but experts predict that they will be catalysts for long-overdue reckonings.[3] A 2020 report card issued by KKS Advisors and research group Test of Corporate Purpose, and funded by the Ford Foundation, evaluated signatories of the BRT Statement performance during the Covid-19 pandemic and racial unrest to see if their commitments to stakeholder capitalism played out in their actions, citing these as "their first test" of real commitment. Candidly, the results weren't positive for many of the signatories, citing payments of dividends to shareholders despite mass layoffs and other actions that seemingly contradicted the statement's promises.[4] Ultimately, the shift to stakeholder-centricity is a long game, and will take years before we can draw evidence-based conclusions about how committed companies are.

And outside the world of organizations, the war for truthful information that barrages us on a daily basis has many of us soul-weary and disgusted. The suffocating skepticism we are fed by the media, political leaders at every level, and experts we once trusted has spread like a bad rash. Most of us are sick of feeling manipulated and lied to, and long to feel like someone is shooting straight with us.

I believe each of us must resolve to *be that person* rather than waiting around for that person to appear. It is my deepest hope that this book will serve as one more arrow in the quiver of courageous leaders who want to use the power of their role and organization to bring about a more honest, fair, and purposeful world... starting with their own teams, divisions, communities, and families.

Truth, Justice, and Purpose: Three sides of the same coin

Three forces are colliding into the business world with increasing intensity.

First, the world is clamoring for insights on ways to live lives of, and become organizations of, purpose. And why wouldn't it be? The data is unmistakable. Purpose-driven companies outperform competitors on many levels, and employees are so eager to have meaning in their work that they'll take pay cuts to get it. Consider the following findings.

As judged by their financial performance on the NASDAQ and NYSE from 1999 to 2019, purpose-driven companies outperformed similar S&P 500 companies by 100 percent.[5] Globally, a study of more than 60 countries conducted by Insights 2020 found that 83 percent of companies that overperform on revenue growth link everything they do to brand purpose, as opposed to only 31 percent of underperformers.[6] And in the UK, certified B Corps are growing 28 times faster than the national economic growth of 0.5 percent.[7]

Purpose-driven companies posted a 9.85 percent compound annual growth rate (CAGR), compared with the 2.4 percent for the S&P Consumer Sector, from 2011 to 2015.[8]

Employees who feel their work is meaningful at work are:[9]

- more productive, on average, by $9,000 per worker per year;

- willing to work extra hours per week and take two fewer paid sick days;

- better retained, and on average, 69 percent less likely to quit within the next six months;

- willing to work for less money, and on average are willing to give up 23 percent of their total future earnings—nearly a quarter of their income—in exchange for work that is meaningful;

- happier, with 51 percent higher job satisfaction than those who don't find their work meaningful.

As far as market loyalty is concerned, the data is even more compelling:

- 77 percent of consumers feel a stronger connection to purpose-driven companies over traditional companies;

- 66 percent of consumers would switch from a product they typically buy to a new product from a purpose-driven company.[10]

Unfortunately, the pursuit of these wonderful results has many companies devolving into "purpose washing," whereby they work hard to create the *appearance of purpose*. Marketers are pulling every lever they can to put halos over their brands and companies, spinning a narrative of goodwill. Employees and consumers aren't buying it, though. While 84 percent of consumers consider trust when purchasing, only 34 percent actually trust the brands they buy from, and 53 percent believe companies purpose wash.[11]

When it comes to purpose, you can't "fake it 'til you make it." You either mean it or you don't, and if you don't, people will see right through it.

The second force is inequality, which has become the moral and ethical issue of the day. The world's sensitivity to how underrepresented identities are treated unfairly is increasing, an important step forward toward true equity. But we have a long way to go before our organizational systems have rooted out their institutional biases and replaced them with justice and dignity. Diversity, Equity and Inclusion efforts, with the best of intentions, are *campaigning* for justice rather than creating more just organizations, meaning they are more focused on advocating for equality rather than creating it. From 1985 to 2015, the proportion of black men in management increased just slightly—from 3 percent to 3.3 percent.[12] And in 2019, 45 percent of Americans reported experiencing workplace discrimination and/or harassment in the previous year.[13]

Third, employee voice—the field of study that looks at the degree to which people freely speak their minds—is becoming an increasing factor in an organization's employer brand. Many internal functions like HR and ethics & compliance are mounting noble efforts to foster "speak up" cultures where people feel psychologically safe enough to share radical ideas that drive innovation, offer candid feedback, raise concerns of misconduct, and openly dissent when decisions lack sufficient rationale. Here, again, intentions and consequences do not always match up. Short training programs and communications campaigns promoting these ideas are nice, but a far cry from having employees practice them daily.

Further, our polarized political climate and a vindictive social media landscape have painfully confused the notion of "speaking *your* truth" with the need to "speak *the* truth." The social gathering places of organizations have become veritable seas of eggshells where everyone is terrified of offending someone, saying something politically incorrect, or being accused of being racist, sexist, judgmental, homophobic, intolerant, hostile, biased, privileged, angry, retaliatory, victimized, or power-hungry. So, we opt not to talk about them at all. The problem, of course, is that these issues do exist all around us, often unconsciously and unintentionally. But since we can't have productive conversations about them within our organizations, we have vitriolic, nasty conversations outside the workplace *about* people we think personify these things instead of *with* those people.

Individually, these three forces seem to fall short of making their intended impact. But what would happen if they joined forces?

- *Purpose*—serve a greater good.
- *Justice*—do the right and fair thing.
- *Truth*—tell it, respectfully and directly, without compromise.

Working together, they create a new, even more powerful capability. Call it "honesty" (see Figure 0.1).

Seems simple. Without all three pieces, honesty is impossible. To be honest, you have to say the right thing. Do the right thing. And say and do the right thing *for the right reason.*

Without an authentic desire to serve, and a genuine belief that serving an organization's purpose enhances their own, an employee has no motivation to contribute toward a more equitable workplace. People will just continue serving their own interests.

Without a hardcore commitment to justice within our organizational systems, employees will never believe their voices matter, because the system will reinforce the truth that only *some voices* matter.

FIGURE 0.1 Honesty

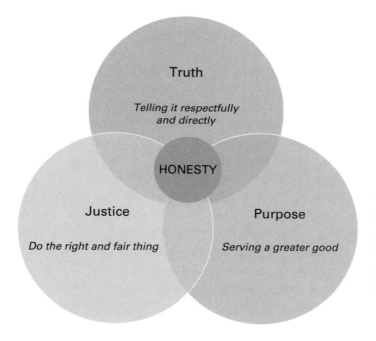

Without the capacity to have hard conversations among the many identity, cultural, and functional differences within companies, we can't build the trust needed to unify our organizations, leaving conflicts and inequities undiscussed and out of view.

Do you see how interrelated these forces are? Indeed, the fundamental conclusion of my research for this book is that to build an honest company, you need a power that can only be harnessed when truth, justice, and purpose operate in harmony.

To have one, you need all three. This is how you build the capability of honesty.

It's important to note that the definition of "honesty" I use here, and throughout the book, may expand on your current understanding of the term, which many think of simply as "not lying." Throughout the book, when I use the word "honesty" I'm referring to the combination of all three factors. When I use the word "dishonesty," I'm referring to the absence of all three.

What You'll Find Ahead:
Four Dimensions of Organizational Honesty

I recently completed a 15-year longitudinal study analyzing more than 3,200 interviews my firm and I conducted during 210 organizational assessments. Interview subjects ranged from individual contributors all the way up to C-suite executives, and they exposed many different types of organizational challenges. To help us make sense of the data, we deployed IBM Watson's artificial intelligence analytics tools to extract patterns across and converted the data into validated statistical models.

Each section of the book is devoted to exploring one of the four major findings from the research. Each has two chapters, one exploring the organizational or *systemic* aspects of honesty and the other exploring the individual or *leadership* aspects of it. There are case studies, stories from history, excerpts from the many interviews I conducted with executives, thought leaders, and regular employees, and stories right from organizations I work with (names and some details have been changed to protect anonymity in those stories).

This book is about exemplars, not villains. The vast majority of stories I've chosen highlight companies I'd want you and your company to emulate. These aren't the stories that typically make headlines, but they are the stories that inspire us to be better. I'll briefly examine a few particularly scandalous stories of dishonesty for contrast, but my hope is to compel you with a front-row seat to some of the most inspiring leaders and organizations for which honesty—truth, justice, and purpose—is fundamental. And alongside these stories, you'll find compelling data from other great researchers that expands on my findings. Here's a breakdown of what you can expect in each section.

Part 1: Honesty in Identity: Be Who You Say You Are

When we don't know who we are, we make things up. When organizations say one thing about themselves but their actions don't match, or when they set lofty goals but don't connect those goals to employees' everyday work, their company identity becomes muddled. A misalignment in mission, vision, values, purpose, and/or brand promises is a big, flapping red flag—for management and employees alike. My research reveals that workers at companies whose statements of identity are unclear or inconsistent with what employees experience day-to-day are almost *three times* more likely to withhold or distort the truth and behave unfairly. You can guess what this means for your bottom line.

The chapters in Part One will show how organizations, leaders, and individuals can align the words they say about themselves with the actions they take to embody those words. You'll see how companies like PepsiCo, Best Buy, and Microsoft have embedded purpose deeply into the core of their organizations. You'll hear groundbreaking research from Contexis, the UK-based B Corp whose purpose is measuring purpose, and the astounding results you can achieve when you activate it yourself. And, we'll take a look at the vital role hope plays in the process of being who you say you are.

Part 2: Justice in Accountability: Putting Dignity First

When we believe we're being unfairly assessed, we exaggerate our contributions to self-protect and cover our asses. Fewer things are more painful in organizations than performance management. When leaders fail to judge performance in ways their employees feel are fair, employees respond by making sure they get the credit they deserve—by whatever means necessary. But instead of inflicting stressful, paint-by-numbers performance reviews, leaders can learn to foster honest and trusting relationships with those they lead, creating an environment where they can talk openly about when contributions were exceptional, and when they fell short. Employees are *four times* more likely to be honest about their results and fair to others when working at a company where they feel they can ask for help without fear of judgment and are empowered to see failure as a learning experience.

Accordingly, the chapters in this section will redefine what "accountability" means. We'll define what it means to build justice and dignity into accountability processes. We'll look at how Microsoft revamped their performance management process to enable employees to learn from mistakes and failure. We'll examine how institutional biases create inequity and hear from renowned experts on how to eliminate them. And we'll look at what restorative justice can teach leaders about engaging people in conversations about their achievements and their shortfalls, making dignity the cornerstone of the relationship between a leader and her followers.

Part 3: Transparency in Governance: Make Trustworthy Decisions Through Honest Conversations

When there are no healthy forums in which the truth can be told, it goes underground, leaving collusion, rumors, and gossip in its place. How decisions get made—or not—in companies is a common source of confusion for people (even the ones who seem to be making the decisions!). When employees don't know or trust how resources are distributed, how priorities are set, or how hard decisions get made, they are more than *three and a half times* more likely to lie or distort the truth. At the core of great governance—the way organizations make decisions—are effective meetings where decisions are transparent and difficult issues can be discussed openly. Every company can learn to do these better.

The chapters in this section will look at governance structures that are especially well-suited to fostering healthy debate and open sharing of ideas, no matter how radical. The chapters will look at the importance of psychological safety, how it's established, and the implications for companies when it is or isn't present. We'll contrast the stories of DuPont and Patagonia, and the stark differences in how they responded to the crisis of learning that their manufacturing processes had potentially lethal consequences. Finally, we'll look at how leaders can create courageous conversations that inspire honest exchanges of challenging feedback and radical ideas, de-risking truth telling for those they lead.

Part 4: Unity Between Groups: Connect Everyone to a Bigger Story

When we fragment an organization, we create dueling truths. The seams of an organization, the places where functions come together to form unique capabilities, hold tremendous but often untapped value; too often, though, these are treated as no man's land, with each party making an exclusive claim. Left unchecked, interdepartmental conflict at a company makes it almost *six times* more likely that workers will lie or distort the truth, or act unjustly. Such conflicts between functions or regions are more than annoying—they create the silos that pit "my truth" against "your truth." Despite these natural tendencies, companies can learn to create healthy collaboration across their seams, fostering partnerships, not rivalries, between people who must work with different departments.

The chapters in this section will take a close look at companies like Cabot Creamery and their remarkable story of creating unity out of long-strained relationships. We take an intimate look at the ways we "other" people who are different than us, the role tribalism plays in dividing people across organizations, and what it means to connect to those outside our echo chambers.

Each of these four sections articulates what it takes to build companies and leaders that integrate truth, justice, and purpose into their actions. Together, they show what it actually takes to be honest.

Honesty Is a Muscle

Of all my findings, the revelation that honesty is more than a character trait or moral principle was the most important. It's more than an aspiration; it's a capability. To be good at it, you have to work at it. And that begins with believing you can be better at it than you currently are.

To be sure, leading this kind of life and team takes work. It demands practice. Embodying truth, justice, and purpose requires real competence. These aren't just ethical qualities you either have or don't. My research revealed that honesty is a muscle, and like any muscle, to make it strong you have to work on it. Regularly. When an athlete leaves the gym or a patient leaves physical therapy, they feel sore but satisfied. Becoming good at honesty is no different. When you declare that you and your organization wish to serve a worthy purpose, you have to eliminate the distractions and contradictions that keep you from doing so. This process takes insight, ongoing feedback, and creativity. It takes grit to deflect the naysayers and courage to remove the obstacles.

When you set out to create a more just organization, you will be tampering with deeply embedded institutional biases that, likely unknowingly, have privileged some people over others. You have to be willing to interrogate your processes of accountability—what you measure, how you acknowledge contributions, how you create opportunities for others to advance and shine, and how you talk with those you lead about their contributions—to make sure everyone has the same chances of being successful, no matter who they are. That may require disappointing some people who've benefited from the biases in the old system and helping them recognize the need to create accountability that is based on dignity and justice for all. It means being vulnerable with those you lead and building sufficient trust with them, as only then will you be in a position to hold them to account for commitments they make and talk openly about when they fall short. And you have to model what it means to acknowledge your own shortfalls and improve.

There are plenty of platitudes I could offer about why being more honest and just is "good for you," though you've undoubtedly heard those since kindergarten. But I deeply believe that understanding the conditions under which we, and our organizations, encourage dishonesty and injustice can bring greater levels of contribution and satisfaction, and ultimately meaning. I want you to discover, painful though it might be, the ways your organization unknowingly encourages employees to withhold or distort the truth or act unjustly, and how to fix the conditions that create this behavior. From there, you will be much more empowered to make different choices. And, as you will see in the following chapters, choosing truth, justice, and purpose can make you and your organization healthier, higher-performing and significantly more competitive, and ultimately, more joyful.

In the end, my hope is that this book will help you live a more honest life—one in which you tell the truth, act with justice toward others, and live your purpose with deep satisfaction and impact. I have no intention of defining your moral compass or value system; that's for you to do. But I want you to feel proud of the people and organizations you lead, knowing that you've created the conditions in which people will choose honesty. That way, when you return home at night, you'll be able to look your loved ones in the eye and know you are exactly the person they believe you are.

What you will find on the pages ahead is the roadmap for doing just that.

Finding Hope in Bigger Stories

At the start of each chapter, I will set the context by "zooming out" with a broader story from an unlikely context in history and life. As leaders, we must be able to learn, find inspiration, and glean hope from stories much different than ours. We have to look at circumstances and challenges we would never face to discover our common humanity and hard-won wisdom from communities and leaders vastly unlike us. I believe that some of the greatest examples of this book's concepts can be found in the most unexpected places if we allow ourselves to be curious and open. Read these stories with fascination. Don't look for their immediate relevance to organizational life, but instead let them reveal a unique form of honesty—truth, justice, and purpose—from people, places, and communities you've likely never heard of but will enjoy the privilege of meeting. You'll probably never face the challenges of these heroes, but trust me, their stories have relevance.

Resist the temptation to compare your story to theirs, making yours feel smaller or less significant. Instead, see how much larger your story could be as you consider the triumphs and tribulations of amazing people and communities from around the globe. For example, we'll travel to South America and learn from how the nation of Colombia made peace after decades of conflict with combatants. We'll explore one man's fight for justice for wrongfully convicted prisoners, and one woman's fight for justice in the Democratic Republic of the Congo. From Baltimore to Thailand, from Oklahoma in the 1930s to Vietnam in the 1960s, from New Zealand to Compton, CA, I will introduce you to organizations and leaders whose stories can enlighten and inspire you. Your job is to open your mind and heart and let them.

Get Busy

Decades ago, during a painful season, I was coming to terms with a part of my story I'd long ignored. A few close friends provided loving support and encouragement as I leaned into areas of my life where I needed help. I decided to confide in my big brother to enlist his support. After all, that's what big brothers are for. As I expected, he listened compassionately as I shared my challenges. He asked questions and shed a few tears of empathy.

I emphasize "a few" because growing up in a New York Italian family of five, I understood "showing emotion" to take many unique forms. We could be loud and intense, and if you were watching from the outside, you might assume we were angry. But within the family, you knew what you were seeing was fierce, uncompromising love. When hard things needed to be done, there was no mincing words or coddling. Empathy looked practical, not sentimental. You said what needed to be said and helped where help was needed. So, in that moment, my big brother leaned over to me, gave me a hug, looked me squarely in the eye, and said, "I love you. Get busy."

Since that moment, I've ended every keynote address I've given by charging the audience with those same words: "Get busy." And throughout this book, I'm going to charge you the same way. You will quickly see that much like my family, I won't be mincing words or trying to make honesty easy for you. To transform our organizations into places of truth, justice, and purpose, we're going to have to dig deep into parts of our stories we have ignored. We're going to have to acknowledge issues we've denied were issues. So, at the end of each chapter, you will see a section titled "Get Busy." Within those sections, I will be giving you practical ideas and advice for how to take the key points from that chapter and apply them in your world. (Hint: You may want to get a notebook to keep all your notes in one place.) Those sections are my way of encouraging you—the way a New York Italian no-nonsense big brother would when there are hard things to be done. So, try to hear the ideas and assignments in those sections—some of which will make you uncomfortable—in that loving spirit, and, well... get busy.

Endnotes

1 Business Round Table Statement of Purpose, reprinted with permission

2 Business Europe (2019) Prosperity People Planet: Three pillars for the European Union Agenda in 2019–2024, http://euyourbusiness.eu/content/uploads/2019/11/2019-11-13-Prosperity-People-Planet_interactive.pdf (archived at https://perma.cc/7QPZ-EKNF)

3 Dorn, A V, Cooney, R E and Sabin, M L (2020) Covid-19 exacerbating inequalities in the US, *World Report*, https://doi.org/10.1016/S0140-6736(20)30893-X (archived at https://perma.cc/P2E4-EVXV)

4 Ward, B et al (2020) Covid-19 and inequality: A test of corporate purpose, https://www.kksadvisors.com/tcp-test-of-corporate-purpose-september2020 (archived at https://perma.cc/VT5S-6NGJ)

5   Sperry, K and Ferran, D J (2020) Ethics + stakeholder focus = greater long-run shareholder profits [Blog] *Torry Project*, 6 April, https://www.torreyproject.org/post/ethics-stakeholder-focus-greater-long-run-shareholder-profits (archived at https://perma.cc/W5QG-PH3V)

6   The Advertising Research Foundation (2015) Insights2020: Facing 2020 with 20/20 vision, 05 October, https://thearf.org/category/news-you-can-use/insights2020-facing-2020-with-2020-vision/ (archived at https://perma.cc/523K-5RMY)

7   Sustainable Brands (2018) B Corp analysis reveals purpose-led businesses grow 28 times faster than national average, 1 March, https://sustainablebrands.com/read/business-case/b-corp-analysis-reveals-purpose-led-businesses-grow-28-times-faster-than-national-average (archived at https://perma.cc/LM7B-6U8F)

8   Korn Ferry Institute (2016) People on a mission, https://www.kornferry.com/content/dam/kornferry/docs/article-migration/Korn_Ferry_People_on_a_Mission_1219.pdf (archived at https://perma.cc/DJT4-5XJU)

9   Reece, A, Kellerman, G, and Robichaux, A (2018) Meaning and purpose at work, https://www.betterup.com/en-us/resources/reports/meaning-and-purpose-report (archived at https://perma.cc/A8HX-D7DA)

10 Cone (2018) 2018 Cone/Porter Novelli Purpose Study: How to build deeper bonds, amplify your message and expand your consumer base, https://static1.squarespace.com/static/56b4a7472b8dde3df5b7013f/t/5c66ce8dfa0d600c4f44d4ce/1550241426931/021319_PurposeStudy_Single.pdf (archived at https://perma.cc/Z4ML-ALUX)

11 Edelman (2019) 2019 Edelman Trust Barometer: Global report, https://www.edelman.com/sites/g/files/aatuss191/files/2019-02/2019_Edelman_Trust_Barometer_Global_Report.pdf (archived at https://perma.cc/4YZ3-PT2L)

12 Dobbin, F and Kalev, A (2016) Why diversity programs fail, *Harvard Business Review*, https://hbr.org/2016/07/why-diversity-programs-fail?registration=success (archived at https://perma.cc/6LQN-YJGG)

13 Porterfield, S (2020) 10 Diversity & inclusion statistics that will change how you do business [Blog] *Bonusly*, 21 February, https://blog.bonus.ly/diversity-inclusion-statistics (archived at https://perma.cc/52J2-A2UB)

01

The Redeeming Power of Honesty

*Set your intention: How can honesty be a force
of transformation?*

Hope From a Bigger Story

In 1964, Manuel Marulanda, a member of the Colombian Communist Party
(PCC), worked with Jacobo Arenas, an ideological thought leader at the
time, to form the Revolutionary Armed Forces of Colombia, commonly
known as FARC. For the previous decade, Colombia had been embroiled in
a brutal civil war. PCC members organized groups of individuals who felt
neglected by the Colombian government and helped them settle throughout
Colombia's vast countryside to create their own viable communities with
opportunities for the working class. Their expressed intent was to create a
society in which the needs of the rural population would be represented and
addressed.

In FARC's early days, the Colombian government attacked these communities, attempting to drive people out of them and re-appropriate the territories under their control. Marulanda realized how outnumbered FARC
was—FARC were fewer than 50 and the Colombian military attacking them
numbered around 16,000. They were forced to retreat into the countryside,
where Arenas' preferences for more extreme and violent tactics took hold.
For the next 50 years, FARC would fund its activities aimed at overthrowing
the government through cocaine trafficking, ransomed kidnappings, extor-
tion, and illegal gold mining, along with other nefarious activities that fueled
their growth throughout the 1980s.[1]

By 1999, FARC had over 18,000 members. That year alone, targeting
largely wealthy landowners, they instigated more than 3,000 kidnappings.

They claimed their goal was to fight for the rural poor of Colombia and protect them from the corruption and violence of the Colombian government. Whether that was their true aim or not, the results of their conflict with the government were devastating. It's estimated that between 1958 and 2013, more than 220,000 Colombians were killed, 45,000 of them children, and more than five million people were forced to leave their homes, 2.3 million of whom were children, creating the second largest population of internally displaced people in the world.[2]

In 2016, a peace agreement was finally reached, ending the 52-year conflict between FARC and the Colombian government. FARC has since transformed into a political party with seats in the Colombian government and has largely disarmed. The agreement was an extraordinary milestone. But it left one lingering, potentially disastrous problem: what to do with the remaining 14,000 FARC guerrillas living in the countryside?

Jaime Góngora—a wildlife geneticist at the University of Sydney and native of Colombia—had a brilliant response to this question. The jungles from where the combatants had waged their war were a rich and unexplored area of biodiversity. Góngora believed that the combatants' knowledge of the uncharted, biodiverse rain forests of Colombia was unparalleled, and if harnessed, could lead to untold scientific discoveries. He decided he would convert the guerrillas into citizen-environmentalists, helping them find new purpose in life while serving their nation. And that's exactly what he did.[3]

Working with scientists and researchers from the United Kingdom, Australia, and ten Colombian institutions, the ex-combatants have since discovered more than 100 new species. Scientists had long desired to study Colombia's immense but inaccessible rainforests, and now they had expert guides to lead them.

Góngora's training program, called Peace with Nature, trains more than 100 ex-combatants three to four times per year. Speaking about the program, he says:

> This is a vital step to enable [ex-combatants] to contribute to environmental projects, improve their livelihoods, and reincorporate into society. We teach them to undertake inventories of biodiversity and protect it, as well as come up with sustainable environment-based business ideas. These workshops have also increased awareness of potential ecotourism projects where they live. We are providing opportunities to develop connections with regional and national institutions to implement their projects.[4]

In some of the workshops, ex-combatants sit alongside members of the Colombian military and police. In one interview, Góngora noted his surprise at how environmental science could become a neutral ground for healing and reconciliation after such a protracted and violent conflict. New ecotourism routes have been cultivated with the ex-combatants' help, and their extensive knowledge of jungle living, such as the identities of medicinal plants and food sources, how to walk the bush without making noise to spot rare wildlife, and other intricacies of the rain forest, has allowed them to embrace an entirely new perspective on their own stories—that the environment that protected them had also molded them into more than just violent guerrillas.

If you had asked the citizens of Colombia in 2015 if they believed the members of FARC could ever do something meaningful and trustworthy for their country, I doubt anyone would have said "yes." Nor were those citizens eager to welcome the ex-militants back into mainstream society. The carnage and heartache created by the country's half-century-long bloodbath might have never earned FARC guerrillas anything more than sneering ill will from their fellow Colombians. But thanks to Peace with Nature, they are no longer seen as just former guerrillas who deserve hatred. The same place they spent most of their lives hiding in fear and rage has been transformed into a highly sought-after treasure trove of knowledge and economic opportunity, and with this, their own stories have been redeemed into ones of purpose and pride.

This story vividly shows the power of truth, justice, and purpose in action. Two conflicting truths needed to be reconciled—14,000 former guerrillas needed something useful to do and the ecologically rich jungles where they lived cried out to be explored. Justice would be served by restoring their lost years and giving them the chance to have meaningful livelihoods while contributing to their country's restoration. On top of this, the higher purposes of scientific knowledge and growing Colombia's economy would both be served.

Góngora's story shows how redemption can be achieved even in the most trying and unlikely circumstances. For this reason, I believe every organization, community, family, and person has their own story of redemption waiting to be uncovered and told.

Harnessed thoughtfully, truth, justice, and purpose become a force for such transformation. That is the redeeming power of honesty. And if organizations can learn to see otherwise difficult circumstances with fresh, creative, empathetic eyes—just as Góngora did—our world will indeed become more honest.

Think this sounds impossible? Well, I've got even better news for you. Turns out we humans come wired for honesty.

Your Brain on Honesty

Our bodies come with factory-installed honesty barometers. The more honest we are, the better we feel. Numerous medical studies have shown that honest people are less prone to illness, have less anxiety and depression, and enjoy healthier and deeper relationships. Clearly, our health thrives when we are honest.

In one revealing series of studies, researchers from the Julius-Maximilians University of Würzburg, Germany, enrolled test subjects in a well-known experiment called "die under the cup." In the experiment, participants roll a series of die under a cup, the results of which only they can see, and then report their results anonymously. Participants were told they would earn money depending on the outcome of their rolls, with higher rolls rewarded more favorably. Each experiment included three rounds of rolls.

To ensure appropriate conditions, the researchers varied the time participants had to report their results. In the first round, they asked participants to report their results immediately. In the second, they were instructed to do so after a short delay. The results were clear, supporting what many researchers have long suspected: the results reported immediately were more honest than those reported after a delay, suggesting that honesty is a more instinctive response and showing that dishonesty takes greater cognitive effort.[5] These findings are also confirmed by a UK-based study undertaken at Sheffield University of fMRI brain imaging studies.[6]

In another study, researchers Haran and Shalvi from Ben Gurion University and University of Amsterdam, respectively, set up a series of experiments in which study participants in Australia, Canada, the UK, and the US received advice and were then asked to make a decision. The purpose of the experiments was to determine what factors influenced participants' decision— whether they took or rejected the advice. To explain the purpose of their experiments, they offer the illustration of a prospective customer asking a car salesman about the fuel efficiency of a car they may potentially buy. In response, the car salesman may recommend one car over another as getting much better gas mileage. But if the prospective customer believes the car salesman doesn't actually know the fuel efficiency of the car inquired about, or has an ulterior motive for suggesting an alternative car, for example he'll be paid a higher commission on that car, the customer's suspicion of bias may now impact the degree to which the customer accepts the advice. The information the car salesperson provides may well have been perfectly *accurate*. So, what determines whether or not the customer *believes it is honest*?

Haran and Shalvi worked to find out through a series of five experiments. In each one, advice was given to various decision makers, and in each experiment, the decision makers were given reasons to be suspicious of bias inherent in the advice. This included subtle cues like telling the decision makers about incentives or what type of prior knowledge their advisors had. It also included inciting overt suspicion, telling the decision makers that their advisors *would* provide inaccurate or false information. The results were conclusive. Decision makers were less likely to change their minds when they suspected the advice as being erroneous or misleading, *even when the advice was accurate*.[7] The implications for anyone wanting to be influential in life are clear: it's not enough to be truthful. You need to be seen as well-meaning (justice) and concerned for something beyond your own gain (purpose).

Both the University of Würzburg and Haran/Shalvi studies confirm: as human beings, we prefer to be honest and receive honesty in return.

And when we do, our bodies reward us. According to the Bloomberg Global Health Index and universities in the US and UK, the most honest countries are also the healthiest. Israel ranks highest as the healthiest country in the world, and the 18th most honest country. Switzerland ranks top as the most honest country and is the sixth healthiest country in the world. Norway ranks #2 for both healthiest and most honest. By contrast, the most dishonest countries are also the most depressed, with China, India, and Russia ranking in the bottom quartiles.[8, 9]

What does this all tell us? That our minds and bodies thrive on honesty.

Unfortunately, unlike our electronic devices, our brains don't come with a "restore factory settings" button. So what happens when those natural instincts are corrupted? If we expose our otherwise naturally honest predisposition to dishonesty, do we resist or succumb?

To find out, researchers and behavioral scientists Garrett *et al* conducted a series of experiments in which pairs of participants worked together to advise each other about the amount of money that was in a jar filled with pennies, estimating the amount the jar contained. Both participants believed they were collaborating toward a shared outcome of an accurate estimate, though in each experiment one of the participants was actually a plant. The incentive structure changed each round such that the outcome would 1) benefit one participant at the expense of their partner; 2) benefit the partner at the expense of the participant; 3) benefit the participant only, with no effect on their partner; and 4) benefit the partner only, with no effect on the participant. The participant believed that their partner (the confederate) was not aware of this incentive structure, nor were they given any feedback on their estimates during the experiment. Over the course of multiple rounds, self-serving dishonesty increased when it benefitted participants, even when it harmed partners.

To understand the brain's response during these experiments, researchers used fMRI images of the participants' brains, and found a neural mechanism in the amygdala—the part of the brain that regulates emotional responses to past experiences. The images revealed that with each passing round of self-serving dishonesty, the signal detection in the amygdala of participants *reduced*, suggesting the brain becomes desensitized to one's own dishonest behavior. Moreover, the amount of reduction in the signal predicted the degree to which one's self-serving dishonesty would escalate. The more desensitized participants became in any given round, the more self-interested they became in the next.[10]

The implications of these studies for leaders and organizations are monumental: if you subject otherwise honest people who prefer to be treated with honesty to conditions that provoke dishonest behavior, over time they will surrender to it. *Even when they didn't intend to do so.*

The remaining chapters of *To Be Honest* will reveal how you might be doing just that. And when that happens, let's look at how disastrous the results can be.

Dishonesty's Carnage

In 2018, Accenture, the global consulting firm, set out to measure the impact of a company's trustworthiness on its bottom line. In a sample of more than 7,000 companies in their Competitive Agility Index, Accenture found that 54 percent had experienced a material loss of trust within the previous two years. They estimated that the loss of trust across those companies equated to a loss of US $180 billion—and that's a conservative estimate.[11] The trust violations included issues like product defects, financial scandals, environmental negligence, and cybersecurity breaches. For their part, Accenture define trust as "a consistent experience of competence, integrity, honesty, transparency, commitment, purpose and familiarity."[12]

Two companies included in the study offer sobering examples. One initiated a campaign to promote their commitment to sustainability. Because they failed to get necessary input from appropriate environmental and social responsibility experts, however, it came off looking more like a PR event. Their revenue dropped US $400 million. Another company was named in money laundering allegations. The following year their revenue dropped 34 percent, or US $1 billion, while their EBITDA (a measure of profitability) plummeted by 61 percent, or US $700 million.[13]

Edelman, the global communications and public relations colossus, conducts an annual study they call the Edelman Trust Barometer. Over the last 20 years they have surveyed more than two million respondents from across the globe and yielded 23 million measures of trust.

The 2020 report, which included more than 34,000 participants of both people in the workplace and average citizens, reveals painful, growing discontent with inequality across the world. Fifty-six percent of respondents believe that capitalism does more harm than good and 74 percent perceive a growing sense of injustice in the world. Fifty-seven percent don't trust the information they get via their media sources.

In the study, Edelman defines "trust" as the combination of competence and ethics. In 2020, no institution was seen as having both. Businesses were seen as competent while NGOs were seen as ethical. That's a stark contrast from their 2019 report, in which businesses were seen as the last hope to create needed societal change. It appears the world is losing faith in businesses' ability to create the positive impact in the world they were once hoped to bring. Only 29 percent of respondents to the 2020 survey believed that business fairly served the interests of everyone equally and fairly.

But people's faith hasn't totally evaporated. Seventy-three percent of respondents still believe businesses can be profitable while serving the communities in which they operate, and 83 percent believe that all stakeholders, not just shareholders, are critical to a company's long-term success.

Most profoundly, 73 percent of employees want their employers to provide them with an opportunity to shape the future of society.[14]

What does this all tell us?

People show up to work hungry to make a difference and believing they can, and honest companies that create an opportunity to do so through truthful, just, purposeful actions far outperform those that don't.

So, between the aspiration of what's possible and the grim realities of what many experience, what is the glue that bridges the gap?

It's hope.

Hope Fuels the Fire of Honesty

In December 2015, Sophie, who was nine years old at the time, arrived with her parents in Sweden as asylum seekers from the former USSR. Three months earlier, she'd witnessed the horrible kidnapping of her father by men in police uniforms. They'd dragged the family out of the car, letting Sophie and her mom flee after brutally beating both parents. Eventually, the father returned home, and the family fled to Sweden. A few days after arriving in Sweden, Sophie's parents noticed she'd stopped playing. Shortly after, the family was informed by Sweden's Migration Board they could not stay in the country. Sophie overheard the entire conversation. After this, she stopped eating and speaking. In the following 20 months, Sophie slipped into a comatose state. She was fed through a feeding tube and wore a diaper. Her vital signs and reflexes were all normal, but her body appeared lifeless.

Since the late 1990s, doctors in Sweden have been reporting cases of this strange phenomenon, called Resignation Syndrome. Approximately 400 cases were reported between 2003 and 2005, and hundreds more have been diagnosed in recent years as well. The syndrome largely affects traumatized children and adolescents whose horrific experiences in their home countries are compounded by the terrifying uncertainty of their status and safety as immigrants.[15]

In 2019, Netflix produced a documentary, *Life Overtakes Me*, chronicling the difficult journey of children in Sweden stricken with Resignation Syndrome. In each case, children had witnessed unthinkable horrors in their homeland and faced an uncertain future in Sweden, making them terrified of returning to the atrocities they'd fled in the first place. Dasha, for example, a seven-year-old girl, witnessed the rape of her mother, an act intended to threaten her father, whose internet business threatened local officials. Karen, a 12-year-old boy, witnessed the murder of a family friend and had to run for his life to avoid the same fate. Like an engine that runs out of gas, or a computer whose hard drive crashes, these children coped with the unbearable uncertainty of their future by simply shutting down. And they remained this way for months, even years.[16]

What is the cure for Resignation Syndrome? According to health experts, it's the restoration of hope. Once families are assured asylum and safety, their children slowly come out of their comatose states and regain the ability to function.[17]

Our brains crave hope to such a strong degree that they are willing to shut young bodies down under extreme distress if they are forced to go without it. What does this tell us about the human spirit's need for this vital emotional nutrient?

More than you may think.

Hope in the Workplace

While the suffering of traumatized children and the irritations of the workplace are certainly not comparable, the loss of hope they share may be instructive. Gallup's well-cited statistic of employee engagement—that approximately 70 percent of the workforce remains disengaged (checked out) or actively disengaged (actively looking to sabotage their companies)—hasn't improved much since the survey began. In 2019, it was reported that the number had dropped to 65 percent—hardly a reason to celebrate.[18] This means that out of the approximately 157 million people in the US workforce,[19] about 102 million aren't showing up at work with any sense of real purpose or commitment to being there.

Employee disengagement represents a loss of hope. And over 100 million people share it. They are walking around in a numbed state, devoid of energy and connection to their work. In some ways, they have shut down. Some are so resentful of their conditions that they actively pursue ways to undermine their employers.

Hope is a key ingredient for organizations and leaders who want to become who they've promised to be. I've never had an executive call me and say, "Can you help our organization build some hope?" I *have*, however, met many executives who *should* have called and asked me that. It's hard to quantify hope's presence, but if you've seen an organization that has lost it, then you know just how bleak things can be. Consider how tumultuous Colombia's relationship with former FARC combatants would have remained had Góngora not inspired the hope that their past could be redeemed into something uniquely meaningful.

Hope is created at the intersections of 1) passion—a desire for something greater; 2) perseverance—the need to prevail against great odds; and 3) faith—the belief that there *is* something greater beyond those odds. When a leader, organization, or even country is facing its darkest days, hope is what gets it through. During times of organizational transition, employees must have confidence that their hopes won't be dashed by broken promises. When an organization declares a renewed commitment to customer service, employees in customer-facing roles who feel starved of resources and empowerment to resolve angry complaints grow hopeful that they will get to do the job the way they've imagined it. When innovation is declared a new competitive advantage, those in product development and R&D roles surge with the hope of getting to use their scientific and technical skills to create things they feel proud of. That hope becomes essential if there's to be any chance of reaching those aspirations.

You may think hope is allegorical or "squishy," but it's not. Researchers Suzanne Peterson and Kristen Byron, who have studied the role of hope in organizations, point out that individuals with a higher capacity for hope are more goal-oriented and motivated to achieve their goals than their less hopeful counterparts. They found that regardless of whether they were talking about sales employees, mortgage brokers, or management executives, high-hope individuals had greater overall job performance. Leaders with reserves of hope facing major cost-cutting pressures, operational setbacks, or customer crises produced better solutions than leaders who lacked hope, suggesting that hopefulness may help employees when facing challenges at work.[20] Relatedly, University of Florida researchers Ambrose, Schminke, and Seabright, in their study on organizational injustice, found that losing hope can be destructive, and that there's a strong correlation between angry employees and sabotage. When workers feel like they've been unjustly engaged—like being given promises that aren't kept—they are far more likely to "get even," extracting their pound of flesh from the organization.[21] Fewer experiences turn people vengeful more than scorned hope.

We've all been burned by organizational hypocrisy and felt tempted to give up hope. We've watched companies start down the path of important change, offering long-overdue management training for unprepared leaders, proclaiming new values to signal culture change, or promising updated technology to replace outmoded tools, only to have those efforts fizzle out before completion. So it's no surprise that when organizations publicly set out to align who they are with how they act, especially in the wake of previous false starts, it takes a huge leap of faith from employees to believe things will turn out as hoped. Hope requires us to place our confidence behind an endeavor *without* necessarily having tangible evidence to back it up. But when things start to falter and that hope is dashed, that's when the most talented people quit and leave—and the mediocre talent quits and stays.

If you want to strengthen the honesty muscle of your organization or team, you'll need hope to get there. If you give up along the way, rest assured, your followers will get even. But if you stay the course, they will handsomely reward you.

Melony offers a wonderful case in point. She's a senior warehouse specialist in the logistics division of a large manufacturing company. I met her in a "team start-up" session I facilitated as part of implementing a new organization design within her company. In the manufacturing industries, automation and technology have been disrupting how companies move the products they make to the markets where they are sold. This means that lots of once-steady jobs are at risk. So Melony became certified in state-of-the-art logistics technologies to ensure that her company saw her as invaluable as machines replaced jobs.

Her company prided itself on delivering products made or assembled in the United States at low cost but with higher quality than competitive goods made abroad. And for the most part, they've kept that promise. But continued cost pressures and the mounting threat of trade wars meant continuously focusing on greater efficiency.

A few years ago, in response to these technological disruptions, Melony was asked to spearhead a major project to integrate two of the company's distribution centers with a technology platform that would move goods from the manufacturing line, to packaging and boxing, to pallets ready for shipping, all with the guidance of just one trained human being. She knew that this conversion would help the company keep its promise to customers of low-cost quality products. But she also feared that for some of her friends, it might mean the loss of their jobs. As she progressed her project, her success was fueling angst. The more efficient the distribution centers became, the worse morale got as people grew fearful of becoming obsolete. In a vicious cycle, the worse those employees' attitudes became, the more management pressured Melony to accelerate the project so they could "cut their losses" on the "disgruntled dead wood."

Melony urged her teammates to improve their technical training to secure their jobs, and even did some coaching to help them. But her supervisors were not interested in saving employees they believed were lost causes. Melony made several appeals. In one email to her boss, she wrote, "I appreciate that we're trying to keep our promise to customers, but what about our promise to employees? Don't we have an obligation to them? We have a chance to save jobs if we make a little effort, and I'm willing to help." But her request for additional resources fell on deaf ears. When I first spoke with her, she told me:

> It's getting harder to stay hopeful. I see amazing progress in our distribution
> center as the technology comes online. At the same time, I see faces I've worked

with for years becoming more bitter and afraid. I don't get why keeping
one promise has to mean breaking others. I'm tired of hearing my boss say,
"Tradeoffs are hard." Especially when they don't have to be.

She sincerely wanted her company to be the honest company she believed it
to be, to *both* customers and employees, and she saw a way to make it
happen. To her, being one way and not the other felt hypocritical. And it felt
like poor judgment and short-sightedness on the part of her supervisor.

As an outsider, I'm usually fairly powerless to do anything in situations
like this. Since my client was three levels above Melony's supervisor, asking
him to reach down that far was inappropriate. But I "might have" suggested
he take a tour of the distribution center to check on progress, "just in case"
morale was beginning to slip as technological change progressed. Which is
exactly what he did. And, what a coincidence! Melony was the one who
gave him the tour. Someone may or may not have suggested to her that she
share her hope for retraining her teammates with him during the tour. And
knowing the man of integrity he was, it came as no surprise to me when he
strongly "encouraged" the head of the distribution center to see that Melony
got the resources she needed to save as many jobs as possible, and that he
wanted her to lead a similar transition at the second distribution center once
this first one was completed.

Melony held onto the hope that her company could be who it had
proclaimed to be and had a clear vision for how to make it happen. She told
the truth, committed to doing the right thing, and served a greater purpose,
and in so doing enabled many of her coworkers to remain and do the same.
Melony wanted her teammates to have the same second chance she gave
herself. Not all of them could make the transition, but with her encouragement and the right training, many did. Hope fueled her commitment to lead
the charge even when things got tough. And hope is what she sustained for
colleagues whose careers hung in the balance.

WALK IN THEIR SHOES

What do you think you would have done in Melony's situation? Would you have
kept hope? Is there anything you wish she would have done differently?

Just like Melony, we all have the capacity to help our organizations be honest about what they are or aren't. Fewer challenges demand hope more than the decision to be an honest organization or an honest person. When we declare a promised identity, whether to our organizations or to ourselves, we ignite hope. We fuel a greater sense of purpose. But we must be truthful about who we are and aren't. And we have to level the playing field so everyone has a fair shot at contributing to the best of their ability.

When we are honest, our sense of purpose is amplified. Every one of us wants to feel like we matter—that our contributions are making a difference, and that we are being true to who we aspire to become. When there is a disconnect between what we say and do, we need hope that we can close the gap. This is true when our organizations promise to be more inclusive, more socially responsible, or more cost-effective. And this is true when we tell ourselves we want to become better leaders, accomplished authors, or successful entrepreneurs. It was certainly true when Jaime Góngora set out to turn former FARC guerrillas into citizen environmentalists.

When it comes to honesty, closing the gap between right and wrong is the simpler journey. It requires a solid moral compass and a reasonable level of resolve. But closing the gap between right and great demands solid doses of hope and organizational grit. By the end of our time together, my hope is to have shown you why that journey is so worth it.

Get Busy: Know Your Honesty Story

Establishing a foundational commitment to honesty is key before you can excel at the four dimensions of organizational honesty described in this book. You may be thinking, "*Well of course I'm committed to honesty. I'm here, aren't I?*" But truth be told, most of us believe we're "honest enough," and that our organizations are "generally honest." Our capacity as human beings to self-justify the corners we cut is nothing short of masterful. So, getting honest about our honesty takes a little digging. For this chapter, I'm going to have you work on both your personal honesty and your organizational honesty. You can define "organization" at any level that works for your role—your team, your department, your division, or your whole enterprise. Find someplace quiet, pull up your honesty notebook (whether it's a device or something more old-school that requires a pen), pour your favorite beverage, and let's get to work.

Your Honesty Story

1 What are the earliest memories you have about honesty? Who was in the story? What did you learn? (It could be a parent telling you about telling the truth or catching you in your first fib; or feeling a sense of betrayal after someone lied to you; or… you get the idea.) As you look back, what impact can you see these stories having on you?

2 What situations draw you to be dishonest (distort or withhold truthful information; act in self-serving ways; ignore when others are disadvantaged; etc.)? What is it about these situations that you find unsettling that leads to your choices? What might you fear or be avoiding? Are there times you resist being dishonest? Have you ever gone back and apologized for your choices?

3 What situations prompt you to be your most honest self (telling the truth even when it's hard; doing the right thing, especially when something is unfair; putting the greater good over your own interests; etc.)? How do you feel when you act this way? What is it about these situations that draws out your strongest honesty?

4 If someone anonymously polled 10 of your closest friends and colleagues and asked them about your honesty, what do you think they would say? How confident are you? (Bonus assignment: approach 10 of your closest friends and colleagues and ask them, even if anonymously, to tell you when they feel you are at your most "honest" [exhibiting truth, justice, and purpose] and when you aren't.)

5 Where in your life have you seen honesty as a redeeming force? Was there a struggle during which truth, justice, and purpose helped change the course of an otherwise unpleasant outcome?

6 What circumstances cause you to lose hope? How do you regain it? To whom could you be a source of hope in your life right now?

Your Organization's Honesty Story

1 Outside of your annually required ethics training, how often do you and your colleagues/team talk about honesty? Do you discuss examples of when it is exhibited and celebrate them? Examples of when there is a breach?

2 When do you feel most proud of your company's behavior? When do you feel least proud or ashamed of it? Is honesty related to either scenario? What determines if your company chooses to be honest or not?

3 Think about the last time there was a major problem that challenged your organization. How did you navigate the honesty aspects of it? What guided your decisions (e.g., values or self-preservation? Transparency or "need-to-know" information sharing? Humility or hubris?)? In hindsight, what would you do differently?

4 Who on your team struggles to have hope in your organization? In you? What factors are making hope difficult to come by these days? What does this person/do these people need from you, or each other, to restore hope?

Honesty Conversations

1 The next time you are at a social gathering among friends, strike up a conversation about honesty. Ask those you're with how they can tell when someone is honest and when someone isn't. Share with each other what determines when you are honest or not.

2 Play "What Would You Do?". In the spirit of the ABC reality TV show, which places people in public, but contrived, situations where they have to speak up in the face of some moral or social dilemma, brainstorm scenarios that would challenge your honesty or require "dig deep" moments to tell the truth, do the right thing, and serve a greater good. Do this with your team or friends (it's actually a LOT of fun and generates amazing conversations).

3 Proudest moments: with your friends or colleagues, have each person share their proudest "honesty" moment—when they had to tell a hard truth, when they stood up for someone being treated unfairly or confronted an unjust policy or practice, or when they sacrificed to serve a greater good. Ask each person to share the story, how it made them feel, and why they felt proud. (Behavioral science has proven that when we talk about these moments, the neuropathways in our brain become stronger, reinforcing our, and others', commitment to honesty.)

Congratulations—you've completed your first workout at the "honesty gym"! Your honesty muscles are looking stronger than ever.

Now let's move on to the first of our four dimensions, honesty in identity—how you and your organization can align your words and actions to be who you say you are.

KEY TAKEAWAYS

- When we declare a promised identity, to our organizations and to ourselves, we ignite hope. We fuel a greater sense of purpose. However, we have to be truthful about who we are and aren't.

- People show up to work hungry to make a difference and believing they can, and honest companies which create the opportunity to do so through truthful, just, and purposeful actions far outperform those that don't.

- Our brains are hardwired to be honest, but when exposed to dishonest behavior over time, our ethical standards become desensitized (loosened). Even when we don't intend to do so.

- It's not enough to be truthful. You need to be seen as well-meaning (justice) and concerned for something beyond your own gain (purpose).

- The journey toward total honesty demands solid doses of hope and organizational grit.

- Behavioral science has proven that when we talk about these moments, the neuropathways in our brain become stronger, reinforcing our, and others', commitment to honesty.

- You need to fully commit to foundational integrity of honesty before you can engage in the four dimensions of organizational honesty that follow. "Honest enough" won't cut it.

Endnotes

1 Mapping Militant Organizations (2019) Las Fuerzas Armadas Revolucionarias de Colombia (FARC) [Revolutionary Armed Forces of Colombia], https://stanford.app.box.com/s/mnkv9b36d5z5qrhdv53wznskqr3crbfa (archived at https://perma.cc/3DET-5J9N)

2 Wikipedia Contributors (2020) Colombian conflict, *Wikipedia*, 3 August, https://en.wikipedia.org/wiki/Colombian_conflict (archived at https://perma.cc/HJN2-SYBR)

3 Joseph, J (2020) Former Colombian guerrillas turn into citizen scientists to protect the country's biodiversity, *Up Worthy*, 15 July, https://scoop.upworthy.com/former-columbian-guerrillas-turn-into-citizen-scientists-protect-country-biodiversity (archived at https://perma.cc/KZ5G-5MP6)

4 Ibid

5 Foerster, A, Pfister, R, Schmidts, C, Dignath, D, and Kunde, W (2013) Honesty saves time (and justifications). *Frontiers in Psychology*, https://www.frontiersin. org/articles/10.3389/fpsyg.2013.00473/full (archived at https://perma.cc/U2A6-GD3M)

6 Spence, S A, Farrow, T F, Herford, A E, Wilkinson, I D, Zheng, Y, and Woodruff, P W (2001) Behavioural and functional anatomical correlates of deception in humans, *NeuroReport*, https://doi.org/10.1097/00001756-200109170-00019 (archived at https://perma.cc/KC7G-S5P5)

7 Haran, U and Shalvi, S (2020) The implicit honesty premium: Why honest advice is more persuasive than highly informed advice, *Journal of Experimental Psychology*, https://doi.org/10.1037/xge0000677 (archived at https://perma.cc/W52L-L93L)

8 Morton, C and Lagrave, K (2020) 10 healthiest countries in the world, *Conde Nast Traveler*, 10 January, https://www.cntraveler.com/gallery/healthiest-countries-in-the-world (archived at https://perma.cc/WJ5X-HGMH); Morris, L and Blumenthal, B (2018) The reinvention of Jerusalem, *Conde Nast Traveler*, 29 March, https://www.cntraveler.com/story/the-reinvention-of-jerusalem (archived at https://perma.cc/MS7K-RPEG); Miller, L J and Lu, W (2019) These are the world's healthiest nations, *Bloomberg*, 24 February, https://www. bloomberg.com/news/articles/2019-02-24/spain-tops-italy-as-world-s-healthiest-nation-while-u-s-slips (archived at https://perma.cc/Y5U4-Q4XY)

9 Chen, S (2019) Chinese score lowest in European–American research team's 'honesty' study—but method may be flawed, *South China Morning Post*, 21 June, https://www.scmp.com/news/china/society/article/3015280/chinese-score-lowest-european-american-research-teams-honesty (archived at https://perma. cc/W4BY-8DM2); Cohn, A, Marechal, M A, Tannenbaum D, and Zund C L (2019) Civic honesty around the globe, *Science*, https://science.sciencemag.org/content/365/6448/70 (archived at https://perma.cc/34GF-YGFC)

10 Garrett, N, Lazzaro, S C, Ariely, D, and Sharot, T (2016) The brain adapts to dishonesty, *Nature Neuroscience*, https://doi.org/10.1038/nn.4426 (archived at https://perma.cc/FE62-7CCH)

11 Long, J, Roark, C, and Theofilou, B (2018) Using competitive agility index to measure trust in business, https://www.accenture.com/_acnmedia/Thought-Leadership-Assets/PDF/Accenture-Competitive-Agility-Index.pdf#zoom=50 (archived at https://perma.cc/4MHS-8NR3)

12 Ibid

13 Ibid

14 Edelman (2020) Edelman Trust Barometer 2020, https://cdn2.hubspot.net/hubfs/440941/Trust%20Barometer%202020/2020%20Edelman%20Trust%20Barometer%20Global%20Report.pdf?utm_campaign=Global:%20Trust%20Barometer%202020&utm_source=Website (archived at https://perma.cc/V7X7-3X4S)

15 Pressly, L (2017) Resignation syndrome: Sweden's mystery illness, *BBC*, 26 October, https://www.bbc.com/news/magazine-41748485 (archived at https://perma.cc/MU9K-ZD9P)

16 Schager, N (2019) The refugee kids entering comas as they face deportation, *Daily Beast*, 14 June, https://www.thedailybeast.com/netflixs-life-overtakes-me-and-resignation-syndrome-refugee-kids-entering-comas-as-they-face-deportation?ref=scroll (archived at https://perma.cc/N2YZ-6WWT)

17 Sallin, K, Lagercrantz, H, Evers, K, Engström, I, Hjern, A, and Petrovic, P (2016) Resignation syndrome: Catatonia? Culture-bound? *Frontiers in Behavioral Neuroscience*, https://doi.org/10.3389/fnbeh.2016.00007 (archived at https://perma.cc/9KND-YRRV)

18 Harter, J (2020) 4 factors driving record-high employee engagement in U.S., *Gallup*, https://www.gallup.com/workplace/284180/factors-driving-record-high-employee-engagement.aspx (archived at https://perma.cc/L492-NXF2)

19 DeSilver, D (2019) 10 facts about American workers. Fact Tank, 29 August, https://www.pewresearch.org/fact-tank/2019/08/29/facts-about-american-workers/ (archived at https://perma.cc/S9DJ-28ZZ)

20 Peterson, S J and Byron, K (2008) Exploring the role of hope in job performance: Results from four studies, *Journal of Organizational Behavior*, https://doi.org/10.1002/job.492 (archived at https://perma.cc/5CM6-6CCL)

21 Ambrose, M L, Seabright, M A, and Schminke, M (2002) Sabotage in the workplace: The role of organizational injustice, *Organizational Behavior and Human Decision Processes*, https://doi.org/10.1016/s0749-5978(02)00037-7 (archived at https://perma.cc/ECW6-7FMX)

PART ONE

Honesty in Identity

02

Be Who You Say You Are

Set your intention: How do my company's values and mission shape my daily choices?

Hope From a Bigger Story

In 2007, Marin Alsop was appointed to lead the acclaimed Baltimore Symphony Orchestra (BSO), becoming the first woman in the United States to ever be appointed to lead a major American orchestra. This wasn't her only trailblazing feat, however. Two years earlier, she became the first conductor ever to receive a MacArthur Fellowship, commonly known as "the MacArthur genius grant," awarded to those who have demonstrated uncommon originality and creativity in their field.[1]

Alsop grew up the child of musicians in NYC and studied violin at the Juilliard School. When she was young, she was told she could not be a conductor because "only men" were. But given how transformative music had been in her life, and the sense of confidence and possibility it had instilled, she learned early on to interpret "you can't" as "I must"—not as an act of defiance, but as an invitation to possibility. Her successes drove her to work for the democratization of quality musical training, making it accessible to children from all walks of life, not just to those with privilege.

When Alsop arrived in Baltimore, she was quickly struck by the wide range of socioeconomic issues plaguing underserved communities in the city—crime, poverty, drugs, and lack of access to opportunity. Alsop decided that the BSO needed to step into the breach in some way. She had long been inspired by the work of maestro José Antonio Abreu, a Venezuelan conductor who began El Sistema in a poor barrio in Caracas back in 1975 with just 11 children in an underground parking garage. El Sistema is a publicly funded, volunteer-driven music education program whose motto is "Music for Social Change." El Sistema programs, now worldwide, provide free classical music education that promotes human opportunity and development for impoverished children. Abreu believed music could act as a force for social change, especially in the lives of children. "Music has to be recognized as an agent of social development in the highest sense because it transmits the highest values—solidarity, harmony, mutual compassion," he said in a book written about El Sistema, crediting it with the ability to "unite an entire community and express all emotions."[2]

Alsop's team flew to Caracas in 2007 to study El Sistema's approach, spending two weeks observing how the children in the barrios and regions of the Venezuelan countryside it drew from had been changed by playing music. They observed the power of consistency in the children's lives and the power in having a reliable place to belong. They saw children feeling proud to be part of an ensemble—a profound metaphor for community and leadership—and what it meant to rely on one another. They saw children whose lives might have otherwise felt meaningless filled with possibility.

Since Caracas faced some of the same plights Alsop found in Baltimore, she decided to be the first conductor to bring El Sistema's approach to the United States. "We're using music as a vehicle to create a future of possibility for these kids," she said in a BSO fundraiser video.[3] She felt so strongly about this mission, in fact, she chose to personally fund its start with $100,000 of her MacArthur Fellowship; inspired by her vision, other donors stepped in to help as well. Dan Trahey and Nick Skinner, music educators both hailing from Michigan, were hired to run the artistic, educational, administrative, and operational aspects of the program.

The first task was to find schools willing to partner with them. Early on, there were (not altogether unexpected) struggles to translate the El Sistema approach to fit the context of Baltimore and the United States. Cultural differences, like building rapport with parents and the rarity of extracurricular participation for kids from underserved neighborhoods, had to be accounted for. Plus, the predominantly Black and minority neighborhood wasn't immediately willing to give two white men from Michigan its trust just because they offered a free music program. "The first year was nothing like we thought," Skinner told me. "We had a lot to learn about how the community actually functioned, how they supported each other, and what it took to gain their trust." The families of West Baltimore looked at this and thought, "The system [has] failed me, and it failed my children. Why should I trust the system?"[4]

The first school Trahey and Skinner approached was Harriet Tubman elementary school in West Baltimore. The school was terribly run down, with broken glass in the sandbox and graffiti on the walls. "It's going to be very difficult to get kids to take pride in their education if they can't take pride in where they receive it," says Skinner. As a good-faith gesture, the BSO sponsored a community-wide beautification program with members of the BSO and the community coming together to paint, repair, and clean up the school inside and out.

In September of 2008, OrchKids was officially launched with 30 first graders. It didn't take long for another challenge to present itself: four months into the program, the Baltimore city public school system announced that Tubman was slated to be closed at the end of the school year, and students would be moved to one of four other elementary schools. To ensure the program's continuity for a second year, Trahey and Skinner had to convince the Baltimore city public school system to transfer the 30 program participants to the same school—along with their siblings and other relatives. "It was a miracle but nearly all 30 students were relocated to the same school," says Skinner.

The first year had a steep learning curve for the small OrchKids team. Some parents used the after-school program as a babysitting service with free snacks, often failing to pick up their kids at the conclusion of the program. Educating the community on the importance of consistency, commitment, and discipline was critical. Eventually, though, they started to make progress. "When parents came to the school and saw every corner of it filled with music, and even more importantly, saw their own child playing a violin or a trumpet, their faces lit up," says Skinner. "They caught the vision. Their suspicions softened and they let their kids stay."

The program grew to meet kids' needs, much of them unrelated to music. It added meals, in-school music training in addition to the after-school program, tutoring for kids who were struggling academically, and an entire fabric of social engagement where kids felt safe, wanted, and hopeful. But that first year wasn't easy. "We did a lot of soul searching," says Skinner. "We questioned our purpose, and sometimes doubted we could succeed. But Marin never doubted. She remained committed to OrchKids staying a central part of the BSO's relationship to Baltimore." At the end of the first year, OrchKids hosted its first concert at which members of the BSO played alongside kids from the program. A packed gymnasium full of proud parents and community members were now certain that something special was happening in their community.

In the second year, volunteers came out of the woodwork to support the program. Interns from universities would come to study it. Older kids volunteered to tutor younger kids in math and reading. Parents volunteered to make snacks and meals and helped with the basic running of the program. The program grew from 30 to 120 children almost overnight.

One of those new kids was Keith Fleming, who joined OrchKids when he was in first grade. One of four children to a single mom, Keith struggled almost daily. He got into fights. He would kick chairs, cry and yell, and throw tantrums at OrchKids. "I could have just thrown him out of the program, but what message would that have sent him? That he doesn't matter? That would contradict everything OrchKids stands for," says Skinner. "When we have kids like Keith who struggle, we lean in. We mentor and get close to them. We help them feel like they belong. Marin's vision for OrchKids was precisely for kids like Keith; I knew if we stuck with him, he'd stick with us, and he'd make it."

Keith eventually decided he wanted to play the tuba. He liked it so much, in fact, that he played it all the way through high school—and beyond. During his time in OrchKids, he got to attend the Peabody Conservatory Preparatory, which is part of one of the country's most selective music schools, and play in prestigious music festivals such as Interlochen, Yola National, and the Alpine Brass Festival. In his later years, he began mentoring younger musicians. When he graduated high school, Keith received a substantial scholarship to the University of Miami to study music.

He credits OrchKids for helping him when he needed it most. "They showed me that through hard times, they always had my back, and I want to do that for other kids," says Fleming. "I want to start OrchKids programs around the world and help change kids' lives the way mine was changed."[5] Skinner says there are many stories like Keith's in OrchKids. "We go the extra hundred miles for each kid because we know they are worth it. I remember waiting around until 9.30 pm with a kid whose parents hadn't shown up to pick them up because that's how much we care."

Despite its affiliation with the BSO, an august institution, OrchKids caters to a broad taste in music. "We play everything from Beethoven to Beyoncé because this is about building great musicians, not just great technicians. They have to play music they love. Ultimately, our goal is to create great musicians and great members of society who see their futures with hope and possibility," says Alsop. "OrchKids isn't just a music program. It's about envisioning and realizing one's dreams. My dream is to see Baltimore represented by an orchestra of these kids and become known as the 'City of Music.'"[6]

Today, OrchKids serves over 2,000 K-12 students throughout the greater Baltimore area. They have a staff of 60 full- and part-time team members. It has also inspired similar programs throughout the United States.

What can OrchKids teach us about what it means to be who we say we are?

- It provides a model for how an organization embodied a stated purpose with concrete actions and hard work, not flowery words.
- It was formed amidst real need and started by a leader who saw the opportunity to meet it.
- It serves a good far beyond the cultural benefits of the Baltimore Symphony Orchestra—it is changing young people's lives.
- Its purpose felt so imperative that people clamored to be part of it; it created coalition out of a community.
- It brought together people of vastly diverse backgrounds to join forces, set aside their differences, and amplify their efforts.
- It helped create more just outcomes for those for whom life had not offered equitable opportunity.
- OrchKids' work has inspired many others to embody their purpose in new ways, and numerous cities have now adopted their model in the United States.

To Alsop, the BSO was meant to be so much more than just Baltimore's symphony. It is a force of transformational change for the city it serves; music is as much the means as it is the ends. She and the BSO staked a claim on who they intended to be and backed it up through tangible acts.

Closing the Say–Do Gap

My research revealed that when a company is strategically clear on who it is and where it's headed, and its actions match its words, people in the organization are *three times* more likely to tell the truth, act justly, and work purposefully. Clarity in your identity—being who you say you are—means that who you tell your employees and marketplace you are and who you *actually are*, meaning your actions match what you say, are completely consistent. It means that people in your organization are held accountable for embodying your stated values, and that the objectives you set cascade down through the organization so that every employee incorporates them into their job. When these things don't happen, the stage is set for dishonesty.

When a leader says that she wants her team to model the high value the company places on innovation by questioning the status quo, but then dismisses ideas her team offers in meetings, she signals that she doesn't really mean what says—*even if her intentions were genuine.* When an employee tells his boss he will commit to being more accountable after he's reprimanded for being unreliable, but then misses the next two deadlines, he's made an empty commitment. And when major strategic goals are set for an organization, a department, or a team, but remain disconnected from every employee's daily responsibilities, once again, the message is, "We proclaim commitments we don't really intend to keep."

Every day, companies announce new "strategic priorities" nobody believes are possible. Mission and vision statements are unveiled to privately rolling eyes. Slogans proclaiming, "We're going to be #1 in…" (fill in the blank) are trumpeted to cynical employees who have no idea what it means for them. And each time, leaders and their employees are inevitably forced to collude in a silent pact acknowledging *they will say one thing but will do quite another.* What if I told you it was ultimately easier, and a whole lot more beneficial long term, to simply do what you say you will? (Or relatedly, not make commitments you know you can't keep.)

Ironically, this may be less obvious than you think.

When organizations fail to do the work to *actually become* who they've said they are, their statements of mission and values are viewed as, well, nothing more than slogans. Worse, this normalizes duplicity, as everyone in the organization now has to pretend what's been declared is true when the evidence suggests otherwise. Tragically, this seems to be the standard in too many organizations. In a 2014 Australian study, conducted by Leading Teams, of more than 500 employees, only 20 percent of them found their missions and values to be inspiring, and nearly half didn't even know what they were.[7] One major study by the Gallup organization found that only 27 percent of employees believe their company's values and only 23 percent believe they could actually apply them to their jobs.[8] Another study conducted in 2013 across several major academic institutions including the University of Chicago and Northwestern University, in partnership with the Great Place to Work institute, found that there was strong correlation between the financial performance of the organization and the extent to which employees felt the organization practiced the values it espoused.[9] The implications are clear—if you're full of it, everyone will know it, and your organization will underperform.

Living the Words

Despite the common disconnect between their promises and actions, many companies are rapidly learning that embodying the purpose they claim, despite requiring a lot of hard work, has tremendous upsides. Consider market leaders like Seventh Generation, a cleaning and personal care products company whose purpose is "to inspire a consumer revolution that nurtures the health of the next seven generations,"[10] or Plum Organics, a leading childhood nutrition company, whose purpose states, "We deliver nourishing, organic food to our nation's little ones and raise awareness and advance solutions for childhood hunger and malnutrition in the United States."[11] India's Tata Steel company declares integrity, responsibility, and unity as core values, and has been widely recognized around the world for how its actions embody those commitments, most notably in the area of sustainability and ethics, winning international awards and being ranked on the Ethisphere Institute's most ethical companies for eight years.[12] Guatemala's Cementos Progreso, a cement production company, committed to environmental stewardship through innovation and to an inclusive global economy. They've backed up those commitments with tangible actions, have won awards for clean production innovations, and were the first Guatemalan company to adhere to the United Nations Global Compact, an initiative through which the United Nations calls on the world's companies to work together to achieve a common goal: a more sustainable and inclusive world economy.[13] These companies have put their money where their mouth is and are living out their purpose through their everyday actions.

Many companies have taken their commitment to living their words to a new level by becoming certified B Corporations, a rigorous evaluation process that requires a company to demonstrate commitment to its purpose through meeting verified standards of performance in creating value for all their stakeholders: communities, employees, customers, suppliers, and the environment. All of these certified B Corps, and thousands of other companies, have adopted what is called a benefit governance structure that expands their legal duty beyond just maximizing profits for shareholders to benefiting multiple stakeholders. Ryan Honeyman is the author of *The B Corps Handbook: How you can use business as a force for good,* and partner at LIFT Economy, itself a certified B Corps. In my interview with Ryan, he told me:

> The rigor it takes to become a certified B Corps, or to pass the requirements
> of earning the legal classification, signals to customers and employees that you
> are a company people can trust. That you put your money and resources where

your mouth is. Your purpose is more than just words. People love the idea of associating with brands like Patagonia, Ben & Jerry's, Allbirds and Danone, North America, knowing these brands are part of a community that's advancing the idea of using business to serve a greater good.

Honeyman went on to explain that many companies use the B Corps certification process to align their purpose to their actions even when they don't pursue final certification. He said, "Just the act of trying to meet the rigorous standards moves a company closer to putting real teeth behind their purpose."

Many established companies look at upstarts like those that become B Corps from their beginnings, that have purpose built into their DNA, and think, "Well, it's easy to start out with purpose, but what about large, complex corporations that never considered purpose when they were founded?"

Understandable question. Let's find out by looking at an organization that has proven it's possible to transform a large, legacy company into one that discovers its purpose and lives it out every day.

When Indra Nooyi took over as CEO of PepsiCo in 2006, the company's transformation was probably not anticipated by many people. As one of the world's largest soft drink and snack food companies, PepsiCo had a portfolio of products that was under attack for contributing to childhood obesity and diabetes. When people thought of companies committed to health and well-being, sustainability of people and planet, PepsiCo wasn't top of mind.

Nooyi announced early in her tenure that she would be changing things. She acknowledged that consumers had long been making their purchasing decisions based on the principles of the brands they consumed, and top talent was increasingly choosing employers who served a greater good in the world, not just whoever paid the best. She committed to shifting the organization's portfolio of products to more healthful choices, focusing on increasing access to clean water in the developing world, reducing PepsiCo's overall carbon footprint, and empowering women around the world in the communities they serve and in their workforce. She believed companies needed to do more than deliver exceptional financial returns—they needed to make a positive contribution to the lives of *all* the stakeholders they served. Nooyi introduced the concept of *Performance with Purpose* as a new trajectory for the company.

For Nooyi, the commitment was personal. Having grown up in the developing world, where access to clean water was a challenge, she watched people standing in long lines to collect and store it. She believed that for a leader's commitment to be authentic and not cosmetic, it needed to be personal.

Her opening moves signaled to the PepsiCo workforce, especially the skeptics, that she meant what she'd said. In 2007, for example, she appointed a new head of R&D and chief science officer, Mehmood Khan, an endocrinologist from the Mayo Clinic. Though the economic downturn began just the next year, Nooyi gave him all the resources she'd committed to help him build a global R&D powerhouse.

Khan hired more than just the usual food scientists one might expect at a food and beverage company; he also brought in molecular biologists, pharmacologists, and nutritionists, including many women, to ensure PepsiCo had the capability to overhaul their product portfolio. They soon saw a dramatic reduction in salt, sugar, and fat from many of their core products without a loss of taste. They added numerous healthy snack and beverage companies to their portfolio, including Naked Juice, Bubly sparkling water, and Kevita, a line of probiotic beverages. To their snack line-up they added healthier options like Health Warrior plant-based nutrition bars, Stacy's Pita chips, Bare Snacks fruit and vegetable snacks, and Off the Eaten Path veggie puffs. Not only that, but they shut down products in the pipeline, like one caffeine-enhanced snack, that risked belying their commitment to Performance with Purpose. When Cheetos got pulled from school menus for not meeting nutritional standards, they worked for two years to invent equipment that enabled them to introduce whole grains into their snack products.

As far as sustainability went, PepsiCo dramatically redesigned their packaging, replacing it with plant-based biodegradable materials, cut waste, invested in ways to reuse wastewater, and increased their use of renewable energy sources. Today, 100 percent of US PepsiCo facilities operate with renewable electricity, which accounts for more than half of its global electrical load. Eighty-eight percent of their packaging is composable, recyclable, or biodegradable, with the goal of 100 percent by 2025. They've invested nearly $40 million in programs to provide women with needed resources for workforce readiness and in programs that empower women in the food system and in the farming industry. They've also improved their water usage efficiency in areas with high water scarcity while delivering access to safe water to 44 million people in high-risk areas.[14]

To sustain the company's commitment using management processes like capital allocations, Nooyi required that every capital investment must get a sustainability sign-off. Performance with Purpose goals were set for everyone at PepsiCo, from the top of the organization all the way down to mid-level managers. Celebrations and awards were given to exemplary leaders who met or exceeded those goals, further reinforcing the company's long-term commitment to its purpose.

Nooyi believes that it's not enough for companies to simply give large amounts of money to worthy charitable causes. To do good in the world, companies need to *change the way they make money*. Her intention from the outset was clear—to set PepsiCo up to be purpose-driven long after her tenure as CEO was completed. She stepped down in 2018, after 12 years at the top, and in the time since, the company's commitment hasn't wavered.[15, 16, 17, 18]

Nooyi would be the first to admit that the journey to becoming a purpose-driven company is grueling. It takes unwavering commitment, hard choices, and the compelling conviction of top leaders to transform a company to one rooted in a larger purpose, especially a sprawling legacy company like PepsiCo. But what she proved is undeniable.

While transforming a global company to be more purpose-driven may be difficult, it is entirely possible.

And those that make the expedition are reaping the rewards. Brands that have a clear commitment to improving their consumers' quality of life outperform the stock market by 120 percent. Over the last decade, purpose-driven brands have seen their valuation skyrocket by 175 percent. In one study of 28 companies over a 17-year period, purpose-driven companies grew by 1,681 percent in comparison with the S&P 500 average over the same span, 118 percent.[19] Indeed, investors are increasingly migrating to ESG (Environmental, Sustainability, Governance) investment funds whose companies are assessed against rigorous criteria. And these funds also have outperformed the S&P 500, suggesting a strong correlation between stakeholder-driven commitment and shareholder-driven results.[20]

When Actions and Words Don't Match

In a complex and noisy world, one where disruptive change is a daily occurrence, achieving consistency is a tall order. Trustworthiness in organizations is hard to come by, which is why employees are hungrier for it than ever. According to the Edelman Trust Barometer, discussed in the previous chapter, 74 percent of respondents, citizens around the world from many walks of life and professions, say it's critical that the organization they work for includes them in strategic planning processes, gives them a voice in key decisions, and fosters cultures that are inclusive and consistent with their stated values. When organizations live up to these expectations, employees trust them. And when that happens, the results are indisputable: the Trust Barometer revealed that in organizations where employees trust their employers, 83 percent of employees are committed to doing great work, 74 percent are loyal to the organization, and 78 percent actively advocate for the organization. In contrast, when employees don't trust their organization, only 52 percent of them are committed to doing great work, 36 percent feel a sense of loyalty, and just 39 percent will advocate for the organization.[21]

Think about those implications for a minute. If you own or lead an organization, how would you feel if you were told only *half* of your people are committed to doing great work and only about a third feel loyal to you and would stick up for you given the chance? Sadly, too many organizations settle for the bare minimum from their employees, inevitably setting themselves up for getting their worst.

When an organization asserts its identity—what it aspires to do, who it intends to serve, and how it intends to operate—without doing everything to ensure its actions match its words, the outcomes can be disastrous. People want their company's mission and values to be sacrosanct. And when they aren't, the logical conclusion they draw is that the organization doesn't mean what it says—and behaving in ways that contradict the mission or values is perfectly acceptable.

Here's an example. The following comes from the Values Statement of a prominent US corporation, a onetime leader in its industry: "Customers can be better served when they have a relationship with a trusted provider that knows them well, provides reliable guidance, and can serve their full range of financial needs." The company declared that this promise was built on three foundational pillars: "Relationships that last a lifetime; expertise and guidance to help customers make confident decisions; and going the extra mile to do what's right." Sounds inspiring, right? After all, who *wouldn't* want to do business with such a principled organization?[22] Indeed, in 2015, the company was honored as the 22nd most admired company by *Fortune*, and the seventh most respected company by *Barron's*.[23]

This all sounds great until you learn we're talking about Wells Fargo. Just two years after its accolades in *Fortune* and *Barron's*, the company settled with federal regulators for $185 million for opening thousands of fraudulent customer accounts.[24] Despite the company's lofty statements, prosecutors found that more than 5,000 of the bank's employees, under the objective of improving cross-selling across their product lines, opened up fake checking, credit card, and other accounts for customers without their consent or knowledge.[25]

Wells Fargo's public statements of mission and values—their identity—were contradicted by a set of short-term objectives that led thousands of employees to act dishonestly. Did some of the employees try to blow the whistle? Yes. Some even quit. But thousands still participated. As a result, they must live with the consequences to their careers and consciences. The investigation conducted in the aftermath of the scandal pegged the top causes to be "a misalignment between stated and actual organizational vision and values" and "a high-pressure and cut-throat sales culture created by aggressive sales management, and performance management systems and unattainable incentive mechanisms."[26] So much for "going the extra mile to do what's right," which was in their mission statement.

From Purpose Washing to Purpose Activating

It's very common for chronic bad behavior, poor performance, or a scandal to provoke a renewed focus on things like mission or values. Mergers or acquisitions also commonly spark a rethink to create a fresh start for two combining companies. But statements of identity that aren't supported by actual efforts to change merely create an illusion of change.

Consider a company from my research that overhauled its values after a significant merger. The cultures of both organizations were very different, making integration much harder. One of the organizations, for example, had more formal processes for making decisions while the other relied on informal information channels. The more formal organization had a more "serious" feel to it while the other prided itself on having a "fun vibe." The one thing they did have in common was that they both had very "polite" cultures—that is, people were deferent to leaders, avoided conflict, and genuinely very helpful to one another. The downside was that they weren't bold in their sales activities, they didn't hold people accountable for underperforming, and took forever to make decisions because everyone waited for "someone in charge" to make them. So, the new values statement included well-meaning but vague language like "We hold each other accountable," "We challenge each other and the status quo," and "We take ownership." Not surprisingly, everyone felt these were "nice" values to have, but they ended up being cosmetic only, failing to provoke real changes in employee behavior. A year into the integration, employees from each company were still operating less cohesively, less accountably, and without any significant change in people's level of "ownership". Because the integration just bolted together legacy pieces from each organization and painted on a new identity over two old ones rather than doing the work to embed that new identity into the organization, people remained mostly confused about how exactly they should act.

Turns out, such cosmetic attempts to brush on the appearance of change have a name.

All too often, companies sidestep the hard work of real change and reach for a seemingly "easy" solution: purpose washing. Some are genuinely lost, with little idea how to articulate and become their best selves, while others are making a deliberate choice to merely campaign for their stakeholders. Their goal is to claim the benefits of being a genuinely purpose-driven company and/or cover up disreputable behavior while not actually making any substantive change. Across the world, marketers and corporate strategists are clamoring for ways to create the appearance of purpose and convince their markets they are committed to serving a greater good. Marketers are pulling every lever they can to put halos over their brands and companies, spinning a narrative of goodwill. Unfortunately for them, employees and consumers aren't buying it. While 84 percent of consumers consider trust when purchasing, only 34 percent actually trust the brands they buy from, and 53 percent believe brands are purpose washing, meaning they aren't as committed to a greater societal good as they claim.[27]

Purpose isn't something to which you can apply the mantra "fake it 'til you make it". You either mean what you say or you don't, and if you don't, people will see right through it. According to Edelman:

> Purpose defines an organization's authentic role and value in society that allows it to simultaneously grow its business and positively impact the world. It must be deeply embedded within the organization, the brand and the experience that is delivered.[28]

In my quest to learn how companies can work toward aligning their purpose with their actions, I spoke with John Rosling, CEO of the Contexis Group, a London-based global consulting and research firm dedicated to helping companies understand and measure purpose as a way to drive strategic growth. I wanted to talk about Contexis's work measuring the impact of purpose on an organization's performance. For the last five years, in partnership with the University of Cambridge and Plymouth University, Contexis, a certified B Corp, set out on an audacious quest: to prove the connection between purpose and performance. Rosling told me, "What is clear in the data is that having a purpose isn't sufficient. Your people won't *trust* your purpose until they see it *activated*. People may intellectually understand your purpose. But they won't believe it until the company's actions follow closely behind the words." It's clear that words matter; Contexis's comparison of companies that had no purpose at all vs. those that had one they failed to activate should be a wake-up call for anyone who doubts this. According to Rosling:

> What we found is that where companies say anything purposeful, it has
> almost no impact at all. Where they say something purposeful and then do
> the opposite, the situation becomes worse. You see higher levels of cynicism
> and disengagement. Employees can tolerate a company that is just driven by
> financial performance. They might prefer a company that is also driven to serve
> a greater purpose but they'll settle for one that just focuses on the bottom line
> if that's all they can get. But if you claim to serve a purpose that your actions
> deny, now you've lied to people. And once you've done that, you have lost their
> trust and turned their behavior toward their own interests.

Contexis's research has additionally shown that companies genuinely embodying the purpose they claim have higher levels of innovation, which is fueled by greater degrees of trust between employees and leaders, which in turn leads to higher levels of financial returns. Purpose-driven companies also spur more ownership over results because employees believe they have the autonomy to act in the interests of those the company serves. Conversely, the less a company's stated purpose aligns with its actions, the more distrust and cynicism (and reduced opportunity) reign.

In one financial services company Contexis worked with, efforts to better understand the gap between their purpose and their lack of results yielded astounding insights. The leaders who called in Contexis believed their issue to be one of communications—that despite having crafted a compelling purpose statement, they'd simply failed to properly communicate it down through the organization so that everyone clearly understood it. Rosling said, "What really mystified them was the more they talked about their purpose, the worse things appeared to get." Clearly, they assumed that *talking about* their purpose was synonymous with actually *living* their purpose. But all the talk was doing was sharpening the contrast for employees between words and actions.

On Contexis's Purpose Index, the instrument they use to measure the impact of a company's purpose on its performance, Rosling said he would have expected the division in the financial services company they were working with to score around a 70—an average score within the index. This division scored an 18, the lowest Contexis had ever seen. Within the group, the lowest-scoring employees were a very cynical group of long-term middle managers who had no trust in upper management's commitment to the company's stated purpose. These employees clearly *understood* the company's purpose statement. They just didn't *believe* it. Management hadn't failed at *communicating* it—they'd failed at *living* it.

Through a series of carefully facilitated conversations between middle and senior management where leaders disclosed some of their frustrations about management and their feelings of betrayal after watching friends and colleagues lose their jobs, middle managers began to *discover* the relevance of the purpose in their own lives. One manager became irate during a session, exclaiming, "Look, I'm getting really angry about all of this. I don't see any point. The reason I come to work is to protect my kids and put food on the table." And someone else in the session said, "Isn't making that possible what we do for our customers? Isn't the purpose of our bank ultimately to protect society and help everyone do that too?"

Over the course of just seven months, the division's revenues grew by more than 15 percent and trust dramatically increased. "They went from being ranked near the bottom of all the divisions in the company to being ranked near the top," said Rosling. People began personalizing the company's purpose in practical ways. For example, one credit manager said that when someone turned in a sloppy credit report, he would have simply returned it, denied it, or told the person to redo it, after demotivating them with harsh feedback. If this happens now, he simply asks the employee, "How does a shoddy credit report like this help us make life better for our customers?" Employees then *want to* redouble their efforts.

As this story shows, the gap between having and living a purpose is often one simple behavioral degree of separation. Here's another example, involving an executive I worked with; we'll call him Alex. When Alex and I first met, he expressed deep concerns about a market downturn that was creating severe cost pressures. When I asked how his team was dealing with the threat, he looked puzzled. He said, "Well, they don't *know* how bad it is, because if I alarm them, they'll panic and the best ones will bail."

Now *I* was puzzled. "But one of your core values is transparency. Why wouldn't you engage them to rally the best ideas and strongest commitment to making sure you can weather the storm?"

His response was telling: "Well, transparency doesn't mean telling people *everything* does it? Isn't it better to withhold some information if sharing it would lead to chaos?" I reminded him that the inherent promise behind the value of transparency was trust—that he would *trust* people with information. Even *unpleasant* information. He wasn't trying to be deceitful. He genuinely believed he was living up to the promise of that value and hadn't considered the horrible consequences of what could happen when people found out how long he'd withheld the fact that the company was in trouble. So he decided on a do-over. He chose to share the company's financial challenges with his team, and in a way that genuinely appealed to their sense of commitment. Working together, they found ways to substantially trim costs without any job losses—solutions he would have never found on his own. It wasn't enough for him to *genuinely mean* to be transparent. It meant *becoming transparent*, especially when it was hard and things felt precarious.

WALK IN THEIR SHOES

If you had been in Alex's position, how transparent do you think you would have been? If you had been on Alex's team, what would you have wanted him to do differently?

Misalignment: Take It Personally

When a company genuinely recognizes its failure to live up to its identity, it should acknowledge that failure with honest humility and resolve to change. Similarly, when you recognize that your own actions and words haven't aligned with your own, or the company's, purpose and values, go out of your way to reconcile them. My client Alex, above, offers a positive example of course correcting. Once he realized his actions didn't match the value of transparency he espoused, he wanted to do the right thing for his organization; he just needed help learning how to align his choices with his values. But without self-honesty, leaders feel compelled to simply *appear* resolute. Instead of amending their actions, they amend the mission or values in a reactive way by writing down good behaviors that sound corrective of the bad behaviors they want to eliminate. "Urgency" suddenly becomes part of a mission when time to market takes longer than the rest of the industry and pressure from the board is mounting. "Transparency" becomes a value when there's been a cover-up. "Diversity and inclusion" becomes a priority after too many discrimination lawsuits.

When a new statement of identity is created with the unspoken intention of fixing the people asked to embrace it, you can bet embracing it is the *last* thing that happens. As was the case with the merged companies discussed above, using new statements of identity this way ends up shielding an organization *from* honesty. Like great magicians who use sleight-of-hand deflection to trick audiences, campaigns touting new identities arouse the illusion of commitment to change while the real sources of bad behavior remain lurking in the background. This is true for both individuals and organizations. When we know, consciously or subconsciously, that our actions and words don't match, our resulting shame triggers the universal need to keep up appearances: to hide. But trying to cover up our hypocrisy is similar to putting a blanket over a pile of rotting food. Eventually the foul odor permeates. As leaders and organizations, we need to value authenticity more than we value the illusion of it. And that means when we find a gap between who we say we are and what we do, we need to expose it and deal with it.

Talk Isn't Cheap

Not all gaps between a company's stated identity and actions are as egregious as Wells Fargo's were. They don't make headlines, they don't result in criminal charges, and they don't destroy the organization's reputation (though they may certainly damage it). But everyday choices like exaggerating results, "forgetting" to invite an organizational nemesis to a critical meeting, omitting important facts in a report, or taking credit for another's work, and the rationalizations we concoct to justify them, are just as toxic. And sadly, more prevalent than we want to believe. See if any of this next story sounds familiar. My hunch is that it will be for more than a few of you.

In 2015, the newly appointed CEO of a $16 billion US global consumer products company who we'll call Blake reached out to me to ask for help. "I feel like every day I come to work to referee another knife fight or street brawl. Short of firing everyone, I'm out of options for how to rehumanize this place," he explained. The company's portfolio of home care products was underperforming across the board as consumers had new and better choices. Much of this was due to self-inflicted wounds; three years earlier, out of desperation, the previous regime had adopted the then-admired Jack Welch-ian approach to competitive focus, declaring they would be either #1 or #2 in their markets across their portfolio. Unfortunately, the definition of what #1 or #2 meant was left painfully unclear. The more people tried to protect their careers by meeting this ambiguous aspiration, the more self-involved they became.

While the company's identity grew increasingly unclear, the environment eventually became so internally competitive that the worst form of dishonesty took hold, and sabotaging fellow employees became routine. Misreporting of a rival's performance, withholding information that colleagues needed to solve problems, and making outlandishly false allegations of misconduct were common weapons of choice. To avoid career suicide, divisional leaders resorted to aggressive means to achieve competitive superiority, or at least the appearance of it. Leaders were contorting data in creative ways to stake their claims as #1 or #2. The resulting environment became cutthroat. If a finance director didn't like a divisional leader, his weekly sales and revenue report could mysteriously be a day or two late. If a brand marketer learned that a colleague in charge of a different brand was launching a new creative campaign, she might call the agency working on it with an "emergency project" to delay her colleague's launch.

To stem the hostile tide, Blake's predecessors established new operating principles to try to shape a more collaborative, respectful environment: "We succeed together"; "We value our differences"; "We put others first"; "We operate with the utmost of integrity"; and "We build partnerships across the organization." The entire campaign was branded with breathtaking creativity. Hallways in every building had stories of people "living the principles" and screensavers that said "I'm Principled" flashed across sleeping computers. The usual swag of t-shirts, ball caps, and, for the especially privileged, leather backpacks, all proudly bearing the campaign's logo, was everywhere. Senior leaders facilitated workshops to discuss the importance of the principles.

But underneath the largely cosmetic campaign still lurked a toxic culture of extreme individuality and competitiveness. After one business review, Blake said to me, "They've learned to use the words, now we need to get them to live by them. I don't believe half of what I just heard in those business reviews, and I know they don't either." Why not? Because the way the organization planned and budgeted didn't change in a way that encouraged sharing resources. This made "partnerships" almost impossible to form. Nor were accountability systems changed to encourage and reward new behaviors. That meant "we succeed together" was still going to mean "I will succeed even if you don't." Leaders weren't expected to adopt behaviors like self-awareness and empathy. Without these, "valuing differences" was a pipe dream. The inevitable consequence was that old toxic behaviors simply took on new forms. Leaders quickly learned that if you wanted to sabotage a colleague now, all you had to say was, "I really don't feel like she lives the principles," usually delivered with blustery indignation for effect to *really* ostracize her. Instead of shaping healthier behavior, the new principles became weaponized, subversively perpetuating old behavior. Blake's story offers a sobering look at what happens when you unveil new promises without doing the hard work to change an organization so those promises can be kept. I can't count the number of times I've been asked to help define new missions or values for an organization that had no intention of doing more than putting them on a colorful poster.

Fortunately, this story has a happy ending. Blake found the courage to acknowledge the complicated situation and decided he wasn't afraid of the long journey and hard decisions ahead. He did the hard work all leaders must do if they are committed to becoming who they say they want to be. He removed senior leaders who were unable to lead in a more collaborative, unified way. He designed a new organization, beginning with an honest assessment of its competitive positions, and set realistic goals for its future. He included many voices in the process of transforming the company, taking a transparent and holistic approach. Cross-functional teams spent months working through the best alternatives to organizing the company to deliver the new strategy. They designed every function and region of the company to make sure it had a clearly defined purpose, simple metrics to track performance, and clarity about the boundaries of their decision-making authority. They focused especially on ensuring every employee's behavior was aligned with what the company was trying to do and the principles by which they said they would operate.

Blake incorporated accountability for living the company's stated promises into the company's selection, rewards, assessment, and career advancement processes. He made it part of everyday conversations. He created a monthly town hall with the top 300 leaders of the company; in each one, he had to come prepared to answer the question, "What meaningful actions have you taken in the last month to advance our stated mission and values?" And he expected everyone in the town hall to have an answer as well—people knew that if he called on them, he expected an honest response.

This is what it looks like to *really* align a company's actions with its words.

From start to finish, the transformation took two and a half years. By the time it was over, Blake calculated that the price tag, which included the previous regime's failed attempts to change, lost market opportunities, unwanted talent defections and re-staffing costs, and Blake's investment in overhauling the company, was in the vicinity of $340 million. He also calculated that the company would have gone out of business within five years had he not completed the transformation. By no means was it perfect, but Blake was determined to hold the organization accountable for being who it said it was, and this was his best shot. When we reflected on the differences between using merely words to bring clarity to strategic identity vs. words *and* actions, Blake quipped, "Whoever said talk is cheap never had to transform a company that overvalued it."

WALK IN THEIR SHOES

If you worked in Blake's organization, how do you think you'd have supported, or not, his efforts? Is there anything he did you'd want to emulate? If you were coaching Blake, what might he have done differently?

Your work may not be as sweeping as Blake's. Perhaps you are focused on a small team or one department. Regardless of the extent to which you're looking to align your words and actions, the lesson from these stories is that you have to embed your promises into every aspect of your and your team's work if you want to make sure the promises are actually fulfilled by everyone's actions.

The great news is that small wins count. Our statistical models show that if you improve alignment between who you say you are and what you do by even 25 percent, you can increase employees' truth telling, just behavior, and purpose-driven actions by 10 percent. This isn't an all-or-nothing proposition. Incremental improvements across your entire organization will be tangibly felt and appreciated.

Get Busy: Be Who You Say You Are

Take Stock of How Well You Are Keeping Your Promises

Dissect your company's various statements (vision, purpose, mission, brand, values, etc.) and identify the implied promises to yourself, colleagues, employees, and customers. What commitments are being honored? If you say you value inclusion and respect, evaluate how your employees would grade you on these metrics. How diverse is your workplace? How is that measured? What should your customers experience? If you say you want to inspire people to reach their full potential, how often do you mentor others? How much do you invest in people's development?

Here's a simple tool you can use to evaluate how well you and your team are living up to the standards your company has proclaimed. For *each* of your company's statements—your purpose or mission—as well as *each* of your stated values, answer the following questions:

1 What does this statement mean to me personally?

2 How do I intentionally try to live by it in my daily work or leadership?

3 How does my team try to live by it together in our daily work? (Another way to think about this is, "How often do we actually talk about this?")

4 Where have we shined in living out this statement?

5 Where have we fallen short?

6 What's one thing we could do to more consistently embody this statement?

Incorporate Your Commitments into Daily Practices

Use these statements to form the basis of how you set priorities, invest resources, and guide meetings. Set aside time to talk with your team and colleagues about where you are being true to these commitments, and where you could improve. Use the list of promises you identified in the step above to appraise your calendar and see if you're dedicating enough time to ensure that the promises are kept. How confident are you that those you work most closely with see you as an example, and not a contradiction, of the promises your organization has made? What do you base your conclusion on?

Cascade Commitments Through the Organization

To be sure that every employee understands how their work contributes to the organization's most important objectives, make sure that those objectives are carefully translated down through every level, to every employee, in a systematic way. Be certain every individual and team goal is directly relevant to the broader organizational strategy it serves. If you can't make a clear connection, change their goals so you can.

Get Feedback

Use a basic survey feedback tool to ask others around you to assess the degree to which they see you, your team, or your whole organization living up to the statements of identity. Allow them to rate you against each of the promises you identified. You can use a simple tool like SurveyMonkey or Qualtrics to turn your identified promises into assessment items others in your organization can evaluate. For example, if one of your promises is "valuing creativity," you might assess this by asking respondents to rate a statement like "Our organization/my leader supports new ideas from a variety of places."

Take Responsibility for Gaps

If you've identified places where you have not been true to who you've claimed to be, or your organization has not been true to who it's claimed to be, it's likely others have borne the consequences of the gap. If you say you value empowerment, but you're still involved in making decisions you shouldn't be making, ask your team to help shift decision-making rights that should be theirs away from you. If your mission or purpose infers that you are serving a specific set of stakeholders (patients, families, women, children, etc.) but you never talk about how your work impacts those stakeholders, add a standing segment to your meeting agenda where you solicit stories of helping them, or even invite one of them in as a guest to speak. If your team has let down key internal stakeholders who rely on them for critical work, make amends and apologize where needed. Make a commitment to closing the gaps, and ask others to hold you accountable for doing so.

Have the Hard Conversations

No company is perfect, and your honest assessment will inevitably reveal problematic gaps, some of which are outside your control. You could choose to conclude, "Well, I can only control what I can." Or you could muster the courage and engage executive peers, or even leaders more senior than you, in hard conversations about contradictions and hypocrisies they likely notice as well. You don't have to be harsh or judgmental. Be empathic and curious, assuming that nobody is intentionally trying to be hypocritical. Your courage to at least start the conversation everyone is probably thinking about but avoiding could be the catalyst that sets change in motion.

Identify a Greater Good to Serve

If your organization hasn't formally declared a purpose-driven cause to be part of its mission, that doesn't mean you can't do so for your team. Whether you are an accounting team or a geographical division of a technology company, you can "zoom out" and identify a reason for your organization to get out of bed in the morning eager to make a difference. Don't think cosmetically, or you may run the risk of purpose washing. Rather, think deeply about how the organization you lead or are part of is enriching the lives of others—whether customers outside the organization or stakeholders inside of it. Create the compelling reason for you and your team to contribute your best work—for the good of someone else.

Dream Big

Think about what would happen if everyone in your organization *actually believed* that the things you claim about your company were sacred and true. And because they did, they came to work every day passionate about personally embodying those claims. What would that look like? What would be different from today? How would it feel to work at such a place? How does it feel *not* to?

Defining *and embodying* your organization's strategic identity takes courage, self-honesty, and perseverance. The decision not to, or to simply assume things "are close enough," is a decision to risk being the headline story in your worst nightmare. While I'm not a fan of justifying this work as a form of "scandal avoidance," any sort of motivation is better than leaving things to chance. But setting out to be who you say you are because you *want* to be seen as an organization of integrity, a company where actions and words align, is the ideal reason to make changes. It may well be the hardest thing you ever do, but I can promise you fewer things in your professional (or personal) life will be more rewarding or transformative.

Ok, now let's make this conversation *really* personal: let's talk about *your purpose.*

KEY TAKEAWAYS

- It is not enough for an organization to have mission, vision, and values statements, however masterfully written. An organization's purpose must be easily observable in the everyday actions of its employees.

- Your people won't *trust* your purpose until they see it *activated.*

- The marketplace can handsomely reward being honest about who you are as a company; purpose-driven companies financially outperform their competition by means of trusting, motivated employees who produce innovative solutions.

- The marketplace, and employees, are growing increasingly intolerant of hypocrisy. When words and actions don't match, performance and engagement will suffer.

- "Purpose washing" doesn't produce results and may even exacerbate existing problems. A recommitment to purpose needs to be supported by structural changes like new incentive programs, performance evaluation criteria, selection processes, etc.

- The great news is that small wins count. This isn't an all-or-nothing proposition. Small improvements can lead to stronger levels of honesty.

- To align words and actions, create rituals and practices in which you and your team talk directly about how you can improve, where you are doing well, and where you are falling short.

Endnotes

1 Wikipedia Contributors (2020) Marin Alsop, Wikipedia, 07 August. https://en.wikipedia.org/wiki/Marin_Alsop (archived at https://perma.cc/8H95-Y96Z)

2 Tunstall, T (2012) *Changing Lives: Gustavo Dudamel, El Sistema, and the transformative power of music*, W. W. Norton & Company, Inc., New York

3 Baltimore Symphony Orchestra (2018) 10 years of OrchKids, https://www.youtube.com/watch?v=n8yaXHQEEzo (archived at https://perma.cc/98ZA-DNKN)

4 I had the privilege of interviewing Nick Skinner in September, 2020—all of his quotes are from that interview.

5 ICM Speakers (2017) Marin Alsop OrchKids Gala 2, https://www.youtube.com/watch?v=k-22Wm-McNg (archived at https://perma.cc/N5DM-N8HK)

6 Baltimore Symphony Orchestra (2018) 10 years of OrchKids, https://www.youtube.com/watch?v=n8yaXHQEEzo (archived at https://perma.cc/98ZA-DNKN)

7 Grime, K (2014) Australian organisations' mission statements fail to inspire their staff, Leading Teams, 24 September, https://www.leadingteams.net.au/mission-statements-values-study/ (archived at https://perma.cc/6XSS-UE2A)

8 Dvorkak, N and Nelson, B (2016) Few employees believe in their company's values, *Gallup Business Journal*, 16 September, https://news.gallup.com/businessjournal/195491/few-employees-believe-company-values.aspx (archived at https://perma.cc/29U8-4UF4)

9 Guiso, L, Sapienza, P, and Zingales, L (2014) The value of corporate culture, *Journal of Financial Economics*, http://economics.mit.edu/files/9721 (archived at https://perma.cc/57JY-CW62)

10 Seventh Generation (n.d.) Inside Seventh Generation, https://www. seventhgeneration.com/Inside-Seventh-Generation#:~:text=Our%20 mission%20is%20to%20inspire,we%20believe%20in%20future%20 generations (archived at https://perma.cc/ZP78-JGZT)

11 Plum Organics (n.d.) Plum, PBC? What's a public benefit corporation? https:// www.plumorganics.com/benefit-corp/#:~:text=Plum's%20public%20 benefit%20is%20to,malnutrition%20in%20the%20United% (archived at https://perma.cc/G3EK-RHC2)

12 Tata Steel (n.d.) Vision, mission & values, https://www.tatasteel.com/ corporate/our-organisation/vision-mission-values/ (archived at https://perma. cc/RZ9N-DW78)

13 Global Cement (2019) Environmental awards for Cementos Progreso, 16 August, https://www.globalcement.com/news/item/9737-environmental-awards-for-cementos-progreso (archived at https://perma.cc/3WLY-5C78)

14 PepsiCo (n.d.) 2019 Sustainability Report: Goals and progress, https://www. pepsico.com/sustainability/goals-and-progress (archived at https://perma.cc/ 8NE6-NMYL)

15 Ibid

16 Nooyi, I K and Govindarajan, V (2020) Becoming a better corporate citizen, *Harvard Business Review*, https://hbr.org/2020/03/becoming-a-better-corporate-citizen (archived at https://perma.cc/RK2L-T2CC)

17 Schawbel, D (2019) Indra Nooyi: Achieving both financial growth and purpose at PepsiCo, *Forbes*, 21 November, https://www.forbes.com/sites/ danschawbel/2017/11/21/indra-nooyi-achieving-both-financial-growth-and-purpose-at-pepsico/#78bcca5aeaa6 (archived at https://perma.cc/GLR5-XMNF)

18 Freeland, G (2020) Indra Nooyi's passions: People, performance & purpose at PepsiCo and beyond, *Forbes*, 24 February, https://www.forbes.com/sites/ grantfreeland/2020/02/24/indra-nooyis-passions-people-performance–purpose-at-pepsico-and-beyond/#2400e243457c (archived at https://perma.cc/C5ZH-2JNA)

19 Business of Purpose (n.d.) Statistics, https://www.businessofpurpose.com/ statistics (archived at https://perma.cc/J2QP-TNV6)

20 Whieldon, E, Copley, M, and Clark, R (2020) Major ESG investment funds outperforming S&P 500 during COVID-19, *S&P Global*, 13 April, https:// www.spglobal.com/marketintelligence/en/news-insights/latest-news-headlines/ major-esg-investment-funds-outperforming-s-p-500-during-covid-19-57965103 (archived at https://perma.cc/4Y72-HA2M)

21 Edelman (2019) 2019 Edelman Trust Barometer: Global Report, https://www. edelman.com/sites/g/files/aatuss191/files/2019-02/2019_Edelman_Trust_ Barometer_Global_Report.pdf (archived at https://perma.cc/UYG8-TT4C)

22 Premachandra, B and Filabi, A (2018) Under pressure: Wells Fargo, misconduct, leadership and culture, Ethical Systems, https://www. ethicalsystems.org/wp-content/uploads/2013/07/files_WellsFargoCaseStudy_ EthSystems_May2018FINAL.pdf (archived at https://perma.cc/J8G6-LCKF)

23 Ibid

24 Ibid

25 Ibid

26 Ibid

27 Edelman (2019) 2019 Edelman Trust Barometer: Global Report, https://www.
edelman.com/sites/g/files/aatuss191/files/2019-02/2019_Edelman_Trust_
Barometer_Global_Report.pdf (archived at https://perma.cc/BWH7-NNSH)

28 Ibid

03

Joining a Bigger Story: Connecting *My* Purpose to *Our* Purpose

Set your intention: How is my job a pathway to living out my purpose in the world?

Hope From a Bigger Story

In June 1987, Walter McMillian, a Black logger from Monroeville, Alabama, was convicted of murdering Ronda Morrison, a white 18-year-old dry-cleaning clerk. He was sentenced to death. At the time of the murder, McMillian was 11 miles away at a fish fry, in the company of dozens of witnesses who could vouch for his alibi. That didn't stop the Alabama criminal justice system from railroading him, however. In a shocking miscarriage of justice, McMillian was immediately sent to Homan State prison, Alabama's death row, to *await his trial*, as if a death sentence were a foregone conclusion. His trial began on August 15, 1988 and took just a day and a half. It had been moved from a county that was predominantly Black to one that was primarily White. He was found guilty of first-degree murder despite a gaping absence of evidence and coerced testimony from career criminals and sentenced to life in prison. When sentencing occurred, using the highly prejudicial and controversial "judicial override," the judge presiding over the case, Robert E. Lee Key, Jr., ignored the jury's sentencing recommendation of life in prison and sentenced McMillian to death.[1]

About four years prior to McMillian's arrest, Bryan Stevenson, a 23-year-old Black law school student at Harvard, was interning with the Southern Prisoners Defense Committee (SPDC), a non-profit organization formed to protect the civil rights of people of color and poor people. For his first assignment, he was sent to inform a prisoner on death row in Georgia named Henry that he was not at risk of execution within the next year because a date for his execution hadn't been set. Stevenson was extremely nervous and stammered when he spoke, as he assumed Henry would not be pleased that Stevenson's only news was that a date hadn't officially been set for his execution.

Henry, however, was struck with sheer joy. He'd been avoiding having his wife and children visit him in prison, fearing what it would be like to face them, knowing the date of his death had been scheduled. Now he felt free to see them.

At the time, Stevenson was deeply ambivalent about what he wanted to do with his life, and uncertain if he even wanted to become a lawyer. But his brief time working in Georgia representing Black men unjustly prosecuted and wrongfully convicted to death changed the course of his life.[2]

Stevenson grew up poor in rural Delaware and experienced segregation until the second grade. Even after the Civil Rights Act was passed, he experienced the same inequity and mistreatment the legislation was intended to end. Not only that, but he suffered deep personal tragedy. When he was 16, his grandfather was murdered in his Philadelphia home. His murderers were sentenced to life in prison.

His grandfather's murder proved to be a seminal moment in Stevenson's life, as he called on the deep principles of his faith to weather the heartache and loss. Stevenson later said in an interview with *People* magazine, "Because my grandfather was older, his murder seemed particularly cruel. But I came from a world where we valued redemption over revenge."[3]

And redemption is exactly what Stevenson has dedicated his entire life to.

In 1985, after graduating from Harvard, he moved to Atlanta to join the SPDC, now renamed the Southern Center for Human Rights, as a full-time attorney, and was assigned to run their Alabama operation. Stevenson discovered two crises in the state. First, it had the fastest-growing population of prisoners condemned to death in the country, with nearly 100 people on death row. Second, it had no public defender system. That meant an enormous number of prisoners, largely Black and poor, had no representation whatsoever while facing a death sentence that—as far as Stevenson could tell—could well have been wrongfully issued.

While Stevenson was visiting with multiple convicted, unrepresented prisoners, he crossed paths with McMillian. His emotional insistence of his innocence struck a nerve with Stevenson, and they began their long relationship and journey to exonerate McMillian. Between 1990 and 1993, the Alabama Court of Criminal Appeals denied four of McMillian's appeals despite substantial evidence of judicial misconduct on the part of prosecutors and no evidence of his guilt other than the falsely coerced testimony of convicted criminals.

Finally, in February 1993, on McMillian's fifth appeal, the Alabama courts ruled that the state had denied him due process and remanded his case for a new trial. The following week, Stevenson filed to dismiss all charges, and on March 2, 1993, McMillian was exonerated.

In 1989, Stevenson founded the Equal Justice Initiative (EJI) in Montgomery, Alabama, a non-profit organization that provides legal representation to people who have been illegally convicted, unfairly sentenced, or abused in state jails and prisons. Since then, McMillian's is just one of the many wrongful convictions the organization has helped overturn. Stevenson has argued and won many cases in the US Supreme Court, including a 2019 ruling protecting condemned prisoners who suffer from dementia. In 2012, he won a landmark ruling that banned mandatory sentences of life imprisonment without parole for all children aged 17 or younger. He and his team have won reversals, relief, or release from prison for more than 135 wrongly condemned prisoners on death row, and relief for hundreds of others who were unfairly sentenced or wrongly convicted.[4] Stevenson's work, and his relationship with McMillian, are chronicled in his bestselling book, *Just Mercy: A story of justice and redemption*, and inspired a 2019 major motion picture of the same name.

Stevenson believes that inequity underlies many wrongful convictions. He's stated numerous times, "Our criminal justice system treats you better if you're rich and guilty than if you're poor and innocent. Wealth, not culpability, shapes the outcomes." Additionally, for decades Stevenson has been shedding critical light on the violence the African American community has faced (and continues to face). This culminated with the opening in 2018 of the National Memorial for Peace and Justice, "The nation's first memorial dedicated to the legacy of enslaved Black people, people terrorized by lynching, African Americans humiliated by racial segregation and Jim Crow, and people of color burdened with contemporary presumptions of guilt and police violence."[5]

One of the most formative moments that shaped Stevenson's remarkable journey came at the end of his first meeting with Henry when he was still an intern. The guards abruptly ended it by shoving Henry, his body shackled, out of the cell where they met, Stevenson recalls in *Just Mercy*. He looked kindly at Stevenson and began singing a hymn they both sang as children in church. After the meeting, Stevenson reflected on the life-changing impact it had on him. He returned to Harvard with a newly discovered purpose:

I had come into the prison with such anxiety and fear about Henry's willingness to tolerate my inadequacy. I didn't expect him to be compassionate or generous. I had no right to expect anything from a condemned man on death row. Yet he gave me an astonishing measure of his humanity. In that moment, Henry altered something in my understanding of human potential, redemption, and hopefulness.

Developing the skills to quantify and deconstruct the discrimination and inequality I saw became urgent and meaningful. My short time on death row revealed that there was something missing in the way we treat people in our judicial system, that maybe we judge some people unfairly. The more I reflected on the experience, the more I recognized that I had been struggling my whole life with the question of how and why people are judged unfairly.[6]

Whenever people ask me who my heroes are, people whose lives and stories have profoundly impacted me, Bryan Stevenson is the first name I respond with. To me, his life is an inspired emblem of what living an honest life of purpose looks like. His dedication, perseverance, sacrifice, and suffering on behalf of others is an epic story I can only hope to emulate by even a small fraction. Equality and justice for the defenseless have remained the plumb line of his life for four decades.

Discovering Your Purpose

There's a famous quote, often misattributed to Mark Twain, that goes, "The two most important days of a person's life are the day they are born, and the day they find out why." This is a riff on the timeless existential question haunting most, of "Why am I here?" Sadly, many of us spend a lifetime searching for the answer.

I was fortunate to discover a deep sense of purpose relatively early in my career. Oddly, it was by choosing the wrong one. I began my profession in the performing arts and studied diligently in a prestigious school in New York City to cultivate my craft. Unlike many aspiring artists I was lucky to actually earn a living at it while studying. But while my friends expressed envy at my good fortune, I suffered silently with a gnawing sense of unease. Though I couldn't quite name it at the time, I was overcome by boredom. Doing the same performance eight times a week indefinitely was the dream of many of my friends, but to me, it felt like a life sentence of monotony. So, I decided to take a break from NYC and travel the world with a non-profit company that used the arts as a medium to educate. The vast array of material and audiences with whom we worked assured me I would never be bored. And the opportunity to live and travel all over the world early in my career felt like a once-in-a-lifetime privilege.

The organization had contracts with the US Military and State Department. In the mid-1980s, prior to Germany's reunification and the fall of the Iron Curtain, I found myself working in (West) Germany doing a program for a very disparate group that included both American and German military soldiers and officers, official State personnel, their families, and other civilians. The term "diversity and inclusion" didn't exist then, but if it had, it would have been included in the program name. It was being held in the chapel at Dachau, the former Nazi concentration camp. The multiple levels of painful irony—performing in a chapel, a place symbolizing love and compassion, inside a death camp, the very essence of hate, while conversing about tolerating differences—weren't lost on anyone in the room.

During the group discussion, a young American soldier, probably only a few years older than me, stood up, and with vulnerable courage expressed to the group, "I'm just so tired of being trained to hate." The room fell quiet. As the leader of the discussion, I was stunned. My first thought was, "How on earth did something we did up here make him think *that?*" We proceeded to process his feelings in an emotional and authentic discussion with the group.

I wanted to know more about this soldier, so after the program I asked him if he wanted to get a beer—we were near Munich and it was almost Oktoberfest, so that seemed like the logical thing to do. We spoke for hours about his experience fighting for his country, why he'd joined the military, what he was proud of, and where he struggled. I learned about his internal battle between his values and being trained to kill, feeling forced to see others as the enemy first, humans second. I was fascinated and endlessly curious about all that our program had provoked within him, and he was deeply grateful for the material we'd presented and the chance to talk about it with me. After we parted ways, my mind was ablaze with an entirely new view of my work. Like Bryan Stevenson after his first meeting with Henry when he was still in law school, I knew this conversation had changed the course of my life—I just didn't know how, at least not yet. All I could conclude was, "Telling great stories is interesting, but having the chance to engage others in *their own stories*, that was inspiring and lifegiving." And I knew I'd never get bored with it.

And for nearly 40 years, I never have.

All of us have formative moments that shape the trajectory of our lives. Bryan Stevenson's experiences in Georgia during law school certainly shaped his. Sometimes we can read and follow the signs, and other times we blast right past them. Self-help and business literature is teeming with formulas and templates for discovering your life's purpose. They infer that finding purpose is akin to following a difficult soufflé recipe—it's hard, but if you follow the instructions, it won't fall in. Nothing could be further from the truth. Finding your purpose, and then connecting it to the larger purpose of the organization you're a part of, is an ongoing pursuit. It's a messy process of trial and error. There are triumphs—moments of crystal clarity where you do your best work, feel proud, and make a difference for others using the gifts and talents you've worked hard to develop. And there are misfortunes— moments of heartbreaking failure, horrific bosses, endless struggles to cultivate skills you feel you'll never grasp, years trying to get someone to notice your passion and contribution while feeling invisible, and dark, lonely nights spent feeling inadequate, rudderless, and futile. That's all part of the journey toward finding and living our purpose.

It's all necessary. And if you want to live a gratifying life of meaning, it's all worth it.

But rest assured, your determination to live purposefully will get tested early, and often.

When Purpose Gets Tested

As the last few stragglers hustled into the conference room, now about 350 people full, the final session of *Taking It Personally: Learning to embrace our values* began. At the ripe old age of 29, I was part of the team tasked with redefining my company's culture. Every employee had been given a comprehensive guidebook on how these new values should shape our future behavior. As a company in the energy industry facing huge disruption, refocusing on values like teamwork and innovation was meant to spur us on to new ways of working together and successfully navigating change. My presentation was on how to use the guide.

During the Q&A session, as had been the case in previous sessions, an employee asked, "Do you honestly think this book is going to change how people behave? I mean, the people in the plants who don't act anything like this today—do you actually think they're going to give a crap?" My palms were sweating as I glanced down into the first row and saw the CEO and his team waiting to see how I responded. I desperately wanted him to jump up, grab the mic, and give the same compelling speech that he had given our team after we devised the values. "I intend to make these values a personal matter for every employee," he had said, and he did.

As I was about to speak, I flashed back to one of the most important moments of the entire project. During the year-long initiative, I became a father for the first time—right as we were coming up on a major deadline which I feared I might miss. The CEO called my home several days later. I assumed it was to ask about progress on the deadline. After I picked up the phone I nervously launched into a clumsy explanation of where things stood and when I'd get the work done. But before I got very far, he interrupted me with his characteristic chuckle, and said, "That's not why I'm calling, Ron. I just wanted to check to see how you, your wife, and son were doing. I'd heard there were some complications and I was concerned." In that moment he showed me a type of integrity I'd not seen in a leader before. He ended the call by telling me that he'd extended the deadline for my section by two weeks. Coincidentally, the section of the guidebook I was working on was about integrity. Its title? "Our actions match our words."

I was jolted out of the flashback by the glares of an impatient audience. I steeled myself and responded to the cynical employee's question: "Look, nobody believes this culture change is going to be easy. But we have to do it. If we want to be proud of our company again, if we want to learn to compete differently as our industry changes, we need to live by these values. And I believe that if we work together, we can all make it happen." I glanced down again, saw the CEO and his team smiling, and breathed a sigh of relief, knowing I'd "carried the flag" well. But deep inside, I knew there was a big problem.

I had just lied to 350 people. And they all knew it.

While the CEO was a good, principled man who genuinely believed in living by these values, the rest of his team did not. Some gave them lip service, while others mocked them behind his back. Furthermore, the rest of the organization was incapable of making this kind of change, and I knew it. There was significant division among the company's nine plants and its two headquarters locations. Our customer base and how we could best serve them had greatly shifted as our industry deregulated and environmental resistance mounted. And none of those fundamental challenges was being addressed by the changes I was involved in recommending. We were just rolling out a new set of values accompanied by a beautiful workbook on a glitzy road show tour. We'd spent more than a year of hard work defining the "dream culture" for our organization, and it wasn't going to make any meaningful difference.

Now you might be thinking, "Well none of that was your fault. It wasn't fair that you were put into that position. You didn't have control over those things. You answered the question as best as you could given the difficult circumstances you were put into." Some of that may be true. And it may partly *explain* why I lied to those people. But it doesn't *excuse* it.

Just a few months prior, I'd attended a workshop on "writing personal mission statements," prompted by my mentor, a woman who has deeply shaped the path of my life. I agreed to go because she'd urged me to but thought it was a waste of time and that writing personal mission statements was a New Age-y gimmick for weak people. My arrogance and immaturity were proven wrong. By the end of the workshop I had scratched out these words in the back of a notebook: "To be a great agent of change, and to help make other great agents of change." Without knowing it at the time, I'd etched out what would be the plumb line of my life for the next three decades. And in moments of career angst and at pivotal crossroads, that line has guided me with distinct clarity.

WALK IN MY SHOES

If you had been me, what would you have done? How would you have coached me? Anything I should have done differently?

Having stood up in front of a room full of people and belied my plumb line, I knew what I had to do. If I wanted to be true to my purpose, I could no longer work at that company—whose well-intended duplicity put me in a position where I chose dishonesty. I'd become a living example of a statistic I would later discover, in the research for this book: when a company's actions and words don't match, people are three times more likely to be dishonest and behave unfairly. I feared that if I'd compromised once, I would do it again if I didn't leave right away. So I left.

That moment revealed two fundamental, often warring needs we humans come hardwired with. First is our deep-seated need to *matter*. We want to know that our existence has significance. And second, when that need goes unmet, we default to indulging the other need: to *look like we matter*. Looking smart, put together, competent, and "good" to others becomes the need we pander to when the former isn't satisfied. And when you confuse one for the other, compromise becomes all too easy, and you have stepped onto that slippery slope.

And what happens when we don't back away from the slope? We slip.

What Fashion Knock-offs Reveal about Self-honesty

Acclaimed behavioral science researcher Dan Ariely set out to understand conditions under which people are likely to be dishonest, which he has devoted his career to learning about. In one experiment, which he described in his 2012 book *The (Honest) Truth About Dishonesty: How we lie to everyone—especially ourselves*, he convened three groups and then assigned each a task to complete—a mathematical matrix problem where they needed to find numbers that added up to 10 from among a grid of fractional numbers, like 1.82 or 2.63. During the task, one group was wearing knock-off fashion accessories and knew it, a second group was wearing genuine fashion accessories of the same high-end brands, and a third group was not told either way about the accessories they were wearing. The results were illuminating: those who knew they were wearing fake accessories reported achieving results from their assigned task that were 71 percent better than they actually were, whereas those wearing the bona fide accessories overreported their performance by only 30 percent. Those in the neutral group overreported by 42 percent.

Ariely's conclusion was that once people know they've behaved in a counterfeit way, moral constraints loosen, making it easier to continue down the path of dishonesty. He explained it this way:

> Social scientists call this self-signaling. The basic idea behind self-signaling is that despite what we tend to think, we don't have a very clear notion of who we are... we observe ourselves in the same way we observe and judge the actions of other people – inferring who we are and what we like from our actions."[7]

When people knowingly behave in duplicitous ways, they see themselves as dishonest. This then makes it much easier to make more dishonest choices when the opportunity arises. Things like sandbagging forecasts, minimizing mistakes, negotiating unfair deals with customers, and even more severe choices like taking bribes eventually just seem "okay."[8] Most people don't start out making such dishonest decisions. It takes time, and increasingly loose constraints, to get to that point.

In my interview with Ariely, he told me, "We have slippery slopes. We don't have slippery ascents. Once an environment has had dishonesty introduced, that new normal spreads." When employees witness contradictions between the values of their organizations and the day-to-day actions of their managers and peers, they naturally feel complicit in that deception. This feeling is intensified when workers knowingly act in ways that contradict not just the organization's values, but their own. For example, when customer service representatives are given rote scripts to repeat at angry customers, they feel their personal violation of the company's public promise of (good) service. We've all been on the other end of an infuriating customer service call and heard the insulting words, "I'm not authorized to solve that problem. I don't make the rules, I just have to follow them. Sorry, but that's our policy." It's hard to have compassion for the disempowered call-center representative when we're stuck with a defective product or poor service. But imagine what it must feel like for her, day in and day out, to say those words while staring at a poster that says, "Our customers are the most important part of our business and it's a privilege to serve them." When an organization proclaims to do one thing but does another, they are putting their people in the position of feeling like frauds. That's the slippery slope toward people *acting like* frauds. "You can take someone who is basically an honest person, put them into a system where the person running the system is corrupt, and they conform," Ariely told me. "They cheat more, and start stealing. It reveals the power of the situation and the context."

My own research bears this out. In one professional services firm I consulted with, interviewees told me stories about male senior executives routinely having affairs with women in the organization, who in turn received undeserved career advancements. The firm was extremely successful in its field, but internally, it was a disaster. One executive confided in me:

> We emphatically tell our clients that they can trust us. That the services they've come to rely on us for are the most honest, reliable analyses they can get anywhere in the industry. But I also know some divisions have gambled with that trust by fudging some of their analyses. If our clients knew what went on inside our organization, I doubt they'd still trust us. Everyone knows how you get ahead here. You either sleep your way to the top, or you subtly threaten to expose those who have. Heck, I got promoted last year just after I casually

mentioned to my boss that I'd seen the CEO leave the office late one night with my coworker. And I knew exactly what I was doing. Sure, I felt disgusting after I did it. But when the raise hit my paycheck, I got over it. I've crossed lines I swore I'd never cross. At some point, this whole thing is going to come crashing down around us.

Ariely calls what was happening here the "what the hell" effect. After a while, those who already feel complicit in deceit conclude, "What the hell, I'm already a cheat. I might as well get the most out of it that I can."

Duplicity sets the stage for further dishonesty because it leads to shame. Nobody likes feeling they are living a lie, and when we do, we feel inherent shame. Note the interviewee's statement above: "I felt disgusting after I did it… but I got over it." Plenty of behavioral research shows that when people feel shame, they are more likely to act shamefully. Cultivating an immovable sense of self-honesty—being true to your beliefs and principles—is vital when navigating environments that will test those beliefs and principles. The only context in which the allure of deceit will struggle to survive is one in which everyone believes their work matters and feels a proud sense of purpose about their contributions. In such an environment, dishonesty's charm offers little appeal.

So how do you create this environment for yourself and others?

Inviting Purpose to Thrive

When Satya Nadella took the helm as Microsoft's CEO in 2014, he inherited a divided, competitive culture of highly individualistic, disheartened employees. The company's stock had been largely flat for years, and Microsoft was losing competitive ground. As he walked onto the stage to make his opening address as CEO, he writes:

> I vividly remember looking into the eyes of hundreds of Microsoft employees in the audience waiting for my presentation, their faces reflecting hope, excitement, and energy mingled with anxiety and a touch of frustration. Like me, they'd come to Microsoft to change the world, but now were frustrated by our company's stalled growth. They were being wooed by competitors. Saddest of all, many felt the company was losing its soul.[9]

Nadella spent the better part of his first year listening deeply to many of Microsoft's 100,000+ employees all over the world. He heard their frustrations and their dreams. He heard what they believed needed to change, and what they hoped he would preserve. He challenged his senior leadership team to answer the following question:

> At the end of the next year if we were tried in a court of law and the charge was that we failed to pursue our mission, would there be enough evidence to convict us? Just saying interesting things wasn't enough. I, all of us, had to do them. Our employees had to see how everything we did reinforces our mission, ambitions, and culture. And then they needed to start doing the same.[10]

Notice his goal—not to just ensure that the company embodied its mission and purpose, but that employees did as well. In an all-company email, he rallied the organization in terms of "we":

> In order to accelerate our innovation, we must rediscover our soul—our unique core. We must all understand and embrace what only Microsoft can contribute to the world and how we can once again change the world. I consider the job before us to be bolder and more ambitious than anything we have ever done.[11]

Nadella knew that making this bold purpose personal to every employee would take intentional work. He understood that lofty goals are easy to see when you're the CEO, but when you're an engineer in Europe or a marketer in Asia, such ideals can feel distant and irrelevant. At the close of one of his speeches at Microsoft's global sales conference, he asked employees to "identify their innermost passions and to connect them in some way to our new mission and culture. In so doing we will transform our company and change the world." Many employees were wiping away tears when the presentation was over. At that moment, writes Nadella, "I knew then we were onto something."[12]

In 2019 I spoke with Kathleen Hogan, Microsoft's Chief People Officer and Nadella's partner in their culture change effort. She described an early offsite Nadella had with his team, during which they sat around casually on comfortable couches instead of around a conference table. During one conversation, Nadella asked them each to reverse the notion of working for Microsoft, and to instead consider that Microsoft *worked for them*. "How can Microsoft be a platform for you to live out your purpose in the world?" he asked. They each had to answer, sharing personal stories of how they hoped to impact the world using their technical abilities, their leadership roles, and the innovation of Microsoft. About that experience, Hogan told me how sustaining it is to feel your own purpose connected to the Microsoft mission. She notes that it's especially energizing during day-to-day challenges to step back and see the collective impact the company is making. She told me:

We're feeling like a united team more than ever. While strategy will evolve, your culture and sense of purpose should be long-lasting. Culture paired with a purpose-driven mission allows your employees to use your company platform to realize their own aspirations and passions.[13]

Microsoft's intentional effort to help employees (now more than 140,000 strong) connect their individual purpose to the company's collective purpose offers a roadmap for leaders wanting to do the same. The scale of the organization you lead doesn't matter; even on the smallest of teams doing the most menial of tasks, a sense of purpose can be ignited. It's simply a matter of inviting people to see their purpose reflected back in the work of the organization.

Consider an experiment conducted by Harvard Business School researchers in a cafeteria in 2016. In most cafeterias, the cooks who make the food and the diners who eat it don't interact. Associate Professor Ryan Buell wanted to test whether or not the cooks would behave differently if that anonymity was removed. As in any ordinary cafeteria, diners approached the grill station, placed their order, and the order was taken to the kitchen to be prepared. But as part of the experiment a video feed was set up between the grill station, where diners placed their orders, and an iPad in the kitchen, where the food was prepared. There was no sound, only video.

Buell and his team conducted the experiment three different ways. In the first experiment, the chefs could see the diners ordering; in the second, the diners could see the chefs; for the third experiment, each group could see one another.

When the chefs could see the diners they were preparing food for, there was an almost instant change. Suddenly they were no longer preparing foods like eggs in batches, but preparing them freshly, and more efficiently. The chefs reported greater levels of satisfaction, as did customers when they could see the kitchen, by almost 15 percent. With this change, the chefs' work felt more meaningful and fulfilling.[14]

As Buell's experiment shows, even routine tasks can help those performing them derive a sense of purpose when it's clear that those tasks matter to someone. Creating a direct line of sight between work and the greater purpose that work serves is critical for leaders to enable others to live out their own purpose through their jobs.

Does your team know how their work contributes to the greater good of those your organization serves? Can they "see" for whom and how their work has impact?

Because if neither you, nor they, have a line of sight to how they want to contribute, and how they actually do, you may be starving a fundamental hunger hardwired into us all.

Your Brain on Purpose

In his book, *Alive at Work: The neuroscience of helping your people love what they do,* Dan Cable describes the parts of our brain that naturally seek meaning. He explains:

> Our seeking systems create natural impulse to explore our worlds, learn about our environments, and extract meaning from our circumstances. When we follow the urges of our seeking system, it releases dopamine—a neurotransmitter linked to motivation and pleasure—that makes us want to explore more... When our seeking system is activated, we feel more motivated, purposeful, and zestful. We feel more alive.[15]

As humans, we're meaning-seeking machines. Our brains crave a sense of significance, and when we feel insignificant, our souls begin to shrivel. As I said in Chapter 1, disengagement is the resignation syndrome of organizations. And meaninglessness is the virus that causes disengagement. Our hunger for meaning is why, in the privacy of our bathrooms, we turn our hairbrushes into microphones and belt out the song streaming on our device. It's why we stand on our coffee tables during the Olympics and bend over as the imaginary gold medal is placed around our neck, our national anthem blaring as our flag is unfurled and tears stream down our faces. It's why, during the Academy Awards, we easily imagine our own acceptance speech. We are hardwired with the capacity to imagine our lives as something more. And the seeking systems of our brains drive us to pursue it.

Leaders would do well to understand just how important this is to those they lead. In LinkedIn's 2016 Global Report on Workplace Purpose, they found that 74 percent of LinkedIn members seeking employment place a high value on finding work that delivers on a sense of purpose.[16] A 2015 study from Spain's Universidad Católica de Valencia of more than 180 college students proved a direct correlation between a sense of meaning in life and psychological well-being. The more purpose one feels, the greater one's mental health.[17] The 2017 Great Places to Work Report states that employees who report that their job has a "special meaning" and that it "is not 'just a job'" are four times more likely to give extra, 11 times more committed to staying with their organizations, and 14 times more likely to look forward to coming to work than employees at peer companies.[18] If a satisfied employee's productivity level is 100 percent, an engaged employee's level is 144 percent, but the productivity level of an employee who is truly inspired by a sense of purpose is a mammoth 225 percent.[19]

Unfortunately, we've got a long way to go before leaders get a passing grade for creating environments in which people are thriving with a sense of purpose. Only 28 percent of respondents in a 2019 PricewaterhouseCoopers survey reported feeling fully connected to their company's purpose. Just 39 percent said they could clearly see the value they create, a mere 22 percent agreed that their jobs allow them to fully leverage their strengths, and more than half weren't even "somewhat" motivated, passionate, or excited about their jobs.[20]

Despite this grim state of affairs, igniting a deep sense of purpose and unleashing it during even the bleakest of circumstances is more than possible. Let's look at one last example of what it takes to make the journey from an environment of despair to one rich with purpose.

Best Buy Defines "At Our Best"

When Hubert Joly took over as CEO at Best Buy in 2012, the retailer was on life support, struggling to compete with the prices of online retailers like Amazon. Most believed he was crazy; some even called him "suicidal" for taking the job. Employee turnover was high and morale was dismal. But eight years later, it's not unreasonable to say that Joly has led one of the most remarkable turnarounds in retail history, the likes of which many other retailers are now scrambling to emulate.

In my interview with Joly, his kind, warmhearted nature shined through his charming French accent. He said, "I spent the first weeks just listening, because I knew I had so much to learn. I spent time in many stores, and I would see customers walking out empty handed after talking with an associate for 30 minutes. When I found out why, that led us to the decision to empower employees to price match, which proved to be an important breakthrough at the start of our turnaround." During Joly's visits to stores, one manager implored him to fix their search engine, noting that if you searched for "Cinderella," you got Nikon cameras. Since losing sales online to competitors was one major threat, they fixed it quickly. Another store manager complained to Joly that headquarters was barraging him with

40–50 KPIs (Key Performance Indicators), and felt he was unable to keep up or able to succeed. Joly could feel their pain. He told me:

> All of this told me we absolutely had to simplify. I boiled the early part of our turnaround down to two problems we had to fix: declining revenue and declining margins. I thought, "How hard could it be to fix just two problems?" If it were five, it might be hard, but two? And if you asked anyone at Best Buy during that season what our two problems were, they all would have told you the same thing.

At the outset, Joly set the stage for a purpose-driven turnaround by laying out all the stakeholders to focus on—customers, employees, technical suppliers and partners, and shareholders. But a more deliberate focus on purpose came later, once the company's performance stabilized. In his letter to shareholders, Joly wrote, "We will do well by doing good"; the company would "[enrich] lives through technology." "Price competitiveness was just the price of entry to the game. I wanted us to win on advice, convenience, and service," Joly told me.

To reach that goal, Joly concentrated squarely on associates in the stores:

> I know it sounds overly simple, but I just wanted people interacting with our customers to be human. We told them, "Be yourself. When you interact with the customer, get to know them. Don't be mechanical, don't go after their wallets. Think of the customer as your grandmother or your best friend. How would you interact with them?"

To make it feel real, Best Buy conducted workshops across the stores and asked people to tell their stories of being human. They heard both heartbreaking and inspiring stories. Joly said, "Everyone's story matters. And for them to bring their best human self to the floor, they needed to feel safe. And to feel safe, they had to trust we knew their story."

Joly also spoke about gathering managers together from multiple levels of the company. At one meeting leaders asked everyone, "What drives you?" to really understand their personal motivations. They added questions like, "What's your favorite charity?" or "Tell us about your family or community." As people shared their answers, their responses were projected for all to see. Joly told me:

> You don't start with a corporate purpose, you start with what drives the individuals. That's the big mistake that companies make now. Purpose is a

fad, so they want to be on the bandwagon. You can't "force purpose" into an organization. You need to start by asking people, "So, what does our purpose mean for you?"

As Best Buy rolled out their new brand campaign, Building the New Blue, they again conducted a series of workshops on the floors of the stores. The core question employees were asked this time was, "What does it look like when we are at our best?" "It was such a simple yet brilliant question because it allowed people to feel proud and describe the standards we all want to emulate," said Joly. "Then we followed with another prompt, 'Let's talk about what's possible.' These are the conversations that make purpose come to life for everyone." Joly described how this approach has cascaded down into the far reaches of the organization. He told me about a Boston store manager who asks his employees, "What's your dream?" Upon hearing the answer, the manager says, "Write it down in the breakroom for everyone to see. My commitment is to help you achieve it."

To live up to their commitment to serve communities, Best Buy has opened Teen Tech centers across the US to help kids in disadvantaged communities learn technology skills that enable them to advance to higher-level jobs and education. Joly says, "It was important to do as part of our purpose to enrich lives through technology while supporting the communities in which we do business."

The results of Joly's leadership and turnaround speak for themselves. Over his eight years at the company, Best Buy's stock price grew from $11 per share to about $100 per share. Employee turnover was cut from 50 percent to 30 percent, which is substantial for retail. Customer satisfaction ratings were at an all-time high. And they achieved their 2021 revenue goals nearly a year early.[21, 22]

Joly's story is a stunning example of what it means to invite people to join their purpose to their organization's. In practical, simple ways, he invited every associate to serve the greater good by finding out what it would take for them to be at their best.

WALK IN THEIR SHOES

If you didn't know how things turned out, how do you think you would have responded to Hubert Joly's approach if you'd worked at Best Buy? What misgivings might you have had?

Get Busy: Join Your Purpose to a Bigger Story

Know Your Story, Know Your Purpose

If you are still searching for an answer to the question "Why were you born?" consider that the answer can be found in the crevices of your own stories. Cultivating self-honesty requires that you look at your story accurately—the painful parts and the beautiful parts. Take the time to write out these stories. Make sure to include vivid details so you can detect important patterns. As you engage your own storytelling, avoid writing that is purely "stream-of-consciousness" or "feelings-based" like a personal diary or blog, or "just the facts" writing that is typical of newspaper reporting. Writing a good story integrates all of it: facts, emotions, thoughts, contributing details concerning characters, details about the location, description of objects, specific dialogue between key characters, etc. Bring yourself into the contours of the story. Usually the scenes that come to mind first as you consider each type of story are likely the ones eager to be told:

Origin story 1: My views of myself. During your formative years, what messages did you receive about your significance in the world? About your potential? About your abilities? What messages did you hear about your limitations? Pick one or two scenes that come to mind and write them out. Consider experiences with your parents, teachers or others in authority that shaped how you see your importance.

Origin story 2: Me at my best. We all have record-setting performances. When was yours? What do you look back on as your greatest accomplishment? When you felt most proud of your talents and the impact they had? Pick one or two scenes that come to mind and write those out. Consider major achievements, periods of time requiring painful levels of perseverance or weathering self-doubt.

Origin story 3: Me at my worst. We all have at least one "why do I keep doing that?" behavior—the thing we do or say at the most inopportune time that reveals our worst. Well, there's an answer to the question of "why" you do it: you learned it. Most unwanted behavior originates in formative moments of pain. Think about when you "learned" the behavior in question. Pick one or two scenes and write them out.

Origin story 4: What I hold sacred. At our core, we all have deeply held values or principles that guide our lives and decisions—compassion, integrity, service, ambition, getting results, earning money, being productive, etc. Think about the sacrosanct values you most hold dear and write out the stories of how they came to be so important. Are those values serving you well today? Do some of them need to be reconsidered? Under what conditions are you tempted to compromise any of them? Where do they feel aligned with your organization's values and where do they feel misaligned?

Look across all the stories you've written. What patterns do you see? What recurring themes stand out? When are you most fulfilled? Least fulfilled? Find a trusted friend or family member and read the stories out loud to them and ask them to reflect back to you what they observe. What patterns do they see in your language or tone? What resonates with their own experience of you? Our stories often find their richest meaning when interpreted through the perspectives of those who know us best.

Identify Where You Fit into Your Organization's Story

Whether or not your company explicitly serves a greater good, identify the stakeholders that benefit from the work your company does. Whose lives are made better by your company's purpose? Even the most menial services and products improve someone's life or work. Where does your contribution fit into the story? Remember the classic story of how the janitors at NASA all said of their work, "I'm helping to put a man on the moon."

Ask Those You Lead about Their "Why"

Set aside a substantial period of time for you and your team to talk openly about their "why" of work. Have each person share the driver behind why they love what they do. And if they've stopped loving it, find out what it would take to reignite their passion. How can you support one another in living your best life and purpose? How does your shared contribution support the organization's bigger story?

Now that we've finished Part One, honesty about who you are, let's turn to the next finding from the research, justice in accountability.

KEY TAKEAWAYS

- Since "purpose" lives in the dopamine-rich reward system in our brains, seeing the connection between personal and organizational goals leads to psychological fulfillment and successful achievement of organizational goals at the same time.

- The only context in which the allure of deceit will struggle to survive is one in which everyone believes their work matters and feels a sense of proud purpose about their contributions.

- If organizational culture allows people to knowingly behave in duplicitous ways, they see themselves as dishonest. This leads to behaviors like sandbagging forecasts, minimizing mistakes, negotiating unfair deals with customers, and bribery.

- While business strategies can change, passion and purpose remain consistent and can help ease anxiety through periods of transition.

- Purpose needs to be personal. Invite employees to describe the way(s) in which their job helps them fulfill their life's purpose. Don't explain it for them, but you can help them connect the two.

Endnotes

1 Wikipedia Contributors (2019) Walter McMillian, *Wikipedia*, 22 June, https://en.wikipedia.org/wiki/Walter_McMillian (archived at https://perma.cc/5J6P-W9QS)

2 Wikipedia Contributors (2020) Bryan Stevenson, *Wikipedia*, 30 July, https://en.wikipedia.org/wiki/Bryan_Stevenson#cite_note-people-5 (archived at https://perma.cc/VZ5Y-FDAX)

3 Grant, M (1995) A stubborn Alabama lawyer stands alone between death and his clients, *People*, 27 November, https://people.com/archive/bryan-stevenson-vol-44-no-22/ (archived at https://perma.cc/9CSD-XD98)

4 Equal Justice Initiative (n.d.) Bryan Stevenson, https://eji.org/bryan-stevenson/ (archived at https://perma.cc/K8PJ-N6H4)

5 Legacy Museum and National Memorial for Peace and Justice (2017) The national memorial for peace and justice, https://museumandmemorial.eji.org/memorial (archived at https://perma.cc/Q5Y8-NF64)

6 Stevenson, B (2015) *Just Mercy: A story of justice and redemption*, Spiegel & Grau, New York

7 Ariely, D (2012) *The (Honest) Truth About Dishonesty: How we lie to everyone–especially ourselves*, HarperCollins Publishers, New York

8 Ibid

9 Nadella, S (2017) *Hit Refresh: The quest to rediscover Microsoft's soul and imagine a better future for everyone*, HarperCollins Publishers, New York

10 Ibid

11 Ibid

12 Ibid

13 Carucci, R (2019) Balancing the company's needs and employee satisfaction, *Harvard Business Review*, 01 November, https://hbr.org/2019/11/balancing-the-companys-needs-and-employee-satisfaction (archived at https://perma.cc/R37H-V7GW)

14 Buell, R W, Kim, T and Tsay C (2017) Creating reciprocal value through operational transparency, *Management Science*, https://pubsonline.informs.org/doi/10.1287/mnsc.2015.2411 (archived at https://perma.cc/PKF2-CMRE)

15 Cable, D M (2019) *Alive at Work: The neuroscience of helping your people love what they do*, Harvard Business School Publishing, Massachusetts

16 LinkedIn and Imperative (2016) 2016 Global Report: Purpose at work https://business.linkedin.com/content/dam/me/business/en-us/talent-solutions/resources/pdfs/purpose-at-work-global-report.pdf (archived at https://perma.cc/2JH9-ZZVN)

17 Garcia-Alandete, J, Martinez, E R, Nohales, P S, Lozano, B S (2018) Meaning in life and psychological well-being in Spanish emerging adults, *Acta Colombiana de Psicologia*, http://www.scielo.org.co/pdf/acp/v21n1/0123-9155-acp-21-01-00196.pdf (archived at https://perma.cc/4G2A-SKUD)

18 Fortune (2017) Great Place to Work Report: Three predictors for the workplace culture of the future, https://www.greatplacetowork.com/images/reports/Fortune_100_Report_2017_FINAL.pdf (archived at https://perma.cc/6EFG-AB5W)

19 Garton, E and Mankins, M (2015) Engaging your employees is good, but don't stop there, *Harvard Business Review*, https://hbr.org/2015/12/engaging-your-employees-is-good-but-dont-stop-there (archived at https://perma.cc/WU68-L69M)

20 PricewaterhouseCoopers (2019) Our research on the connection between strategic purpose and motivation, *Strategy&*, https://www.strategyand.pwc.com/gx/en/unique-solutions/capabilities-driven-strategy/approach/research-motivation.html (archived at https://perma.cc/EZC6-Z47P)

21 Hirsch, L (2019) People thought Hubert Joly was "crazy or suicidal" for taking the job as Best Buy CEO. Then he ushered in its turnaround, *CNBC*, 19 June, https://www.cnbc.com/2019/06/19/former-best-buy-ceo-hubert-joly-defied-expectations-at-best-buy.html (archived at https://perma.cc/D4YC-FXM9)

22 Bolger, B (n.d.) Hubert Joly, Best Buy, Winner of the ISO 10018 Honorary CEO Citation for Quality People Management, *Engagement Strategies Media*, http://www.enterpriseengagement.org/articles/content/8630677/hubert-joly-best-buy-winner-of-the-iso-10018-honorary-ceo-citation-for-quality-people-management/ (archived at https://perma.cc/QGZ2-XM9A)

PART TWO

Justice in Accountability

04

Nurturing Dignity in Accountability

Set your intention: How can I fairly and equitably honor the contributions of others?

Hope From a Bigger Story

In December 2019, the eastern part of the Democratic Republic of the Congo (DRC) was stricken with heavy rains, causing severe flooding. One morning in January 2020, after the floodwaters started to recede, Julita, a 60-year-old woman living in the small village of Kiliba, noticed something disturbing on a flood-damaged area of her property: trees. They weren't hers, she hadn't planted them, and most infuriating of all, they marked the boundary of her property line—10 meters short of where her property actually ended. Her neighbor, Katabazi, a wealthy 43-year-old businessman, had planted the trees there to expand the property he used for his business. Enraged, Julita ripped the trees out and threw them onto Katabazi's property.

For the past quarter century, the DRC has been torn apart by two wars, conflicts stemming from government corruption, extreme poverty and genocide, and some of the worst human rights atrocities in history. During the second war in the early 2000s, the city of Goma was named the rape capital of the world, as the invading M23 militia used rape as a tool of war. As of 2008, more than five million Congolese had lost their lives as part of what has been named "the great African War."[1] At this time the country's justice system all but collapsed, leaving local villages and territories to fend for themselves when conflicts arose. Women, especially poor, older women, had little voice or opportunity for justice.

In such a world, a wealthy businessman appropriating 10 meters of an old woman's land would hardly be noticed. Indeed, people in the DRC have grown painfully accustomed to having what's theirs taken from them. The terrible irony of the DRC's destitution is that when it comes to minerals and natural resources, it is one of the wealthiest nations on the planet. Corrupt governments from other countries (and at home), along with the eager hand of multinational companies, have benefitted handsomely from the country's rich supply of minerals like cobalt, gold, uranium, and coltan, while citizens of the country serve as little more than the cheap labor that excavates for them.

Julita's situation was made worse by the fact that when you have very little to begin with, your land is everything. In places like the DRC, your land is your heritage; it represents your family and birthright. Your history. Julita had inherited her land from her grandmother. And she wasn't going to let it go without a fight.

Fortunately for her, the Foundation Chirezi (FOCHI), a local non-profit supported by the Peace Direct global NGO,[2] had established community "peace courts" throughout the DRC. The foundation even created community courts led entirely by women to ensure that women were given a fair opportunity to be heard and to find justice. Far from a new invention, these courts are a continuation of the area's tradition of justice-dispensing, where chiefs gathered members of the community "under the tree" to hear all sides of a conflict, weigh the facts, and come to a decision, ensuring that the community was not fractured, but restored and strengthened through the process.

At first, Katabazi was unwilling to participate in a peace court to resolve his conflict with Julita, but the villagers persuaded him to. So, for more than two days, the court heard testimonies from villagers who knew Julita and her family and told stories of being guests in the home; most crucially, they confirmed where her property line was supposed to be. Julita hoped the court would rule for her, but as a poor, elderly woman, she feared the odds weren't in her favor.

Justice prevailed: the peace court ruled that Katabazi was wrong for appropriating the land and had to return it. Julita's joy and relief were short-lived, however. Participants in communal peace courts have the right to appeal verdicts to the official magistrate of the city, and that's exactly what Katabazi did. Unfortunately, Julita couldn't afford the costs of challenging such an appeal, assuming her land would be forfeited when the magistrate overturned the community's ruling.

The community was outraged by her inability to take on the appeal, and local residents committed to paying for her appeal costs. But, in a surprising turn of events, the magistrate threw the case out. He said that the community peace court had already made the decision, and that the parties needed to abide by it.

Peace court interventions are concluded with a formal reconciliation ceremony in front of the entire village where both parties in conflict must drink from the same cup; in this case, a local beer was used, as a sign of their commitment to restoration. To date, Mrs. Julita and Mr. Katabazi live in peace as neighbors, "rubbing shoulders" without any issue.[3]

What could a story like this possibly teach us about accountability within our organizations?

Everything.

Peace courts in the DRC are an example of restorative justice, an ancient practice of community engagement to address conflicts between community members, and to ensure fair accountability while maintaining communal unity. It has been practiced all over the world with remarkable success. In South Africa, after Apartheid ended, the new government used multiple models of restorative justice to reconstruct a divided nation, with thousands of formerly violent perpetrators coming forward to acknowledge their crimes through the nation's Truth and Reconciliation Commission, a tribunal set up "to enable South Africans to come to terms with their past on a morally accepted basis and to advance the cause of reconciliation."[4] In Kenya and the Democratic Republic of the Congo, many local NGOs have worked to restore traditional concepts of community justice where attempts at more formal, state-sponsored judicial processes have failed.[5] Infractions such as land ownership disputes after displaced people return home, as well as payment and debt disagreement, have effectively reconciled using these practices. Even in the case of extreme violations, such as the atrocities of mass murder and rape in war-torn countries, some degree of healing and restoration has been found in special applications of restorative practices. Indigenous people throughout North America have used restorative practices for generations as a core part of their justice system.[6]

In the United States, school systems have successfully used the approach to help children learn how to resolve conflicts. Even within our traditional justice system, the practice has helped restore the mental health of many victims of violent crime. For example, Stephen Watt, a former Wyoming State trooper and state legislator, was shot multiple times by a fleeing bank robber in 1982. As part of a difficult reconciliation process, the two met, Stephen shared his story, and ultimately forgave his perpetrator. Since then, the two have even cultivated an amicable friendship.[7] Similarly, after

Baltimore councilwoman Rikki Spector was brutally attacked by two teens in December of 2016, a local community group who had been working with the teens approached Spector and asked her to participate in their rehabilitation. She agreed to do so, setting the stage for the two teens to acknowledge their wrongdoing and commit to their ongoing restoration.[8]

There seems to be widespread agreement among justice experts, even those who advocate for retributive justice approaches, that most cultures have developed some form of restorative practice, and that a common set of principles undergirds them all.[9] These universal principles include:

1 *Truth telling*—there must be an honest account of what happened by all those involved.

2 *Taking responsibility*—the person(s) who committed the wrongdoing must acknowledge the effect it had on others and that it was their choice to do it.

3 *Listening to the story*—those harmed in the process of wrongdoing will have their story heard by those who harmed them.

4 *Rehabilitation*—the person who caused harm must commit to learning and change and be given the opportunity and resources to do so.

5 *Reconciliation*—accountability isn't just about meting out consequences for wrongdoing (retributive justice), it's about restoring relationships and communities that have been broken as a result of the wrongdoing. Although it doesn't always happen, sometimes forgiveness can result from reconciliation.

6 *Restoration*—there must be appropriate consequences for the perpetrator or reparations made to compensate the injured party for harm done to them.[10, 11]

At the core of restorative justice lies nurturing the dignity of all involved. Throughout the process, community is maintained—often strengthened. Those who committed wrongdoing work to learn from their mistakes and commit to not repeating them without being shamed into doing so.

While justice systems in many parts of the world have realized the powerful benefits of restorative approaches to accountability, our corporate workplaces have lagged. In most companies, "accountability" is maintained by a punitive system of blaming and fault-finding. It's an antiseptic process devoid of humanity and rife with inconsistent, either overly lenient or overly penalizing practices that prompt people to hide their mistakes, embellish their accomplishments, and point fingers when something goes wrong. While the circumstances at even the most tumultuous companies don't match those of divided, war-torn nations across the globe or violence-stricken regions in the United States, the emotional and psychological conditions at play may be more similar than we want to believe. Both encourage high levels of anxiety and self-protection; a perspective that views those in authority as villains whose power will cause harm; constantly justifying and defending your actions; automatically assuming others are rivals out to get what you have; and the fear that mounting, unspoken tensions could erupt at any moment.

And what's been the result?

The Grim Accountability Landscape

Few words in management vernacular induce a tighter wince than "accountability." And for good reason: companies and leaders have grappled with what it is, and how to tackle it effectively, for decades. One 2015 HR Dive study on workplace accountability shows that 82 percent of managers surveyed acknowledge they have "limited to no" ability to hold others accountable successfully, and 91 percent of employees surveyed would say "effectively holding others accountable" is one of their company's top leadership development needs.[12] Despite our best efforts, the concept has devolved from a high-minded practice to spur improvement, to a synonym for the blame, judgment, and shaming processes that keep people defensive and nervous. Ask anyone if they look forward to their performance appraisal or the monthly check-in with their boss, and most will give you an emphatic "no."

Research confirms how unimportant today's accountability systems make employees feel. A 2017 Gallup Report found that only 14 percent of employees surveyed felt their performance was being managed in a way that motivated them to improve, 26 percent got feedback less than once per year, only 21 percent felt their performance metrics were within their control, and only 40 percent of employees felt that their manager held them accountable for goals they set.[13] In another 2019 study from Reflektive, 70 percent of surveyed employees felt their managers were not objective in how they evaluated their performance.[14] Yet another 2017 study reported that a staggering 69 percent of employees don't feel they are living up to their potential at work.[15]

One interviewee in my research repeated to me, nearly verbatim, what I've been told by so many others in the organizations I've worked with over the years: "I honestly don't know why I work as hard as I do. My boss doesn't have a clue what I do or how hard I work. I fill out the stupid performance appraisal forms for him at the end of the year, he signs them and sends them on to HR. And then we start all over. It's a completely rigged system, but I don't have the energy or luxury of changing jobs right now. So, I just suck it up."

His pessimism is hardly unique. The Corporate Executive Board, a management resource arm of the Gartner Group, found similar sentiments in their 2014 study of 1,000 companies: 66 percent of employees surveyed said that their accountability processes *interfered with* productivity, 65 percent said the way performance was managed wasn't relevant to their jobs, and 90 percent of HR professionals—those assigned to steward accountability processes—said their performance assessments did not actually provide accurate information to employees about their contributions.[16]

Another interviewee expressed, with no small amount of frustration, the capricious nature of her experience of "accountability":

> My boss is constantly changing her mind about what she wants. No sooner do
> I clarify one set of expectations than she pulls the rug out from under me and
> changes direction. We play the classic "bring me a rock" game until the deadline
> is looming, she panics, we scramble through a few all-nighters to get something
> done, and then we start the process all over. Some days I think she appreciates
> my heroics to save her ass, and other days I think it's all a carefully calculated
> plot to get me to quit. I never really know where I stand or if what I do even
> matters.

Her experience is apparently widely shared. The Gallup report noted earlier found that only 50 percent of employees clearly know what is expected of them and only 26 percent agree that their manager continually helps them clarify priorities.[17]

Sadly, comments like these truthfully depict how too many people experience accountability in organizations. And when people believe things aren't fair, it's more than just irritating. It's damaging to our mental health. A 2014 Danish study of 4,237 public employees found that organizational injustice leads to depression, anxiety, and burnout.[18]

When people spend most of their waking hours at work, the last thing they should feel is ambivalent about their contribution, uncertain of their value, and depressed from believing things aren't fair. But the result of this accountability mess has led to just that. When it comes to providing constructive, dignifying accountability, we indisputably suck.

So, how on earth did we get to such a grim place?

Like many outdated processes, it all started with good intentions.

Scaling Sameness Like Fairness

Some historians trace the management of performance back to 221 AD, when Wei Dynasty emperors rated their family members' performance. But its more modern roots can be traced back to Scotland in the 1800s, when cotton mill owner Robert Owen hired secret monitors to observe and scrutinize the performance of his workers. Later, at the end of the 20th century, as the Industrial Revolution took hold, business owners sought to maximize the returns on their investments by getting the most out of their laborers' contributions. Early management theorist Frederick Winslow Taylor's approach to task monitoring and reinforcing productivity, and later, Peter Drucker's introduction of "management by objectives" in the 1950s, solidified the importance of ROI in the minds of US companies.[19] The intent was to ensure efficiency and productivity in how employees were managed as companies scaled into large, complex enterprises.

Along the way, the idea of accountability was created as a well-meaning way to ensure fairness to workers across an organization. Rather than leaving accountability to the judgment of individual managers, making companies vulnerable to lawsuits from disgruntled employees and susceptible to uneven efforts and results, "standardizing" how we hold people accountable and measure contribution attempted to ensure everyone was treated the same, or "fairly." That may have worked fine when many workers were responsible for similar outputs, but that's not the case today. The Industrial Revolution gave way to an economy based not on productivity but on ingenuity, creativity, and insight. The outputs of today's employees are far from standard, but rather as unique as the employees themselves.

To combat the diminishing returns of standardized performance management, some companies have decided to do away with formal evaluation processes altogether,[20] but without a viable alternative, this often backfires. Employees complain about feeling rudderless without reliable feedback. Some companies have moved to more frequent encounters, like monthly or quarterly check-ins between leaders and employees. But if those interactions aren't any more dignifying, they just spread the misery out over the course of a year instead of saving it all up for one big annual insufferable moment.

The fact is that people *want* and *need* to be held accountable. But what's needed are processes that focus on the dignity of people as unique humans and contributors. Leaders should be less concerned about the uniformity with which that process is carried out. Their attempts to neutralize inconsistency have ended up neutering individuality, resulting in a dehumanized version of accountability. Ironically, accountability *should* be the most inspiring process in a company—the one that honors an employee's unique contribution and motivates them to become even better. Unfortunately, today's approaches to accountability are more designed to avoid litigation through documentation and eliminate a company's liability exposure. They have removed far more *individuality* than they have variation. And that is exactly what makes them unfair.

Worse, the workplace has become so litigious, with some people's self-interest swelling to such unimaginable heights, that to rein in misconduct (or even just excesses) companies have had to establish monitoring and whistleblowing functions for employees, among them anonymous ethics hotlines and employee relations groups. After a complaint is lodged, extensive investigations are conducted, while the accused often has no idea who has even accused them. Sadly, these mechanisms are used for anything from serious misconduct to retaliation against a boss for giving someone else the promotion we wanted. In other words, our ability to hold ourselves and others accountable has been reduced to inflexible, legalistic processes that serve mostly to find or eliminate blame while accomplishing little except protecting against lawsuits.

The good news is it doesn't have to be this way.

Turning the Tide

Making dignity and justice (fairness) more central to our accountability processes would allow two very important things to change. First, the connection between *contribution* and *contributor* could be re-established. In an economy of ideas and insights, we can no longer say things like "It's not personal, it's business" or "I have to evaluate the work and results." The value of subjectivity has significantly risen as the contributions people make have increasingly become reflections of who they are—their creativity, their analyses, their imaginative ideas. Thus, accountability becomes *fair* when managers grow the unique talents of their employees as individual people, with the realization that cultivating someone's abilities is as important as the fruits of those abilities. Accountability has dignity when it requires assessing and honoring the *integration* of unique contributions with their contributors. Fairness no longer equals sameness.

At the core of accountability with dignity must be an honest, caring relationship between a leader and those she leads. When that happens, the unique requirements of individuals and teams can be considered and honored. Too often, unfortunately, what makes people distinctive stays hidden behind rigid processes that nullify the very uniqueness needed to bring out their best contributions and performance.

So, what does accountability with dignity look like? Let's look at an example from one of my clients.

Angela is the president of a $6 billion division of a $25 billion apparel company, the largest and highest profit-earning segment of the company. Her industry is facing constant disruption, and her division is under constant pressure to deliver results that are increasingly difficult to come by. Despite this she is upbeat, energetic, and driven.

Every two years her company conducts an employee engagement survey to assess employees' degree of satisfaction and attitudes about their work experience. To ensure the process is taken seriously, a portion of all management bonus compensation is tied to divisional and regional performance as measured by the survey, *as well as* the level of improvement since the previous survey two years earlier. In the 2019 survey, the performance of Angela's division, which had traditionally returned high engagement scores, took a dip, particularly in the career development dimension of how employees perceived "opportunities for learning and advancement." Perplexed, her first instinct was to search for disconfirming data. She asked HR for all of the division's promotions, training and development, and career data for the previous four years so she could compare current and previous survey results. There were no material changes over the last four years in analysis of their HR practices to explain the sudden decline in their survey results.

Being conscientious about such things, she vowed to get to the bottom of the results. At this point I stepped in and encouraged her to consider an alternative approach to "investigating" what could have led to the disappointing engagement scores. Instead, I suggested she ask each member of her leadership team to take responsibility for learning what the organization was telling them through the survey feedback. I also suggested she not require any specific tactic, but empowered her team to choose their own approach. She followed my advice, letting the team members know they would be accountable for returning to her what they discovered within three weeks.

Her team of five VPs embarked on their mission to better understand the survey results. Two chose to have informal conversations with folks one and two levels below them, which returned very little useful insight on what the data indicated. The lower-level managers said things like, "My people were just as surprised as we are by this feedback" and "People I talked to think we're really good at the career stuff." Two other VPs embarked on comprehensive "road shows" throughout their regions using the HR data that Angela had initially commissioned. In multiple town hall-style gatherings that felt like pep rallies, the VPs presented the data with great confidence to show that, in fact, the division was very effective at creating opportunities for advancement and learning, essentially refuting the survey results. The VPs returned to the office proudly declaring that whatever the misunderstanding had been, it was now cleared up within their respective groups, and that their employees once again understood just how effective the division was when it came to offering opportunities for development and advancement.

Helena, the fifth VP, took a very different approach than her peers. She conducted a series of 14 small focus groups she called "listening circles." She prefaced each by saying, "Whatever we think we're doing to empower your careers isn't working, and you are not feeling as though the opportunities you'd like are accessible to you. I'd like to know more so I can better understand what you are feeling, and how I can fix it." Helena heard many stories of employees having their ideas dismissed or ignored by their boss, being pulled out in the middle of training programs for trivial problems, and in general, a culture that prized results at the expense of people. The message employees were sending Angela's team wasn't, "You don't *provide* opportunities for advancement or learning." What they were saying was, "You are all so busy driving us to get results and *telling us what to do* that you leave us no room, energy, or desire to *care about* our development or careers, nor do you ever *ask us about them*."

As Helena shared her findings with the team, Angela's expression sank. The other four VPs attempted to dismiss Helena's findings and defend the division, but Angela cut them off. And in a stunning reversal of her own instincts, she surprised the team with the following response: "Helena, I owe you a huge debt of thanks for having the courage to do what you did. If you hadn't, we would have marched forward having never learned that we have a cultural cancer growing in our midst." To the two VPs who used the HR data to wave away concerns in the town hall-style meetings, she said, "As I listened to your feedback, I found myself fluctuating between thinking what bold leadership you showed taking the initiative to 'educate' your people and feeling sick to my stomach at how utterly insulted everyone in those rooms must have felt after you finished. But I can't blame you for that because you were just following my example." To the whole team, her message was:

> We've been given the amazing gift of a second chance here. If we'd waited to the next cycle of our survey, this toxicity would have spread, and we'd see it in our performance. I spend too much time *telling* and *pushing*, and not enough time *listening* and *caring*. Helena gave her people what our whole division is telling us that they need. We have to be accountable to them if we expect them to be accountable to us. We need to listen to them. And we need to apologize for whatever we've done that has made them think we don't care. So, the rest of us are all going to do what Helena did for her group. Only I'm going with you. And then we're going to come back together and figure out what we each have to change about ourselves and our organizations.

For the following month, Angela accompanied the four VPs in listening circle conversations, during which she heard the same complaints Helena did. Even more courageously, Angela shared with her boss (the company CEO) and her peers what she'd learned about herself, her survey results, and how her division was responding.

In effect, Angela had held herself and her team accountable in ways that modeled a restorative approach. These were the steps they took:

1 They searched for the true meaning of the survey data, no matter how inconvenient it may have been.

2 They listened to employees' stories and explanations for why they felt the way they did, treating their unique experiences as valid.

3 She and her team rethought how they could truly "lead" their division.

4 They restored trust within the division by taking responsibility for the leadership environment she and her team had modeled and committed to change.

5 They made it safe for leaders one and two levels below Angela's team to take responsibility for their actions and apologize to employees who had been made to feel unimportant.

(These adjustments didn't come about without bumps and bruises, however. The following year, Angela removed nine leaders from the division, including one from her team, who were unable or unwilling to change.)

This story would have had a drastically different ending had Angela instinctively dismissed Helena's findings and joined the other VPs in concluding the data was largely inconsequential. The division never would have realized how badly it needed to change, continuing its downward spiral.

WALK IN THEIR SHOES

How would you have responded to Angela's approach had you been on her team? How would you have coached her to deal with survey feedback data? Are there aspects of her approach you want to emulate?

Fairness and Honesty

Researchers have extensively studied "procedural fairness" as a major factor within organizational justice—the degree to which a process that makes decisions or allocates resources is seen as fair by those who must live with its outcomes. Of the many findings, one stands out clearly across most research: a sense of unfairness among employees sets the stage for sabotage and ethical misconduct.[21] When people feel like processes for judging their work or allocating resources aren't fair—meaning they are applied capriciously by their boss, applied differently to different people, lack transparency, or disadvantage them in some way from being successful—they are significantly more likely to retaliate against their boss or organization.[22] My research also found this to be true: when accountability processes are seen to be unfair, people are nearly *four times* more likely to lie, act unethically, and put their own interests first. A 2018 McKinsey study on fairness in performance management further confirms this important connection. They found that when people perceived their performance management system to be fair, 60 percent also felt it was effective. McKinsey boiled down fairness to three factors:

1 Making sure expectations of employees were clearly tied to the organization's top priorities, and when those priorities shifted, so did expectations.

2 Effective development of managers as coaches and daily arbiters of fairness.

3 Rewarding differentiated high performance where it makes sense.

Their study showed that when these three factors were in place, 84 percent of leaders reported their performance management system was effective.

They were also *12 times more likely* to report positive results from their performance management efforts than leaders at companies who had none of them.[23]

In the last chapter, we discussed the importance of making sure individual and collective purpose are closely aligned. Well, your accountability system is one of the strongest ways to do just that. (In the next chapter we'll dive even deeper into how leaders can become better arbiters of fairness.)

Tiffany Archer is the ethics and compliance officer and corporate counsel for Panasonic Avionics Corporation, and a thought leader with extensive experience in human behavior and ethics. In a 2020 interview I conducted with her, she offered keen insights about why ineffective accountability systems create risk for companies:

> Everyone knows performance can be very subjective. So, when you try and make a quantitative assessment of qualitative work, then put a number to it so it appears "objective," then try and call it fair, you're asking for trouble. I don't believe such processes work to do anything but demotivate people. Peers start anxiously comparing themselves to one another and think, "Wait, why did I get a three out of four and they got a four out of four when I stayed later to get the work done, I worked on the most important projects, and he even got reprimanded for not performing? Why should I bother putting out more effort if I'm never going to get the top rating for it?" People just become resentful and distrustful, and when that happens, you've increased the risk of bad behavior.

Only a Three!?

Tim, an executive in the biopharmaceutical industry I've worked with for several years, showed up to one of our coaching sessions irate—with a level of anger I'd not seen from him before. That week had been his annual performance review, during which he had been hoping to hear news of a promotion for which he'd been the top succession candidate. He pounded his fist on the desk and barked:

> [My boss] gave me a #**$^& three! I've been a four since I've gotten to this company. In my last company the top rating was five, and that's what I was there. I've always gotten the highest rating. Now, just because HR has instituted a stupid quota limiting the number of fours she can give out, I get dropped to a three. How the hell does that make any sense? And she had the nerve to play the victim card with me. She said, "I'm sorry Tim, there's nothing I can do. My hands are tied. This doesn't change the way I or the company feels about you."

Is she serious? It sure as hell changes the way I feel about them! It's honestly one of the most insulting things I've ever experienced in my whole career.

I spent the next two hours walking Tim back from the edge. During our conversation, several things astonished me. First was the degree to which he'd completely lost any objectivity about himself, his boss—who had been a very strong advocate for him—and his company. Second was how little he'd heard or retained from the conversation once he'd seen the number. As I read over his review, I was taken aback by the glowing regard it showed for Tim's contributions, and the comments about areas he needed to work on were fair and accurate. Further, he was still the top succession candidate for the role we'd been working hard to prepare him for, and on track to get it within the next 12 to 18 months. But in that moment, none of it mattered. Tim's sense of contempt for himself, his boss, and his company overshadowed it all. All he could do was toggle between obsessing over areas he should have worked harder in or done more for, paranoia about who could have possibly deserved the coveted fours more than him, and whether or not to ever trust his boss again.

Tim's experience vividly demonstrates the war between sameness and fairness. To him, being treated "the same" as all the other forced-rated former fours—now threes—felt harshly unjust. The experience spiraled him into extreme levels of shame and self-involvement. He became consumed with the offense, and it took nearly a week before a more balanced perspective returned.

As it turns out, Tim's response wasn't extreme, or uncommon after all. Neuroscience explains a good deal of Tim's outrage. Research from the NeuroLeadership Institute has shown that the part of our brain that senses threat, our amygdala, responds with a fight or flight response when we perceive danger. When we are placed into rating categories, we literally feel trapped and in peril, triggering the same survival instincts we feel when we fear our safety is in jeopardy. Additionally, a fixed number signals a sense of permanence, as though we have all of the capability we are ever going to have, discouraging us from believing we can, or should, try to grow.[24] Another neuroscience study, from UCLA, has shown that when we feel unfairly rated or judged we experience a sense of rejection and exclusion, and this registers in the region of our brain that also registers pain. In other words, Tim's experience actually *felt* as if someone had hit him.[25]

If our accountability systems continue to make people feel shame, distrust, rejection, ambivalence, and resentment, driving them to extensive levels of self-involvement, they'll never inspire people to be the best versions of themselves.

To grow and learn, reflect on and take responsibility for their mistakes or skill gaps, and feel proud of their contributions and the companies they work for.

Unless we change the systems, that is.

Your Brain on Dignity

If neuroscience holds a key to understanding why our accountability systems fail, it also reveals why, when working productively, they can unleash the best of human potential. Neuroscientists have found that the part of our brain that regulates self-esteem is a pathway that connects the area of our brain that controls self-knowledge to the area that regulates motivation and reward. The stronger this neuropathway is, the stronger someone's sense of self-esteem.[26] Studies also reveal that the strength of this pathway is strongly influenced by what others think of us.[27] Interestingly, the studies conclude that the weaker this pathway is, the more prone to anxiety, depression, and other mood disorders we become.

Remember how we discussed that in today's economy, the contribution and the contributor are more integrated than ever? That means that when a manager is evaluating *the work* of their employees, the employee is experiencing it as an evaluation of *them*. Accordingly, the thoughtfulness of a manager's feedback—the accuracy of their assessment, the empathy and care with which it is delivered, and the extent to which it sees the employee's work as a reflection of themselves—has the ability to shape how an employee sees themselves and the degree to which they feel motivated to do their best. Through the process of accountability, managers hold the power to strengthen the dignity of those they lead or weaken it in ways that intensify issues like depression and anxiety. As Dr. Michael Gervais and Pete Carroll, head coach of the Seattle Seahawks, say in their book *Compete to Create*:

> When there is dignity to the human experience first, people feel valued for who they are, not only for what they produce. A workplace that recognizes the humanity of the individual rather than seeing someone as a replaceable cog in a machine inspires that workforce to explore the edges of their potential.[28]

Insightful companies like Microsoft have figured this out and shaped their accountability systems accordingly. The culture shift Satya Nadella embarked upon was intended to move the company from "know it alls" to "learn it alls." Historically, Microsoft hired people from top schools who were perceived as the best and brightest in their field. The unintended consequence was to create a highly competitive culture in which a willingness to admit mistakes and learn became impaired. As you might imagine, this created substantial challenges for accountability processes—including stifling the ability to hear feedback and learn, take responsibility for shortfalls, and support others in reaching their goals.

In my 2019 interview with Kathleen Hogan, Microsoft's Chief People Officer, she explained how the company reshaped their accountability systems to expand their definition of success. Traditionally, the largest part of their performance management systems focused on individual contribution, which reinforced a culture of individuality and competition. She said they've now expanded "success" to include the metric "contribution to others," which is meant to gauge how well someone worked collaboratively and the extent to which they helped others. Another metric is "leveraging others," which evaluates the degree to which employees ask for help from others and build on their ideas. Hogan told me:

> By evaluating and rewarding a more cohesive set of behaviors, people are learning to work more collaboratively. In a culture where people struggle to admit they don't know something, calculating risk can be tricky. Being open about failure helps us balance a growth mindset with accountability. We are learning to not just reward success, but also reward people who fell short while getting us closer. We don't need people to show up in meetings having memorized pages of information to look smart. We want it to be perfectly acceptable to say, "I don't have that information, but I can get it." Learning from our mistakes gets us closer to our desired results—that's a new form of accountability for us.[29]

Together, these shifts in performance focus are helping Microsoft's leaders and employees reorient their sense of what it means to contribute. Further, they reinforce a sense of dignity—treating people as human beings first and honoring the idea that both achievements *and* gaps have value. Nadella was clear that shifting accountability would start from the top down. He says:

> One of the big things that we have done at the leadership level is to focus on shared metrics. We make a distinction between what we call "performance metrics" and "power metrics." Performance metrics are in-year revenue and profit and things of that nature. Power metrics are about future-year performance. A large part of the compensation for me and my leadership team is fundamentally based on that.[30]

Today's world craves dignity beyond the workplace, too. In late 2020 I spoke with Michael Sandel, Harvard Law School Professor and political philosopher, about his book, *The Tyranny of Merit: What's become of the common good?* He told me:

> Over the past four decades, as globalization has expanded, the divide between winners and losers has deepened. What's made it all the more galling for those who haven't flourished in the new economy is the sense among the winners that their success is their due—they've made it on their own and therefore deserve their winnings. By implication, the attitude among the successful is that those left behind must deserve their fate as well, that they have no one to blame but themselves, that the work they do is of lesser value to society and if they didn't invest in cultivating their talents (aka, get a four-year degree), then that was their doing.

The result is that society has stopped prizing important work done by the working class. We've equated the compensation someone earns with the value of the work. Sandel believes the populist backlash to meritocratic elites in the 2016 US presidential election wasn't just about feeling left behind from economic opportunity, but from the dignity gained by doing work valued by fellow citizens. In his book, Sandel writes:

> ... we are most fully human when we contribute to the common good and earn the esteem of our fellow citizens for the contributions we make. According to this tradition, the fundamental human need is to be needed by those with whom we share a common life. The dignity of work consists in exercising our abilities to answer such needs.[31]

As workplaces and communities, we must learn to treat one another *and one another's contributions* with dignity and esteem, regardless of what they are. If the COVID-19 pandemic taught us anything, it's that the value of "essential workers," whose contributions we previously overlooked, is critical to how we live our lives, and they are deserving of our respect and regard. Let's widen that esteem to all of our colleagues and neighbors.

Dignity in Action: Restorative Accountability

We started this chapter by looking at the model of restorative justice and understanding how it can nurture an accountability process that treats people with dignity. Now let's look at an accountability system that brings dignity to life within an organization.

Elias, a former client of mine, is the managing director of a technology firm in Denmark with approximately 450 employees. After working in what he felt were the demeaning environments of large corporations, he decided to try his hand in the startup tech world. He grew with the company, and eventually ended up with the top job. Elias knew that if his firm was to continue enjoying successful growth, they had to find ways to create accountability that inspired great performance. But, like scaling any venture, creating large-scale accountability processes that preserved the company's entrepreneurial and human environment without being cumbersome or bureaucratic was challenging. His solution was to empower a team of 25 employees from across the company and at different levels to propose a process to the leadership team that "would make them feel proud of working there and excited to be held accountable." Leveraging the company's technological DNA, one of the first criteria in their design was "no forms or paper." They wanted all data collected and shared digitally, and for that technology to promote more meaningful conversations between bosses and their direct reports. And, as a purpose-driven firm committed to democratizing technology access, they also wanted to make sure any process they devised would remain firmly connected to the firm's mission.

Here's what the team came up with. At the start of the year, every employee meets with their boss and presents their "mission impact statement" for the upcoming year; this is a set of objectives they wish to accomplish that both contributes to the overall growth and mission of the firm while furthering their personal development. Then the employee chooses the metrics they wish to be held accountable to. Finally, each team comes together, shares their respective mission impact statements, makes specific agreements on how they will support one another, and consolidates any shared commitments into a "team mission impact," which integrates their individual efforts. Elias's mandate was that any accountability process needed to leave both employees and the company better at the end of each year.

Through a custom-built app the company created, employees and their managers exchange feedback on a regular basis. Managers and peers give positive and developmental feedback on employees' work contributions as well as their participation in "the community," or team. Employees, in turn, give managers immediate feedback on whether their guidance was helpful, and when it's not, how to improve it. Employees routinely use the app to offer their peers observations like, "You seemed a little impatient in today's product update meeting. Everything ok? Anything I can do to help?" The constant real-time calibration serves to sustain trust and clear up any misunderstandings quickly.

When there are missteps or mistakes, there is a special process for resolving them: "leveling up." Given the firm's need to be constantly innovating, they saw mistakes as an opportunity to help them be more inventive. The person who made the mistake (a deadline miscalculation, a cost overrun, ineffective code, misinterpreting a product specification, etc.) takes the lead in calling a level-up session that includes all those impacted by their misstep. They present their interpretation of what went awry, or if they haven't figured it out, ask for the group's help in doing so. At the end of the session, everyone discusses how lessons learned from the mistake can be applied to help everyone "level up." The team takes time to reassure the person who made the error, who is often harder on themselves than anyone, in a way that *restores* community and confidence in themselves and the team's support. This is what multidirectional accountability looks like.

The process in Elias's company also encourages learning from successes. When a project goes especially well, they come together for what they've named "leaping up." In this case, a peer, manager, or even members of a whole team call a session to celebrate the win, and again, extract insights about "what went right" so that everyone can be empowered to take their own "leap up."

The firm's rewards are largely based on company-wide performance, with a small amount of compensation set aside for teams or individuals who have performed exceptionally and overdelivered on their mission impact statements.

Elias says that this accountability process is one of the things he's most proud of at his firm, and it's a core engine of the company's growth. The firm's clients notice the extra miles of dedication that go into their solutions and services, and the firm's net promoter score for referrals is a 10 out of 10. "If everyone here goes home at night, no matter how challenging the day was, and feels proud of their work, loves who they do that work with, and can't wait to come back the next day, I have done my job," says Elias. "The primary job of any accountability system is for people to know that they and their work matter, and how they matter."

WALK IN THEIR SHOES

What was risky about Elias's approach? How might people have resisted his ideas? What lessons can you apply from his story?

Get Busy: Nurture Dignity

Be Honest About Accountability Today

There is inevitably some injustice lurking within your organization's current definition of accountability. Even if you don't have the power to overhaul the entire process, you have influence over how some experience it. Where is it unfair? Where is it separating people from their contributions? How does it treat mistakes or setbacks? How closely does it tie people's commitments to the organization's strategic priorities and purpose? Pick one place where there is an obvious gap, gather your team to hear their experiences with the process, and together, come up with simple ways you can close the gap. Some of the following ideas may serve as compass headings to guide you.

Connect Commitments to Purpose

Building on the work you did at the end of Chapter 3, examine the connection between your purpose, your team members' purpose(s), and your organization's purpose through the lens of your commitments. How closely do your goals align with your and your company's purpose? To what degree do those goals *encourage* you to embody purpose, by directly supporting the company's most important strategic priorities? To what degree do they *hinder* embodying purpose because they seem disconnected from, or irrelevant to, your company's top priorities? What would you need to change to better align these elements?

Ensure the Process Offers Dignity

This is especially important if your company uses a forced rating scale. If you are in a position to do so, advocate to HR to consider abolishing it, or at least allow you to experiment with alternative "reviews" within your group. If you're granted the leeway, go a full performance cycle without using the old metrics and see if there's any difference. If that's not possible, have an honest conversation with your team about how you can deal with the triggering effects of forced ratings. Ask them to share how they have felt when they've been categorized in ways that don't match their perception of their contributions. Talk openly about what approaches to goal-setting, feedback, development, and ongoing calibration you could take that would help make them feel honored for who they are *and* what they do.

Create Your Own Standard of Accountability

Those you lead need to understand your commitment to fairness and dignity. How would you define accountability in a way that conveys your dedication to your team's best work and highest aspirations? What would you have to do differently so that your team *wanted* you to raise the bar, knowing you would be there to help them reach it? Write out your own standard of accountability, share it with your team, and ask them to hold you accountable to a higher standard of how you hold them accountable.

In the next chapter, we'll take a more personal look at justice and accountability in leadership. To be specific, *your* leadership.

KEY TAKEAWAYS

- Traditional approaches to accountability can be confusing, dishonoring, or punitive. These experiences encourage people to hide their mistakes or blame others for them, rather than take ownership of them.

- Lessons from restorative justice practices offer insights to our systems of accountability. The approach maintains the dignity of all parties by emphasizing that wrongdoers can learn from their mistakes while they actively work to repair damage. Rather than excising wrongdoers, restorative justice supports long-term sustainability by strengthening communities.

- In today's knowledge economy, our contributions are close reflections of their contributor. That means traditional metrics that used to seem "objective" made them fair because they purported to treat people "the same." But when contributions are so unique, sameness no longer equals fairness.

- Accountability processes need to dignify the unique talents and contributions of each individual, and managers need to establish trusting relationships in which they can authentically honor the work of those they lead.

- Three ways to encourage fairness are: (1) make expectations clearly tied to the organization's top priorities, (2) effectively develop managers as coaches, and (3) reward differentiated high performance where it makes sense.

- Companies can reshape their definitions of "success" so that admitting/fixing mistakes, learning new skills, or attempting innovation are not accidentally stifled.

Endnotes

1 Oppenheim, C (2018) Women who survived war where rape was used as weapon tell of its horrors and their struggle since, *Independent*, 25 November, https://www.independent.co.uk/news/world/africa/second-congo-war-women-sexual-violence-rwanda-economic-exploitation-a8647356.html (archived at https://perma.cc/772Y-9NWA)

2 Peace Direct (2017) Chirezi Foundation, *PeaceInsight*, November, https://www.peaceinsight.org/conflicts/dr-congo/peacebuilding-organisations/chirezi-fochi/ (archived at https://perma.cc/ERE5-QXGN)

3 I personally interviewed Floribert Kazingufu, the Director of FOCHI in the DRC, who shared details of the story with me as well as official detailed documents of the case from the peace court.

4 The Truth and Reconciliation Commission (n.d.) Welcome to the official Truth and Reconciliation Commission Website, https://www.justice.gov.za/trc/ (archived at https://perma.cc/H9DX-QCU8)

5 Omale, D (2006) Justice in history: an examination of 'African restorative traditions' and the emerging 'restorative justice' paradigm, *African Journal of Criminology & Justice Studies*, https://www.researchgate.net/publication/326265660_JUSTICE_IN_HISTORY_AN_EXAMINATION_OF'AFRICAN_RESTORATIVE_TRADITIONS'_AND_THE_EMERGING_'RESTORATIVE_JUSTICE'_PARADIGM (archived at https://perma.cc/BH5U-YZ3G)

6 Indigenous Peacemaking Initiative; Native American Rights Fund, https://peacemaking.narf.org/ (archived at https://perma.cc/P7A8-YWVE)

7 Rea, L (2009) Lisa Rea interviews Stephen Watt, *Justice Reparatrice*, 05 November, http://www.justicereparatrice.org/www.restorativejustice.org/RJOB/lisa-rea-interviews-stephen-watt (archived at https://perma.cc/VCW4-75JM)

8 Murphy, J (2018) Restorative justice: healing victims and reducing crime, *Baltimore Sun*, 24 January, https://www.baltimoresun.com/opinion/op-ed/bs-ed-op-0125-restorative-justice-20180124-story.html (archived at https://perma.cc/T7K2-47FT)

9 Omale, D (2006) Ibid

10 The University of Texas at Austin (2020) What is restorative justice? The University of Texas at Austin Human Resources, https://hr.utexas.edu/sites/hr.utexas.edu/files/NEW%20RJ%20in%20WP.pdf (archived at https://perma.cc/5EWC-TQMQ)

11 Office of Juvenile Justice and Delinquency Prevention (2020) OJJDP Report: Guide for implementing the balanced and restorative justice model: Balanced and restorative justice practice: Accountability, https://ojjdp.ojp.gov/sites/g/files/xyckuh176/files/pubs/implementing/accountability.html (archived at https://perma.cc/TD33-LN7X)

12   Starner, T (2015) Study: Workplace accountability requires a specific strategy, *HR Dive*, 02 June, https://www.hrdive.com/news/study-workplace-accountability-requires-a-specific-strategy/400130/ (archived at https://perma.cc/XMX8-582P)

13   Wigert, B and Harter, J (2017) Re-engineering performance management, https://www.gallup.com/workplace/238064/re-engineering-performance-management.aspx (archived at https://perma.cc/Y2EQ-2K6Q)

14   Werder, C (2019) The ROI of modern performance management, https://www.reflektive.com/wp-content/uploads/2020/03/REFLEKTIVE_RESEARCH-BRIEF_FINAL_111219-1.pdf (archived at https://perma.cc/4M88-ZD2L)

15   TINYpulse (2017) The Broken Bridges of the Workplace: 2017 employee engagement report, https://www.tinypulse.com/hubfs/whitepaper/TINYpulse-2017-Employee-Engagement-Report-Broken-Bridges-of-the-Workplace.pdf (archived at https://perma.cc/K3BA-PS8Z)

16   Meinert, B (2015) Is it time to put the performance review on a PIP? *Society for Human Resource Management*, 01 April, https://www.shrm.org/hr-today/news/hr-magazine/pages/0415-qualitative-performance-reviews.aspx (archived at https://perma.cc/BPT3-GCQ5)

17   Wigert, B and Harter, J (2017) Re-engineering performance management, *Gallup*, https://www.gallup.com/workplace/238064/re-engineering-performance-management.aspx (archived at https://perma.cc/Y2EQ-2K6Q)

18   Nielsen, D and Britt, M (2014) How a lack of workplace 'fairness' can cause depression, *Eurofound*, 05 March, https://www.eurofound.europa.eu/publications/article/2014/how-a-lack-of-workplace-fairness-can-cause-depression (archived at https://perma.cc/PK3A-78N2)

19   Workfront (2019) The history of performance management, *Workfront*, 18 June, https://www.workfront.com/blog/history-performance-management#:~:text=Its%20origins%20in%20workplace%20settings,cotton%20mill%20as%20a%20whole (archived at https://perma.cc/N7B9-GR4T)

20   Smith, A (2018) More employers ditch performance appraisals, *Society for Human Resource Management*, 18 May, https://www.shrm.org/resourcesandtools/legal-and-compliance/employment-law/pages/more-employers-ditch-performance-appraisals.aspx (archived at https://perma.cc/WF4L-E2K8)

21   Fiske, S T (2019) *Social Beings: Core motives in social psychology* (4th ed.), Wiley & Sons, Inc. Hoboken

22   Ambrose, M, Seabright, M and Schminke, M (2002) Sabotage in the workplace: The role of organizational injustice, *Organizational Behavior and Human Decision Processes*, https://www.sciencedirect.com/science/article/abs/pii/S0749597802000377 (archived at https://perma.cc/Q845-4YH3)

23 Hancock, B, Hioe, E and Schaninger, B (2018) The fairness factor in performance management, *McKinsey & Company*, 05 April, https://www.mckinsey.com/business-functions/organization/our-insights/the-fairness-factor-in-performance-management# (archived at https://perma.cc/5KAP-2H7N)

24 Rock, D, Davis, J and Jones, B (2014) Kill your performance ratings: Neuroscience shows why numbers-based HR management is obsolete, *Strategy + Business*, 08 August, https://www.strategy-business.com/article/00275?gko=c442b (archived at https://perma.cc/J8GJ-87PG)

25 Rock, D (2009) Managing with the brain in mind: Neuroscience research is revealing the social nature of the high-performance workplace, *Strategy + Business*, 27 August, https://www.strategy-business.com/article/09306 (archived at https://perma.cc/X2KD-VZNZ)

26 Chavez, R and Heatherton, T (2015) Multimodal frontostriatal connectivity underlies individual differences in self-esteem, *Social Cognitive and Affective Neuroscience*, https://academic.oup.com/scan/article/10/3/364/1653348 (archived at https://perma.cc/J6MN-XL6T)

27 Neuroscience (2017) Self-esteem mapped in the human brain, *Neuroscience*, 24 October, https://neurosciencenews.com/self-esteem-brain-mapping (archived at https://perma.cc/697J-SEL4)

28 Gervais, M and Carroll, P (2020) *Compete to Create: An approach to living and leading authentically* [Audiobook] 09 July, https://www.amazon.com/Compete-Create-Approach-Leading-Authentically/dp/B08911JMJX (archived at https://perma.cc/JT9J-BT9A)

29 Carucci, R (2019) Microsoft's Chief People Officer: What I've learned about leading culture change, *Forbes*, 14 October, https://www.forbes.com/sites/roncarucci/2019/10/14/microsofts-chief-people-officer-what-ive-learned-about-leading-culture-change/?sh=44e860ab410d (archived at https://perma.cc/T5V6-8RUE)

30 McKinsey & Company (2018) Microsoft's next act, *McKinsey Quarterly*, 03 April, https://www.mckinsey.com/industries/technology-media-and-telecommunications/our-insights/microsofts-next-act (archived at https://perma.cc/4JSZ-CSDU)

31 Sandel, M (2020) *The Tyranny of Merit: What's become of the common good?*, Farrar, Straus and Giroux, New York

05

Everyday Justice

Set your intention: How can I level the playing field so all those I lead have a fair shot to succeed?

Hope From a Bigger Story

In March, 1968, at the height of the Vietnam War, a unit of Charlie Company had received intelligence that the village of Son My, a small town nested along the southern Vietnamese coast, had been taken over by remnants of the Vietcong (VC), the local communist guerrilla force fighting the government of South Vietnam and their backers, the US military. In the months prior, Charlie Company had lost nearly half its men in brutal attacks from Vietcong snipers and booby traps. Angry at the losses and determined to triumph in Son My, Captain Ernest Medina of Charlie Company, 1st Battalion, 20th Infantry, ordered his men to be "very aggressive" in their upcoming sweep of the village. Within Son My, the hamlet of My Lai was believed to be the stronghold of the remaining Vietcong. Medina told his men that the women and children of the village would be at the market in the morning hours when they planned to invade the village, so there wasn't a concern of killing innocent civilians. They were to assume those remaining in the village were either members of the VC or their sympathizers.[1] They were ordered only to capture prisoners, level buildings, kill livestock, and destroy wells.

In the early morning of March 16, 1968, troops from Charlie Company led by Lt. William Calley arrived in My Lai but found no evidence of VC combatants; instead, they found a village mostly full of women, children, and older men preparing their rice for breakfast.[2] Nevertheless, many villagers were rounded up in groups and their huts were inspected for VC members and weapons. Only three weapons were found. Then, the unthinkable happened.

Calley ordered his men to shoot the villagers.

At first, they didn't take him seriously. But after pushing his company into a firing line, Calley repeated himself, ordering two privates, Meadlo and Conti, to kill the villagers. Meadlo obeyed his orders, and what became known as the My Lai Massacre, the most heinous civilian-involved killing of the Vietnam conflict, began. For the next several hours, the soldiers gathered men, women, and children, put some in ditches, and murdered them.

Just before the massacre, Warrant Officer Hugh Thompson, a helicopter pilot, was assigned to provide air cover to Charlie Company during their mission. As Thompson flew over My Lai with his crew of two at around 6:00 a.m., just like the troops on the ground, he received no enemy fire. He spotted two possible VC suspects and forced them to surrender. Next, he came across wounded Vietnamese civilians, after which he marked the ground area with green smoke, a signal that they needed help. Then he went to refuel.

When he returned to My Lai around 9:00 a.m., he noticed the wounded civilians were now dead. He turned his attention to another location, close to a nearby rice paddy, that he had also marked with green smoke after seeing a wounded young Vietnamese woman. From a low hovering position, he watched as Medina came up to the woman, prodded her with his foot to see if she was alive, then shot and killed her.

He then flew over an irrigation ditch filled with dozens of bodies and realized it was his fellow American soldiers killing the civilians. He radioed command and said, "It looks to me like there's an awful lot of unnecessary killing going on down there. Something ain't right about this. There's bodies everywhere. There's a ditch full of bodies that we saw. There's something wrong here."[3]

Thompson landed his helicopter to investigate what was happening, and more importantly, why. While he was confronting one of the soldiers guarding the civilians in the ditch, Calley stepped in. They had the following exchange:

Thompson: What's going on here, Lieutenant?

Calley: This is my business.

Thompson: What is this? Who are these people?

Calley: Just following orders.

Thompson: Orders? Whose orders?

Calley: Just following…

Thompson: But, these are human beings, unarmed civilians, sir.

Calley: Look Thompson, this is my show. I'm in charge here. It ain't your concern.

Thompson: Yeah, great job.

Calley: You better get back in that chopper and mind your own business.

Thompson: You ain't heard the last of this![4]

As Thompson took off again, his crew noticed that the soldier Thompson confronted was carrying out Calley's order to kill the civilians in the ditch. Enraged, Thompson flew to the northeast corner of the village and saw a small group of about 10 civilian men, women, and children running for shelter; they were being chased by members of Charlie Company. Then Thompson did the unimaginable.

He landed his helicopter *between* the civilians and the American troops advancing on them.

He told his helicopter crew that if the Americans opened fire on him or the Vietnamese civilians, they were to open fire on the Americans. Thankfully, he was able to stop the Americans from firing, and proceeded to rescue the civilians.

Thompson's courage stopped the massacre. But by the end of it, more than 500 Vietnamese civilians had been murdered. The Army tried to cover up the incident, and Thompson was subjected to horrific retribution for his actions, including death threats and dead animals left on his front porch. In a closed hearing of the House Armed Services Committee in 1969, Thompson was harshly criticized by several Congressmen who tried desperately to play down the massacre. They tried to have him court-martialed, unsuccessfully. Calley was court-martialed, and Thompson testified at the trial.

Eventually, however, the tables turned. In 1998, 30 years after the massacre, Thompson and his two crew members, Glenn Andreotta (posthumously) and Lawrence Colburn, were awarded the Soldier's Medal, the Army's highest honor for bravery not involving conflict with an enemy. That year Thompson also returned to visit My Lai with Colburn to commemorate the 30-year anniversary of the massacre and meet with some of the civilians they rescued. They toured a small museum that had previously been opened in his honor, and the two Americans helped dedicate a new elementary school. One of the most poignant moments of the visit occurred when one of the women the men saved asked Thompson, "Why didn't the men who committed these acts come back with you?" Thompson was devastated. But then she finished her question: "… so that we could forgive them?"[5]

During the ceremony, Thompson said, "Something terrible happened here 30 years ago today. I cannot explain why it happened. I just wish our crew that day could have helped more people than we did."[6]

It's hard to know how many more deaths Thompson's courage prevented. But his choice to do the right thing for those who could not defend themselves—to confront the abuse of power and gross injustice right in front of him—is an example for all leaders. Mindful of the painful ostracizing he had suffered, Thompson said in a 2004 interview, "Don't do the right thing looking for a reward, because it might not come."[7]

Thankfully, most of us will never have to risk our lives as Thompson did in the name of justice. And by no means is it my intent to trivialize the atrocities of My Lai by making an erroneous comparison to the injustices we face in organizations. But it would be a mistake to therefore dismiss Thompson's courage and sacrifice for the sake of justice as irrelevant to all of us.

In organizational life, countless injustices happen every day that we have the power to right. Interestingly, we often use wartime metaphors to describe them. "He shoots the messenger," "She got slaughtered in her presentation," "That quarterly review was a bloodbath," "The board meeting is going to be a battle. Can you give me some air cover?" "They killed my project." And the most difficult ones to acknowledge are those that come from people or groups we thought "were on our side." Righting and learning from wrongs, instead of covering them up or shaming people for them, is what lies at the heart of everyday organizational justice. Without that, accountability systems will be forever consigned to the foul perversions we discussed in the last chapter.

For accountability to be shaped by dignity and justice, each of us must find the courage to do our part.

Rooting out injustice

When I interviewed Ed Townley in 2020, he had been CEO of Cabot Creamery, the acclaimed dairy cooperative in New England, since 2015. He told me, "I may have been naïve about what it was going to take to lead the company." He had served as Cabot's CFO prior to taking the helm. Dairy cooperatives can be enormously challenging businesses to run, especially when it comes to balancing the needs of both the dairy farmers trying to get their milk to market at a fair price and the dairy product manufacturers trying to manage raw material and manufacturing capacity, pricing regulations, and the complexities of the many customer segments served. When Townley took over as CEO, he said, the Cabot board decided to build a hiring profile for the role, and "honesty and integrity were the top two criteria." He would immediately be tested on both fronts.

As soon as he began, he realized he would need to replace members of his team who "weren't creating the culture I thought we needed." The problems, though, went a lot deeper: "What I hadn't expected to find was people committing fraud. I found two cases where leaders were doing just that." In one case, a maintenance manager had been ordering expensive manufacturing equipment the company paid for, and selling it through his private business. In another case, the head of technology was purchasing unnecessary equipment and converting it for his own use, or selling it and pocketing the money.

How should he respond? Townley had a very important decision to make, one that would set the tone for Cabot for years to come: "Now, I could have just fired them and swept the whole thing under the carpet, but I knew that was the wrong thing to do. I decided we needed to prosecute them."

After the second case was discovered, Townley had to stand up at an annual meeting in front of approximately 300 farmers and explain what was going on. They were furious. They wondered how someone could have stolen millions of dollars of product[8] right under the nose of the CEO, and worse, where else it may have happened:

> Vermont is a small state, and this became the talk of Vermont. The farmers were embarrassed and naturally felt betrayed. They wanted reassurance that it wouldn't happen again, and given it was early in my run as CEO, I couldn't guarantee that. I said, "I'm not going to shirk away from this kind of offense. If I find it, I'm going to deal with it, and unfortunately, that means you're going to know about it.

Townley knew that if the culture he wanted to create was going to take hold, people had to know he was serious about change. "I couldn't have people wondering if I was condoning such behavior, or worse, concluding that if people in leadership could do this, then it must be ok for them to do it." So Townley took a strict line: no behavior that might give off even a whiff of impropriety would be tolerated, no matter who was involved. This meant that a plant manager ("a very senior leader") who sent $300 worth of product to his family for Christmas was fired. "People really understood I was committed to a culture of integrity," said Townley. Under Ed's leadership, Cabot went on to become one of the most admired companies in the dairy industry, and a certified B Corps.

(Later, in Chapter 8, I'll share the rest of the remarkable story of Ed's leadership, and the extraordinary company Cabot Creamery has become since those early years of his leadership.)

WALK IN THEIR SHOES

If you had discovered what Townley had, what would you have done? What would you have coached him to do differently?

A commitment to justice in your own organization requires that leaders share Ed's conviction about honesty and fairness. Consider how you might navigate moments like these real-life scenarios I've heard from clients or seen happen:

- During a staff meeting, your boss publicly chews out your peer, a finance professional, for missing a mandatory business review. The sales leader on your team, also present, whose function routinely gets away with things others wouldn't because they bring in the revenue, missed the same review but got no admonishment. When the boss isn't looking, the sales leader smirks at you and winks.

- You are in line at the company cafeteria checkout and notice that the cashier stops a Black employee, a close colleague of yours who has worked there for years, and politely asks to see his badge. She asks none of the White people in the area to see theirs. As your colleague walks away, you can see his shoulders slouching and his head slightly lowered.

- At a budget review meeting, your fellow department leads are presenting their budget requests to the review committee that will allocate next year's resources. Having done this numerous times, you give a perfect presentation and your budget is quickly approved. The young woman whose presentation follows yours, a newly appointed department head, is visibly nervous. She stutters during her presentation and you notice people on the committee trying to hide their snickering and eye-rolling. The department she inherited has been in shambles and clearly needs more resources than anyone else. But when she's finished, the committee, largely made up of men, gives her only 75 percent of her requested budget. When you pass her office later, you notice her red eyes and how she avoids making eye contact with you.

- You are choosing who to promote into a vacant manager position, with the choice between several candidates on your team. They are all equally qualified, each with unique strengths and gaps. The Diversity & Inclusion team is urging you to promote the person whose identity is underrepresented in your organization and industry. Your boss has made her top choice known—someone who has been unfairly passed over before but whose close connection to your boss makes you nervous. And the person you feel would be best for the job happens to be someone you are close to and have worked with for years.

Each of the four scenarios above depicts everyday incidents in workplaces across the world. Every time you turn a blind eye to situations like these, however benign you may think they are, you are working against justice.

Our organizational routines are full of choices that appear much less straightforward when seen through the lens of justice. Any time you hear someone protest, "That's not fair!," be on alert for organizational injustice, no matter how small the infraction may seem. And if you want to be a leader of honesty, you can't remain a passive bystander. You need to step in and proactively influence things toward a just outcome.

So, when facing situations like those above, how can you do that?

Use Your Power for Justice

Power is a complicated source of influence within organizations. Most often it's thought of negatively, in the context of headlines touting the many ways it's been abused. But it is the starting point from where leaders can right organizational injustices. The decision to create organizations of fairness starts with a leader's personal conviction that justice is theirs to create. It doesn't just come about via some mysterious force of "fairness pixie dust" being sprinkled over the organization. It takes conviction, courage, and the choice to exercise the power of one's leadership. And to do that well, we need a more instructive understanding of what exactly power is, and how it works.

As part of the research for my last book, *Rising to Power: The Journey of Exceptional Executives*, I wanted to understand what factors determined whether a leader taking on a broader leadership role would succeed or fail. We've known for decades that approximately 50 to 60 percent of leaders fail within their first 18 months after being promoted to a bigger role. One of the biggest surprises in our findings, though, was that their greatest abuse of power did not involve self-interest or immoral gain, as scandalous headlines might have us believe. The greatest abuse of power was the *abandonment* of it—people too afraid or anxious to use it.

Whether for fear of being judged or simply wanting to purchase popularity from others, leaders abdicating their power instead said "yes" too often, giving people their way but in the process diluting the resources and focus of their organization. They often justified their power failure as a desire to create a sense of egalitarianism—to ensure those they led felt valued and included. In so doing, they struggled to make hard choices, including too many others in decisions to the point of paralysis. They ignored poor performance, played favorites, purchased loyalty by divulging confidences, and generally wreaked havoc on their organizations. Our data revealed how unprepared most leaders are to make effective use of their power. Of our respondents, 67 percent struggled to let go of work they'd done in previous jobs—a way of hanging on to the familiarity of past success and avoiding the uncertainty of more ambiguous challenges. Sixty percent struggled with the fact that people ascribed more power to them than they actually believed they had. And 50 percent found that political power dynamics at higher levels made it much harder to trust and work with peers.[9]

You may feel that because of where you sit on your organization's hierarchy you have limited power. That's a common misunderstanding. Organizational power comes in many shapes, not just the formal levels of authority, or positional power. In fact, our research showed that managers at any level have three primary sources of power that can be brought to bear to right injustices and allow others to thrive:

- **Positional power**
  This includes the formal decision-making rights that come with your role, such as budgetary oversight, performance management and career influence over direct reports, governance, the meetings and decisions you participate in across the organization, etc. Most leaders underestimate the degree of positional power within their role. I've had numerous CEOs say to me, "I feel like I have the least amount of power in the organization." That's largely because in today's highly collaborative workplace, positional power can only go so far. It offers one of the strongest ways to correct organizational injustice if you have the authority within your role to instigate change, but it is by no means the only way. But it provides a strong platform from which to ensure justice within the team or department you lead.

- **Relational power**

  Your network of connections is an extraordinary source of power and influence. The degree of trust you have built up, the equity you have gained from contributing to others' success, the reputation you have garnered for being reliable, smart, easy to work with, service-oriented, or goodhearted all create important sources of power that you can use to help create needed change.

- **Informational power**

  Many companies still treat information as a power source—have it and you're powerful, don't have it and you're not. But these days, the ubiquity of most information makes hoarding it rather pointless. The abundance of data has rendered *insight* a greater source of power than just information. A novel *interpretation of the information* becomes a unique form of power that helps cut through lots of noise and piles of raw data.

Armed with these three sources of power, you will be well equipped to bring justice anywhere it may be lacking—you just need to be on the lookout for where that could be. Here are some questions that can help you figure it out:

1 *Who on your team has felt deprived of the chance to shine or advance their skills?* What project assignments could you help them take on that would allow them to learn and gain visibility? (Your positional power could create that assignment, your relational power could network the person to someone who could help, and your informational power could help them learn where in the organization their talents could be best used.)

2 *Who has struggled to have their voice or ideas heard?* What group is feeling marginalized or as if they don't matter? (Your positional power will allow you to listen to their concerns and advocate for them to leaders at higher levels. You could flex your relational power by demonstrating empathy to them and listening to the stories of their struggle to be heard. Your informational power could be leveraged to inform others of the importance of their voice and the value the organization is missing by not hearing it.)

3 *Who is accountable for results that they feel ill-equipped or under-resourced to deliver?* What team or individuals feel "set up to fail"? Every organization inevitably justifies asking more of people than they can deliver, reassuring them that it will be okay, but then punishing them when they fall short. (You could use your positional power to call this practice into question with leaders at higher levels. Your relational power could be

used to help broker support for the person or group that's under-resourced. Your informational power may be able to offer insight into why they haven't been set up for success and offer ideas for how to rectify that).

4 *Who are your organization's bullies?* Which people or leaders have reputations for disrespecting others, being overly harsh, or manipulating people into doing things for them? (You could use your positional power to use the company's HR system to make sure the person is held accountable, and if those processes fail, you can directly confront the person with feedback—yes, even if they are higher ranking than you; your relational power could get you close to this person to win their trust, learn more about the reasons behind their bullying, and earn the right to engage them in a conversation about the impact of their behavior. Your informational power could help you coach those being bullied on how to better understand or effectively stand up to the bully).

Once you focus the lens of justice onto the things that cause people to feel treated unfairly, it's not difficult to see the places of inequity built into your organization. You simply have to be willing to look and act. And like Hugh Thompson did with his helicopter, you must be willing to land yourself between the source of injustice and those on the receiving end of it. Instead of rationalizing that "No organization is perfect," "I can't risk my career to intervene in something that won't change anyway," or "That's not my job, or my place, or my responsibility," we have to resolve, like Thompson did, that if something unjust is happening within your view, and you believe it's unacceptable, then you have to act. When more of us start doing this, systems of accountability across our company, industry, and perhaps the wider world will become fairer, unleashing those around us to do their best work. Moreover, we will strengthen the honesty muscle within our organization by dramatically reducing the risk of unethical misconduct. Even incremental improvements will help. The statistical models in my research show that even a 20 percent improvement in fairness within accountability, as evidenced by employees' belief that their contributions have been justly assessed with dignity, can improve honesty by 12 percent.

Equity and Privilege: Leveling the Playing Field

On 25 May, 2020, George Floyd, a Black Minneapolis resident, was murdered by White Minneapolis police officer Derek Chauvin. His death set off a firestorm of outrage across the world about racial injustice. Millions of people took to the streets in protest as scenes from the horrific video capturing his death flashed across screens of every kind. It appeared that the long-overdue day of reckoning had finally arrived, and much of the world seemed ready to face the deep-seated racial inequities plaguing us. Companies felt compelled to issue statements condemning racial inequality. But protests and public declarations are a far cry from tangible actions. Being outraged is a start, but rooting out inequity in the systems and relationships around us is what will truly level the playing field. I wanted to understand how systemic inequalities that create injustice within our organizations actually formed, and more importantly, how they could be eliminated.

Dr. Tiffany Jana is a renowned expert in the field of Diversity, Equity and Inclusion, and co-author (along with Ashley Diaz Mejias) of the 2018 book *Erasing Institutional Bias: How to create systemic change for organizational inclusion*. I spoke with Jana about the effects of bias and privilege on systems of accountability.

To help illustrate what true accountability looks like, she posed two provocative questions that get to the crux of the matter:

> Regardless of how I show up in your organization, do I have just as much
> likelihood of success as anyone else? Whether someone arrives as male or
> female, white, black, Hispanic, Asian, LGBTQ, with invisible or visible
> disabilities, or regardless from which school, will they get the same mentorships
> and opportunities, will they be given high-profile assignments to prepare
> for advancement, will they actually get promotions on a par with any other
> demographic in your company? Equity in accountability is about making sure
> that your systems, not just your intentions, can answer with a yes. And since our
> systems are built by humans, biases are already built in.

Selection systems, for example, are often biased because they're based on the networks and alma maters of those in power. So, if we keep recruiting and promoting from the same network pools and schools, we're going to keep advancing the same demographics.

Rather than treating underrepresented groups as people who need "extra help" to advance, Jana argues that hiring managers should instead see someone's uniqueness as added value that can benefit all parties:

> I would never tell anyone to hire someone because they are from an
> underrepresented demographic. First, they've got to be qualified to do the job
> and frankly they need to be the most qualified. However, if you've got multiple
> candidates and you've got three that represent demographics that are currently

highly overrepresented in your organization, and you have one or two that come from demographics that you currently don't have strong populations of in your organization, these perspectives on top of their experience are like additional advanced degrees. So being Asian, being Black, being a woman, being LGBTQ, all of these things are going to add so much dimension, so much depth and so much value to your organization that you need to see them as additional line items on a resume and privilege that identity as something that the organization will derive unique value from rather than merely as people to help fill your diversity quota.

If power is an asset you acquire, privilege is one that you inherit, not something you earn. Aspects of your identity, like skin color or gender, may be privileged—meaning you get benefits from them that others don't. It doesn't make you a bad person with ill intent, but it does require that you understand how those privileges affect others. You may have privilege because you are fully able-bodied, or because you went to a certain college, or you are part of a certain religious group. Usually such privilege forms among those within a "majority" group, rendering them least likely to notice it.

It's common for people to have such privilege pointed out and become immediately defensive, insisting that whatever they have, they worked hard for. This is a short-sighted conclusion. When you are part of the privileged group, you're the last one to notice it precisely because you're in the "normative" group. By default, the normative group becomes the unspoken "standard." In many companies, there is occupational privilege. For example, in high-tech companies, engineers are often a privileged role. In companies with iconic brands, marketers are often privileged. In high-growth companies, salespeople are often privileged. In companies with very steep hierarchies, higher-ranking people are often privileged. The important thing is to recognize that having that privilege doesn't make you elitist, classist, racist, sexist, or any other-ist. It's failing to acknowledge the ramifications of that privilege—the benefits you enjoy and the implications for others—that makes you part of the problem.

In her book, *Erasing Institutional Bias,* Jana suggests asking yourself the following reflection questions to begin addressing privilege and bias within your organization:

1 What specific privilege or bias is at issue?
2 How is it affecting me?
3 How am I benefitting from it?

4 How am I hurt or limited by it?

5 How is it affecting my colleagues and this organization's stakeholders?

6 How might it benefit specific demographics?

7 Which groups are hurt or limited by it?

8 How will erasing it help these groups?

9 Who might feel threatened by an attempt to erase it?[10]

Once you've identified the area of concern, determine what role you want to play in change, what allies you can enlist in a coalition, and how you can create a movement of people committed to leveling the playing field for everyone. Jana offers encouragement for aspiring changemakers, suggesting that they (you):

> … give yourself grace as you embark on this journey. Institutional bias can be a really ugly business. Once you begin to see its effects and examine it closely, it is very hard to "unsee" it. It is also hard to avoid becoming angry, bitter, and jaded about the whole phenomenon. It is, however, very important not to lose sight of the goal. Your purpose in this endeavor is to improve opportunities for people. You need to stay strong, maintain focus, and remain as optimistic as possible.[11]

Jana's conclusions are supported by rigorous research from the University of Amsterdam's study on the psychology of justice, where researchers found that human beings have an "undeniable drive to extend justice to fellow human beings."[12] Organizations have to create the context in which people can fulfill that drive.

Now that we've talked about the realities of power and privilege as routes to organizational justice, let's talk about the other area you can influence as a leader—how you treat failure.

Failure as a Vehicle of Justice

I wish I had a dollar for every time I heard a leader pronounce, "We need to learn from our mistakes" or "Fail fast so we can innovate." While you may be genuine in your intent, and even though these platitudes sound nice to say, trust me—nobody in your organization believes you mean it, and they're rolling their eyes behind your back. Still, failures large and small happen every day in organizations and if we understand how to leverage their value, they can lead to justice and honesty in surprising ways.

There's a legendary story about Thomas Watson, Sr., IBM's CEO in the 1950s. Betting on booming post-war growth, Watson kept inventory levels high despite the lack of demand. Without a solid sales pipeline, manufacturing and storing products burns through cash that isn't being replenished. The company's board of directors disagreed with Watson and called for his removal. Every deal counted—inventory levels had to be reduced to keep the company's cash flow healthy. There was a large government bid in play worth nearly a million dollars. Unfortunately, the young salesman overseeing it lost the bid, and he showed up at Watson's office with his resignation in hand. Watson asked what had happened and the young salesman explained everything he had done. Then he thanked Watson for the chance to explain, and got up to leave. Watson handed him his resignation back and said, "Why would I accept this when I just invested a million dollars in your education?"[13] Clearly Watson understood the immense power of failure. That story became folklore throughout the company.

While most of us would like to think we'd have the fortitude to respond to a failure like Watson did, how many of us would?

Amy Edmondson is the Novartis Professor of Leadership at Harvard Business School and author of *The Fearless Organization: Creating psychological safety in the workplace for learning, innovation, and growth*. I spoke with her in mid-2020 about her research and insights about the connection between psychological safety and learning from failure. "Whenever I ask executives how many failures in their organization are truly blameworthy—meaning they were avoidable failures—their answers are usually very low, like 4 or 5 percent," she says. "But when I ask them how many failures are *treated as blameworthy*, they often laugh nervously and say 'like 80 or 90 percent.'" Edmondson concedes that most leaders are genuine when they say they want people to learn from failure. Extensive, often expensive post-mortem studies of mistakes indicate a genuine desire to learn and improve. But, she told me:

> When leaders get fixed on finding fault and placing blame to "make sure failure doesn't happen again," they unwittingly make it unsafe for people to acknowledge, much less learn from, failure. And if your accountability systems are out of whack, where expectation, reward, and punishment teach people that cause and effect simply don't match around here, then you're teaching people learned helplessness by inducing fear. Nobody's going to fess up to failure in that environment.

(You'll hear more from Edmondson in Chapter 7, when we discuss the role of psychological safety in creating environments where people freely speak up about tough issues and offer risky ideas.)

A particularly noxious form of failure occurs when people feel as if they have been *set up* to fail, a topic I touched on earlier. Many leaders believe that setting high standards enables people to reach greater levels of performance. But when those standards become unreachable, people's performance, and spirits, flag. I have a striking example from an interview I conducted with a leader about his boss, the CEO of a large corporation. "Nothing I do is ever good enough for her. We're all starting to ask ourselves why we bother trying," he told me. When I spoke with the CEO to get her side of things, she said, "People consistently disappoint me. It's always been that way. I have high standards. That's why I get the results that I do."

When I raised concerns about the unintended consequences of her high standards, she said it had never occurred to her that she might be undermining the very high performance she sought. As an executive whose standards are excessively high, or perfectionistic, she isn't alone. Research shows that up to 35 percent of high-performing executives fail because of their tendency toward perfectionism.[14] To be clear, your discontent as a leader can be a powerful asset to spur yourself and those you lead on to greater achievement. But you must learn to harness that discontent for good by knowing when and how much to express it. Make sure that when you set the bar high, you also help people reach it. Express confidence in people's ability, make sure you have a clear understanding of what they need to do so that they believe your ask is realistic, and honor their desire for your approval regardless of the outcome. When those you lead are left to question their value in your eyes, your perfectionism becomes a constant source of critique and disregard. Make sure everyone you lead knows what you value about them *and* their contribution.

Fewer environments can suffer from perfectionist-driven failure more than the US Military. For an example of this, look no further than Lt. Commander Erik Nyheim, a naval executive officer and commander of a special warfare team, who wrote about his personal experience with failure in the book *The U.S. Naval Institute on Leadership Ethics*. In his chapter contribution, "Zero-defect leadership is the problem," he explains that:

> Operational pressures from two wars combined with the pressure to be perfect led to poor decisions out of uniform. From binge drinking to questionable behavior, I could have lost the privilege to serve. Were it not for the focused attention of community leaders, expanded education on ethics and behavior, and congressionally directed mental and emotional health resources, I would not have recognized the destructive path on which I was traveling.[15]

Nyheim writes that having sufficient "safe space" to air his failures, reflect on his actions, and learn from them enabled him to bridge failure and success. He also suggests that being a leader who prized honesty and improvement over perfection only deepened his commitment to his oath and values, and to those with whom he served. Much to his credit, Nyheim courageously names the cultural challenge that he was up against and, through his own leadership, set out to change the stigma of failing:

> The expansive effort to rid our service of failure has unintended consequences that detract from performance and character. Specifically, a fear of failure projected across the force robs leaders of the opportunity to teach service members how to learn from mistakes and grow. Rather than fostering a culture that values honesty and creates space to bridge failure and success, members often feel suffocated by the pressures of perfection. Those pressures, manifested in destructive ways, detract from our goal of being the finest Navy in the history of mankind.[16]

Notice his direct correlation between accountability and honesty—they go hand in hand.

Nyheim goes on to lay out his process for overcoming a zero-defect mentality and overemphasis on perfection. First, they had to destigmatize the notion of failure, reorienting its meaning to help people understand its inherent value in promoting growth and improvement, not perfection. Then, they had to work on creating safe spaces where Navy personnel could bridge failure and success by teaching them that failure leads to reflection, reflection to self-awareness, self-awareness to adaptation, and adaptation to improved performance.

Nyheim shares a story of the significant difference this change made. A top-performing petty officer was driven with perfecting his unit's performance to the point of very damaging outcomes. Because of several violations of misconduct, some involving alcohol, the officer had to be relieved of his command. The officer hadn't realized the degree to which the imposed pressure of chasing perfection led to his failure. Through a disciplinary process, the officer got the help he needed, was able to bridge failure to success by learning from his mistakes, and embarked on his journey to turning things around. Though his actions almost cost him his career, the petty officer restored his standing and took on a new command. Nyheim says, "He is thriving again because our leaders allowed failure to be his stepping-stone to success."[17]

Tragically, in most organizations, failure is received with one of two extreme reactions: it's either ignored without consequences, or it is considered fatal. Rarely are people held accountable to learn from it. Nyheim's story and approach offers us a blueprint for how, even in high-risk contexts where the bar is demandingly high, we can create environments where failure offers a pathway to justice in accountability.

Sanyin Siang is the Executive Director of the Coach K Center on Leadership and Ethics at the Duke University Fuqua School of Business. She works with executives as well as sports and military leaders from around the world. In my interview with her, she offered this insightful perspective about the importance of failure:

> You can't isolate the treatment of failure from the rest of a leader's relationship with those she leads. The very essence of how a leader shapes success for others is bound in an agreement, sometimes unspoken, that leaders want others to be their best. When that's the case, there are steady streams of empowering feedback that help people improve while avoiding catastrophe. Small course corrections are easier than major ones. But even when there is significant failure, the only real tragedy is when we don't learn from it. As leaders we have to be honest about our role in others' failure. Were we clear in our expectations? Did they have the right resources? Are we showing them the grace they need to pick themselves back up and keep going? Failure rarely happens in isolation—we have to look at all the factors that led to it. When our children fail, we don't document their mistakes in a performance improvement plan, we sit down with them and lovingly talk through what happened, what we can learn and how we can grow from it. Leaders should approach their people the same way, seeing failure as the first step toward success. We can be both firm and show empathy. We can have high expectations and we can be compassionate when things don't go as planned. If leaders want innovation, experimentation, openness to trying new approaches and resilience after setbacks, honoring failure comes with the territory.

You may wonder if a compassionate response to failure in some way implies lowering the bar or accepting sub-par performance. But it actually raises the bar. Simply shaming someone after failure is easy, and almost guarantees their lost confidence; fear of you and resentment for your treatment won't get you much improvement next time. Allowing others the grace to fail and grow is much harder, but almost always leads to even better performance.

Like using your power to right wrongs or confront inequity, treating failure with compassion takes courage. Because the road to everyday justice is only paved with counter-intuitive leadership. Organizational injustices often appear so routine that the need for justice doesn't naturally occur to us. It takes intentionally looking for it to find it. When something is unfair, true leaders willingly stand in the breach to right the wrongs that cause others to feel marginalized or mistreated. They make sure everyone has an equal chance of success. They use their power to actively seek out opportunities to help others thrive and contribute their best work. They make sure that no one has privileges that unintentionally disadvantage others. And they are purposeful about making it safe for others to fail and learn, so nobody feels they have to cover up mistakes.

Whether or not you have the authority to change your organization's systems of accountability across the company, you do have the opportunity to create a more just environment around yourself. Here's how you can do your part.

Get Busy: Bring Justice to Places of Injustice

Use Your Power to Create a Platform for Others

Organizations can be especially noisy places, making many people feel unheard. Creating opportunities for your peers, or those you lead, to share their ideas, make presentations to important audiences, or contribute to others' learning are all impactful ways to amplify the voices of others. If you host a standing meeting of any kind, consider carving out part of the agenda on a regular basis to showcase the ideas and good work of those who don't have many opportunities to be heard. Host special events that allow people you lead with unique expertise to share their knowledge and skills with others. One executive I worked with planned his department's "Ideas Forum" a year in advance. Throughout the year there were bi-monthly workshops, webinars, and discussions led by various people from across his organization. If you report to someone who leads a much larger portion of the organization, consider challenging them to incorporate a rotating segment of their meeting agenda where they invite employees from around the organization to showcase their work. This also has the side benefit of allowing senior leaders a view of promising talent they would otherwise never get to know.

Level the Playing Field for the Marginalized

Somewhere within your organization there are those who enjoy privileges, and perhaps are even blind to how those privileges disadvantage others. Identify someone in your organization who you believe may feel disadvantaged or marginalized in some way and find ways to level the playing field for them, especially if the unequal field is the byproduct of another person's or group's privilege. Start by picking one person or group and engaging them about how they may feel disadvantaged and the ways they may be suffering in silence as a result. For example, people in support or oversight functions like human resources, finance, or ethics and compliance often feel they lack the "seat at the table" that others enjoy, and therefore feel unable to have the kind of impact the rest of the organization expects of them. Similarly, people from underrepresented demographics often feel isolated and misunderstood. How can you help build a bridge between these employees and those who could most benefit from their skills? Where is ignorance of their value or unconscious bias contributing to their feeling sidelined? Even by raising the question with them, and engaging your team in a conversation about this, you will signal that ensuring fairness for everyone is important to you.

Confront a Bully

Somewhere in your organization is a person with a reputation for being demeaning, exploiting others, and driving their agenda while sacrificing people's dignity. You know who they are. I'm not suggesting you sacrifice your career on a political alter by getting in the CEO's face about his bad behavior. But it could be a peer in another group, or someone a level or two below you. Start by making your intentions known to your organization that you intend to value dignity and fairness. Name the bullying behaviors you won't tolerate. And, as appropriate, engage a bully in a private, safe conversation about your observations of their behavior and its impact on others, and the reputation those have led to. Help them discover the gap between their intentions and their impact (most bullies don't actually intend to hurt others). Make it clear that you expect them to change their behavior.

Manage Your Perfectionism

Make sure you make it possible for people to meet your high standards. Ask for feedback (anonymously if necessary) from those you lead about whether your criticism, dissatisfaction, or continual pushing for "more" ever leads to their discouragement or feelings of inadequacy. Learn to set standards *with them* rather than for them and engage them in honest conversations about what they need from you to be successful.

Treat Performance Shortfalls with Dignity and Learning

Think about the last time someone you led underdelivered against expectations or made a significant mistake. How did you respond? Did you minimize it so they didn't feel bad? Did you react harshly and shame them? Being honest about underperformance is one of the most important places to treat others with dignity. Too many leaders pull their punches when it comes to giving productive developmental feedback to others. They soft-pedal important messages in the interest of being "nice." But withholding feedback that could help others improve is actually not kind, it's cruel. You are protecting your own ego and indulging your discomfort with conflict, and in so doing, hurting the dignity of others. Because they know exactly what you are doing. The alternative, belittling people with demeaning feedback when they fall short, is just as cruel. Treat performance shortfalls with clear feedback about how you believe things went off track. Ask the person you are coaching to lead the conversation with their own assessment so they can restore confidence that they can turn things around. Together, develop agreements for how things will change, what you both can learn from the failure, and what you each need to contribute to get performance levels back to where you both want.

Ask for the Story

Nothing strengthens another person's dignity more than asking them to tell you the story of an important achievement. Far from just routine praise or a high-five, acknowledging that the contribution is a personal reflection of them as the contributor elevates their sense of esteem in your eyes, and their own. Simply saying, "Wow, I'm sure that was more challenging than it looked. How did you do it?" sets the stage for them to share the parts of the story most would never hear: where they struggled, where they doubted, moments they broke through obstacles, and what makes them most proud of the achievement. Without a doubt, an animated retelling of a story to an intently listening ear solidifies the teller's deep sense of significance. Ask questions, jot down a few notes, and remain fascinated. It may only take 15 or 20 minutes, but it may be one of the most lasting experiences of dignity you offer someone.

Now that we've finished exploring the role of justice in accountability, let's move on to Part Three, transparency in governance.

KEY TAKEAWAYS

- The heart of organizational justice is righting and learning from wrongs instead of covering them up or shaming people.

- We all must do our part to hold each other accountable if we want to shape dignity and justice in organizations.

- Leaders in organizations must express conviction about honesty and fairness as a way of showing their commitment to justice.

- Being a leader of honesty requires you to be active in conversations and aware of day-to-day infractions that show organizational injustice.

- Within the first 18 months of being promoted, 50–60 percent of leaders fail. In contrast to what many think, this failure is actually due to an abandonment of power, i.e. people being too afraid or anxious to use their power.

- Organizational power doesn't necessarily come from company hierarchy. While some power comes from positional power, relational power and informational power are critical forms of power that leaders can employ to create more just organizations.

- To see the places of inequity in the organization, try to focus your lens of justice on things that cause people to feel they've been treated unfairly.

- The realities of power and privilege as routes to organizational justice start from identifying the area of concern, determining what role you want to play in change, what allies you can enlist in a coalition, and figuring out how you can create a movement of people committed to leveling the playing field for everyone.

- Failure in organizations is either ignored without consequences or is fatal to a career. Rather, leaders like Erik Nyheim can create environments where failure is a pathway to justice in accountability.

Endnotes

1 Levesque, C (2018) The truth behind My Lai, *The New York Times*, 16
March, https://www.nytimes.com/2018/03/16/opinion/the-truth-behind-my-lai.
html (archived at https://perma.cc/BD43-ULBY)

2 History.com Editors (2009) My Lai Massacre, History, 17 April, https://www.
history.com/topics/vietnam-war/my-lai-massacre-1 (archived at https://perma.
cc/8CLU-TE4L)

3 U.S. Army Warrant Officers Association (n.d.) The forgotten hero of My
Lai: The Hugh Thompson story, https://warrantofficerhistory.org/PDF/
Forgotten_Hero_of_My_Lai-WO_Hugh_Thompson.pdf (archived at https://
perma.cc/7E6Y-DDFP)

4 Angers, T (1999) *The Forgotten Hero of My Lai: The Hugh Thompson story*,
Acadian House Publishing, Louisiana

5 Wiener, J (2018) Op-Ed: A forgotten hero stopped the My Lai massacre 50
years ago today, *Los Angeles Times*, 16 March, https://www.latimes.com/
opinion/op-ed/la-oe-wiener-my-lai-hugh-thompson-20180316-story.html
(archived at https://perma.cc/TD7E-3RWJ)

6 Goldstein, R (2006) Hugh Thompson, 62, who saved civilians at My Lai, dies,
The New York Times, 07 January, https://www.nytimes.com/2006/01/07/us/
hugh-thompson-62-who-saved-civilians-at-my-lai-dies.html (archived at
https://perma.cc/SKK3-WPHX)

7 Ibid

8 Savage, K (2019) Murder suspect sentenced to prison for Cabot Creamery
theft, *VT Digger*, 06 December, https://vtdigger.org/2019/12/06/murder-
suspect-sentenced-to-prison-for-cabot-creamery-theft/ (archived at https://
perma.cc/U8FQ-CHZ4)

9 Carucci, R and Hansen, E (2014) *Rising to Power: The journey of exceptional
executives*, Greenleaf Book Group Press, Texas

10 Jana, T and Mejias, A (2018) *Erasing Institutional Bias: How to create
systemic change for organizational inclusion*, Berrett-Koehler Publisher,
California

11 Ibid

12 Gollwitzer, M and Prooijen, J W (2016) Psychology of justice, in *The
Handbook of Social Justice Theory and Research,* https://www.researchgate.
net/publication/312096640_Psychology_of_Justice (archived at https://perma.
cc/E2F8-D5RC)

13 Greulich, P (2019) On thoughtful mistakes: We forgive thoughtful mistakes,
MBI Concepts Corporation, 30 September, https://www.mbiconcepts.com/
watson-sr-and-thoughtful-mistakes.html (archived at https://perma.cc/B24J-
KVGE)

14 Harrari, D, Swider, B, Steed, L, and Breidenthal, A (2018) Is perfect good? A meta-analysis of perfectionism in the workplace, *Journal of Applied Psychology*, https://www.apa.org/pubs/journals/releases/apl-apl0000324.pdf (archived at https://perma.cc/M3EV-QFKT)

15 Demy T (2017) *The U.S. Naval Institute on Leadership Ethics: U.S. Naval Institute Wheel Book*, Naval Institute Press, Maryland

16 Ibid

17 Ibid

PART THREE

Transparency in Governance

06

Trustworthy Decision Making

Set your intention: How might greater transparency improve my team's decision making?

Hope From a Bigger Story

On January 5, 2020, the World Health Organization (WHO) published news of an outbreak of an unknown, "pneumonia-like" viral respiratory pathogen. According to the WHO, all 44 cases had been detected in Wuhan City, China.[1] Two days later, Chinese health authorities confirmed the cases were associated with a novel coronavirus, later named Covid-19. By January 30, the WHO had declared the outbreak a Public Health Emergency of International Concern (PHEIC). At that point, 9,976 cases had been reported in at least 21 countries, with the first case reported in the United States on January 20.[2]

By March 11, the WHO declared that the world was officially in the midst of a global pandemic for the first time in nearly a century. At this point, 126,599 cases had been reported around the world, along with just over 4,600 deaths.[3] Public health officials, government officials, local healthcare organizations, and people around the world found themselves clamoring for reliable information. How serious was this? Was it just like the flu or worse? Was it only serious for senior citizens? What was the best way to stop it? Did we have enough Personal Protection Equipment (PPE) and ventilators should healthcare systems become overrun?

Like clockwork, politicians immediately hijacked the virus to advance their political platforms. Social media sites were ablaze with memes mocking the virus or mocking those who mocked the virus. Basic but crucial questions remained unanswered. Would social distancing really help or was it all a hoax? Were we really choosing between people's health and economic well-being? How were parents going to work from home while trying to homeschool their kids? Could hydroxychloroquine really work as a surrogate vaccine? Could we actually run out of toilet paper? With no clear answers at hand, the media reported itself into a frenzy of conflicting information. Countries around the world, with little guidance to follow, were writing their playbooks as they went, as cases and death tolls rose. There simply was no precedent to guide leaders through the precarious decisions this crisis required.

There was an exception to the rudderlessness and recklessness, however. Not every politician hijacked the virus for their own ends; a rare few put politics aside and public health first. One such leader was the prime minister of New Zealand, Jacinda Ardern.

In retrospect, New Zealand seemed unlikely to mount a successful, rational response to a once-in-a-century pandemic. In the fall of 2019, the country ranked 35th in the world for pandemic preparedness, scoring only 54 out of 100 points as assessed by the Global Health Security Index.[4] But Ardern was determined to take the strange new virus seriously.

Assembling her team of experts, Ardern set in motion some of the strictest pandemic-response protocols in the world. On February 2, just three days after the WHO declared an emergency, she closed New Zealand's borders to visitors from China.[5] On March 20, the country's borders were closed entirely. And the next day, with only 59 confirmed cases in New Zealand, she announced the country would be locked down; the order went into effect six days later. "These decisions will place the most significant restrictions on New Zealanders' movements in modern history. But it is our best chance to slow the virus and to save lives," she told her nation, emanating resolve and compassion. "Please be strong, be kind and united against Covid-19."[6]

Her goal wasn't to just slow the spread of Covid-19—she was determined to eliminate it from her country.[7] She set in motion a four-level color emergency system, adapted from Singapore, to help citizens understand the current degree of risk, based on assessments her team developed using all available data. There are four levels to the system, with 1 being the least risk of infection and 4 the highest. At the time of the announcement, New Zealand was at Level 2. Each level brings added restrictions on activities or movements. She had her director general of health implement speedy testing, rigorous contact tracing, and stringent isolation. She communicated consistently, clearly, and sympathetically through all her decisions. Her daily briefings for government and private sector officials laid out unfolding plans and decisions she and her cabinet were considering, while her Facebook Live sessions—more intimate in nature given the medium—helped encourage her fellow citizens with sense-making explanations and insight behind the choices she was making. She even held a special press conference just for the children of New Zealand, knowing that their anxious questions needed to be answered to help keep them at ease and in support of concerned parents;[8] she reassured them that the Easter Bunny and the Tooth Fairy were, indeed, "essential workers."

From the outset, she rallied her nation around a common purpose: "We are a team of five million."[9] But Ardern looked beyond her borders as well. Concerned that New Zealand could be a transmission hub to other Pacific islands in the region, where no cases had been reported, the Ministry of Health and Ministry of Foreign Affairs and Trade worked closely with the WHO to support their neighbors in the Pacific. This included procuring supplies and providing training to health staff within those countries and via remote support.[10] Though she had closed New Zealand's borders, she opened its arms to neighbors, recognizing that the decisions New Zealanders made had implications beyond their perimeter.

Ardern's tough, collaborative leadership aligned government and business leaders and the people of New Zealand to achieve a clear, compelling, and unprecedented goal. The nation would have to sacrifice together if they were to succeed.

By mid-May, New Zealand was reporting no new cases of the virus and remained that way for the next three weeks. They shifted from Level 2 to Level 1 on June 8, lifting many of the system's restrictions. They saw a slight rise in cases in early August in Auckland, so Ardern once again elevated the country back to Level 2, and Auckland to Level 3. Auckland moved down to Level "2.5," a modified version of Level 2 with further limitations on public gatherings and mandated mask wearing on public transport, on August 30. New Zealand moved to Level 1 on September 21 while Auckland would move to Level 2 on September 23.[11] The system was flexible and proactively managed throughout the peak months, empowering local regions to adapt the system as needed while still providing clear direction based on scientific data from the national level.

As of September 2020, New Zealand had totaled only 1,683 cases of the virus and 22 deaths. Ardern garnered rousing approval as a result. A poll taken at the time showed that 83 percent of New Zealanders trusted their government to deal with national crises and 88 percent trusted the government to make the right decisions about Covid-19. The overall approval rating for Ardern's Covid-19 response was 83 percent, the highest rating for any leader of a G7 nation; for all the others, the average was only 54 percent.[12]

Media and health experts around the world are hailing Ardern and New Zealand as one of the greatest examples of leadership during a crisis.[13, 14] Her transparency, decisiveness, appropriate inclusion of the right data sources available at the time, and collaborative nature with her key cabinet leaders serve up a stellar example of what organizational governance looks like when it is well synchronized and effectively executed. While we may not have been able to see the rigorous debate and even conflict that went on behind the New Zealand government's closed doors, Ardern's credibility and results tell a clear story: that when all the heated exchanges were done, decisions were made, executed, and communicated in a cohesive, transparent way.

While a business obviously isn't a government, the moral of this story applies just as well in both contexts. Effective *governance*—the processes by which organizations make and communicate decisions—allows a company to do the right thing even when it's also the hardest thing. Convening the right group of people and giving them clear decision rights, appropriate resources, and a well-crafted charter that defines what they are to accomplish sets the foundation of truly exceptional governance—and, ultimately, performance.

This all sounds great, sure, but it's astonishing how infrequently organizations actually operate this way. More often than not, "meetings" feel like random gatherings for show-and-tell updates during which people catch up on email. Most people in the room don't know what, if any, decision they are even there to make, or with what authority and resources. And most of the time participants come to find that a decision was already made prior to the meeting, and that the leader's real agenda is to make it "look like" everyone is being included in it by being "transparent" with information that's already been agreed to in private. I call this "orchestrated theater"—the *illusion* of people participating in decision making. Worse, the conflicting messages emerging from such meetings send followers off to work at cross purposes.

In too many workplaces, the dysfunction that occurs during the decision-making process brings predictable results: people get frustrated or check out, coordination becomes choppy as people leave a meeting with their own interpretations of what happened and go do things as they see fit, and a slow erosion of trust in decision making spreads, increasing the (already substantial) level of cynicism about a leader's competence. This common version of governance is tragic for workplaces and employees. My research shows that when governance is not perceived as transparent, employees are *three and a half times* more likely to lie or withhold the truth, act unfairly toward others, and put their own needs above those of the organization.

And this is just under ordinary circumstances. As if the state of affairs wasn't treacherous enough, imagine what things are like when a crisis hits. That's when you *really* find out whether your organization's governance is fit for purpose or if it's contaminated. Especially when that crisis is one of your own making.

What Do You Do When You Find Out You're Poisoning People?

The Patagonia outdoor apparel company was founded in 1973 by Yvon Chouinard, an avid mountain climber. At a young age he taught himself how to blacksmith, a skill he used to make his own climbing pitons—the metal spikes climbers hammer into the rockface when climbing. Eventually, other climbers wanted him to make theirs, too. Chouinard and his partner realized that their pitons were destroying the rock, given the repeated need to hammer them in and remove them. They found a viable alternative—aluminum chocks that could be wedged in by hand rather than hammered in and out of crevices. Eventually their chock business grew and cannibalized their piton business. The switch from pitons to chocks—to intentionally sunset a successful business for an untested one—was Chouinard's first step in creating a company committed to doing what was right even when it was hard.[15] For this ethos, along with its high-quality product offerings, Patagonia has long been considered one of the world's most admired companies.[16]

Vincent Stanley is Patagonia's Director of Patagonia Philosophy. He has been with the company since the beginning, having served in numerous executive roles, and is co-author with Chouinard of *The Responsible Company: What We've Learned from Patagonia's First 40 Years*.[17] I spoke with Stanley about Patagonia's story, specifically about an episode he characterizes as one of the most challenging inflection points in the company's journey—its switch to organic cotton.

It all started after the opening of their Boston store. Excitement over the opening quickly turned to concern after employees began getting sick with unexplainable headaches. Stanley says:

> We had the air tested: we learned that the ventilation system was faulty and off-gassing formaldehyde was poisoning our staff. A typical business response might have been to fix the ventilation system to make the headaches go away. At the time, all we knew about formaldehyde we remembered from biology class: the chemical in the jar with the sheep's heart. But the source of formaldehyde in the store turned out to be the finish on our cotton clothes, added by the mill to prevent shrinkage and wrinkling.[18]

After they researched the harm formaldehyde could cause, including several types of cancers, they changed some of their manufacturing processes and pre-shrunk the cotton to significantly minimize its use. For most companies, that would have been the end of "being responsible." But their experience with the finish motivated them to question their entire cotton clothing production process, says Stanley: "We honestly had no idea where the cotton being used in our clothing was coming from, or how it was being milled." So, they decided to find out.

By the late 1980s, Patagonia had begun taking environmental concerns more seriously, but the formaldehyde incident kicked things into high gear. In 1991, the company commissioned a major study to gauge the environmental impacts of all the fibers they used in their clothing. What they learned was devastating. They write:

> To prepare soil for planting cotton, workers spray organophosphates (which can damage the human central nervous system) to kill off all other living organisms. The soil, once treated, is doornail dead (five pesticide-free years have to pass before earthworms, an indication of soil health, can return). Such soil requires intensive use of artificial fertilizers to hold the cotton plants in place. Rainwater runoff from cotton fields contributes significantly to the growth of ocean dead zones. Cotton fields, representing 2.5 percent of cultivated land, ingest 15 percent of chemical insecticides used in agriculture and 10 percent of pesticides. About one-tenth of 1 percent of these chemicals reach the pests they target... Cotton fields contribute 165 million metric tons of greenhouse gas emissions every year. A conventional cotton field stinks: its chemicals burn the eyes and nauseate the stomach. Before harvesting in non-frost regions like California, cotton has to be sprayed by a crop duster with the defoliant Paraquat, about half of which hits its target. The rest settles over the neighbors' fields and into our streams.[19]

Stanley told me that once they'd learned the damage cotton was doing to people and planet, the decision to switch to entirely organic cotton was the only one they could make:

> It's one thing to simply be honest about what we were doing, to admit that 25 percent of all of these horrible chemicals are used on 8 percent of arable land, that it's disproportionate and unnecessary. Before World War II, cotton wasn't grown this way. But if you're in a bus and you don't even have the windows open and it smells like a bottle of formaldehyde, and your eyes are burning, that's something else. I've come to realize that in human nature, if you give me facts that counteract my values, I just double down on my values and discount your facts. But experience changes people. And our experience taking key stakeholders out into the cotton fields changed us. And by experience, I mean something that enlarges your sense of the world, that changes your worldview and allows you to expand your mind in some way. It was a critical turning point in our story.

In the fall of 1994, Patagonia committed to switching over their entire line of cotton clothing to organic cotton within 18 months.[20] This sounded great, except for one problem: there wasn't a sufficient supply of organic cotton available through traditional brokers, so they had to work directly with the few farmers around the world who grew their cotton organically. Then they had to convince the vendors who processed the cotton, the ginners and spinners, to clean their machines before and after processing Patagonia's relatively low volumes. They and their partners had to innovate across the entire supply chain of cotton production, but by 1996, they did it: every piece of Patagonia's cotton clothing was made from organic cotton.

Today, Patagonia have extended their commitment to transparency and sustainability in their manufacturing choices through an interactive online portal they call "The Footprint Chronicles." Launched in 2007, Patagonia decided that they wanted to do more than just engage in routine "corporate social responsibility," a term that has, frankly, become a cliché. They wanted customers and partners to know about the entire lifecycle of their products, from design to fiber selection to dyeing and weaving and warehouse delivery. To date, they've traced and published the entire journey of about 150 of their products on The Footprint Chronicles.

What's more, the origins of The Footprint Chronicles illuminate what truly empowered governance looks like. Stanley says:

> There was no budget for it, and no department was "charged" with doing it. Our environmental group is intentionally just two people because we wanted sustainability to be part of everyone's job. So, a bunch of us got together and

just did it. We thought, "This is a fantastic idea, so we're going to do this." It was almost like a volunteer activity. But because it was a project that reflected the values of those involved, we got it done. Once everybody saw its value the company adopted it more fully. We value subsidiarity at Patagonia. If a decision is going to be made that affects people, they need to be involved in it, so they feel ownership for it. That's how The Footprint Chronicles got its start.

It's clear that Patagonia has fostered a sense of transparency and ownership from the beginning. This passage from *The Responsible Company* captures the company's ethos in a nutshell:

> The responsible company owes its employees light-handed, attentive management; openness about the numbers; encouragement to cooperate, across divisional lines when necessary, and to continuously improve processes; freedom to organize workflow with minimal delays or interference from higher-ups; and a penalty-free whistle to blow against wrongdoing.[21]

WALK IN THEIR SHOES

If you had discovered what Patagonia had about your products, what would you have done? What were the risks to their choice?

Patagonia offers a shining example of transparency, governance, and doing the right thing in the face of a crisis. Tragically, however, they are in many ways an exceptional company. The truth is, many other organizations would not have reacted the way they did after learning their products were poisoning or even killing people. They might have easily taken an alternate path, one all too frequently embraced, and buried the truth for decades with the arrogant assumption they were above getting caught. So, to see how things could have played out, let's turn to an example of a company that took this other path (spoiler alert: it's a really bad strategy with a radical boomerang effect).

Earl Tennant was a cattle farmer in Washington, West Virginia. By July of 1996, half of his cows and their calves had mysteriously died, and the rest had been born deformed and dead. Strangely, even buzzards wouldn't eat the carcasses. And it wasn't only his livestock that was dying inexplicably— other wildlife such as birds, deer, and rabbits were turning up dead in the area where Tennant lived, near Dry Run Creek. Tennant suspected they were being poisoned; the foamy green slime floating on top of the water in the creek was the first hint. Despite his pleas to several government health agencies, nobody took him seriously.

Using his own camcorder, he carefully documented the deaths of his cows, the internal organs he'd removed that looked like experiments in a pathology lab, and the deformities they'd suffered. Then he boxed up several dozen videotapes and notebooks full of records and, in October 1998, drove them to Cincinnati and handed them to Rob Bilott, an environmental attorney. Bilott agreed to examine the evidence and get back to Tennant.[22] At that moment, the cattle farmer had no idea he was signing up for a 20-plus-year battle with one of the largest and most successful companies in the world.

Bilott dug into the case. He learned that there was a DuPont plant in Parkersburg, West Virginia, about seven miles from Washington—where Tennant lived and farmed—that manufactured Teflon, the non-stick coating used on many household cooking products. Teflon was discovered in 1938 but became commercially popular in the 1960s because of its various water-resistant and stain-repellent applications, as well as for its ability to create non-stick cooking surfaces. The plant complex was enormous, about 35 times the size of the Pentagon.[23] Bilott soon discovered that Dry Run Creek, the offshoot of the Ohio River that Tennant's livestock drank from, was full of C8, an industry name for perfluorooctanoic acid or PFOA, one of the main components of Teflon. DuPont had been dumping millions of pounds of the chemical into the river for years. Bilott also learned that chemists within DuPont had made several attempts to expose the plant's actions and had been silenced.

DuPont never reported any of the chemists' findings to the Environmental Protection Agency (EPA), as was required. But within their own files, the company had scientific studies going back to the 1950s that showed the dangers of C8 and how it caused cancer in laboratory animals; by the late 1980s, they had evidence it caused cancer in humans. Their files also contained internal reports urging that wastewater from the C8 manufacturing process should never be released into public water sources.

In the summer of 1999, Bilott, a passionate environmentalist and moved by the plight of the Washington-area citizens, filed a lawsuit against DuPont on Tennant's behalf but was met with a quick setback. The veterinarians assigned to the investigation by the EPA and DuPont ruled that the deaths of Tennant's livestock were caused by his poor "husbandry"—as their findings claimed his cattle were undernourished, and had poor veterinary care and fly control.[24] Additionally, DuPont was Parkersburg's major employer, and townspeople turned against the Tennants for suing the company that controlled their livelihoods. In the face of such dire circumstances, however, they persisted.

In 2017, after more than 15 years of comprehensive medical studies, a personal health crisis, and the deaths of the plaintiffs he sought remuneration for, Bilott prevailed. His litigation efforts yielded more than $671 million in damages for approximately 3,500 people. DuPont also settled with the EPA, agreeing to pay a mere $16.5 million fine for failure to disclose their findings about C8, a toxin that is now estimated to be present in 98 percent of the world's population.[25] In a Netflix documentary on the scandal, *The Devil We Know,* Ken Cook of the Environmental Working Group aptly muses, "I'm not sure what the appropriate penalty judgment is for contaminating humanity, but I'm pretty sure it's more than $16.5 million."

While money can't replace the lost lives and livelihoods in that corner of West Virginia, relieve the victims' pain and suffering, or make up for the years of work by countless people, the outcome shows that when there is someone passionately committed to justice, no effort to cover up injustice is likely to prevail.

The battle to expose such corporate malfeasance prompted Bilott to write a book on the ordeal, *Exposure: Poisoned water, corporate greed, and one lawyer's twenty-year battle against DuPont.* His story also inspired the major motion picture *Dark Waters* (Bilott is played by actor Mark Ruffalo) in addition to the Netflix documentary.

I spoke with Bilott to learn more about how such reprehensible behavior could have gone on for so long and what sustained his sense of justice over such a protracted and difficult legal battle. Here's what he had to say:

> Well, it's a combination of things. I think back to the privilege of having met Mr. Tennant. He was somebody that was absolutely passionate about the fact something very wrong was happening. And there was no equivocation, no gray. There was a problem, it needed to be addressed, and we needed to get to the bottom of it. I guess that combined with my view that if people see the facts, they'll get it, they'll understand it. Even when I took the deposition of the CEO, which is depicted in the movie, my goal there was show him the facts. I wanted him to see the reality of what was in his own files—that these things actually happened. That's what has sustained me for the last several decades. If I can just get the facts out to people so they can see what I'm seeing in the documents, in

the medical studies, and in the science. Yet even in the face of hard facts, we saw folks standing up and saying that either this process was somehow flawed or rigged, or they disagreed with the results of the largest seven-year medical study of its kind, or that frankly none of it ever happened at all. That was amazing to me, that people could still be steeped in such denial despite the facts.

I pointedly asked Bilott why he felt the battle was so grueling, and what lessons corporate leaders should heed from the scandal. He offered a sobering reflection in response:

DuPont was a company that had prided itself on being the science company. Its scientific reputation was renowned. They invented a lot of the scientific processes that the regulatory agencies used. DuPont obviously was around many years before the EPA even existed. The US EPA came into existence in 1970. Haskell Labs had been in existence for decades before that, employing thousands of world-class scientists. In fact, the Haskell Labs helped invent the field of toxicology—how you go about sampling animals and how you conduct tests and properly interpret them. So, when the EPA is set up, DuPont is looked to almost as a mentor, training the scientists at the agency. That hubris permeated throughout the entire journey: "We are the science company." They simply thought, "And how could what we say about the science be questioned?" To have ordinary folks questioning the conclusions that their scientists were making, or that their people interpreting their scientists were making, was just incomprehensible to them. They believed, "We invented this field. How dare you suggest that we're not interpreting this correctly." When you create the standards, the tests and the whole system by which these things are judged, it's very difficult to have outside parties telling you you're not seeing things correctly.

But over time, DuPont's initial separation of science from the business begins to blur, and suddenly science is being done only as a driver of business interests. Science for science's sake cedes priority to what's best for the bottom line. So, studies that could show a bad result are no longer conducted.

That level of success and arrogance stops people from being willing to listen. DuPont's own lawyers warned them about how weak their case was in an email expressing their frustrations, but they simply refused to listen. It sounds simplistic, but leaders just have to be willing to listen to people with an open mind and not in the context of some self-created construct in which the data has to fit like a predetermined peg in a hole, and if it doesn't, you don't pay attention to it. You've got to be willing to reassess an entire situation—even everything you believe—if you need to.

You've got to have leaders who aren't personally invested in maintaining systems that must always be "that" way. Leaders who exert a "This is the way we do it" mentality are setting themselves up for risk. If a leader isn't approaching complex problems with a "Maybe there's a different way we ought to be looking at it" mentality, that's when you have reason to be concerned. Your refusal to look at the facts right in front of you tells people not to bring you data that contradicts what you already believe. And when that happens, you should be very concerned.

This story shows that if a single cattle farmer in West Virginia can get his voice and data heard, anyone willing to speak up can change things, even if it may take a painfully long time. Bilott's sense of justice and passion to make a difference, his long perseverance against enormous resistance, is an example all leaders can follow.

That's not the only important lesson to take from this story. DuPont's track record of reckless harm wasn't isolated to Teflon, and their widespread negligence, harm, and fines resulting from numerous violations over the years are well documented.[26] Today, it has all but disappeared as a company, broken up with its pieces acquired by various other corporations, and one small division retaining the DuPont brand. The legacy of this once-hallowed company has been forever stained by the damage they've done to the world.

Patagonia and DuPont represent polar opposites on the spectrum of transparent governance. Your organization likely resides somewhere between the two. If you detect any hints of DuPont's hubris or denial and find yourself minimizing the risk by comparison—"Oh, we could *never* do anything as scandalous as *that*"—you've already started down the slippery slope. None of us is immune to DuPont's denial. In fact, our success is the greatest blinder to our fallibility: the more certain you are of your convictions, the more you should open them to the scrutiny of others.

Transparent governance means more than providing visibility into how decisions are made. Transparency requires clarity, agility, and empathy, which when combined create the credibility behind decisions, enabling them to be executed with confidence across an organization. So how do you design decision-making systems that provide clarity on where people's authority starts and stops, the agility to invite multiple, even competing, viewpoints to the table, and enough empathy to ensure decisions can be communicated in ways that build ownership among those impacted by them? Many people, literally or metaphorically, shake their fists at the sky in frustration at the painful absence of these seemingly basic things.

But you might be surprised to learn just how much control you have over creating them.

Clarity: Know What, Who, and How Much

The data suggest we have plenty of room to improve in the governance department. For example, a 2011 McKinsey global study of 2,207 executives found that only 28 percent of respondents believed their company made good strategic decisions more frequently than bad ones, 60 percent thought that good decisions were made about as frequently as bad ones, and 12 percent thought that good decisions were altogether infrequent.[27]

If our meetings are any indication of our decision-making abilities, these statistics should hardly come as a surprise. Despite the fact that we spend $37 billion annually on meetings, and spend more than a third of our work time in them, according to one 2014 study by Meeting King, 47 percent of people consider them the biggest waste of their time, as evidenced by that fact that 70 percent of people bring other work to do during them and 39 percent report dozing off during them.[28]

Fortunately, there is a way out of this mess through—you guessed it— clarity and honesty. The McKinsey study noted just above found that an effective decision process that rooted out bias and engaged people in honest conversation was the primary factor in improving decision quality, not an improved analysis of the data. To get that outcome takes a meticulous design process. To choreograph and synchronize the countless decision pathways into a cohesive, transparent, and functional set of decision-making processes requires effort. But as we've discussed, the results of *not doing so* can be disastrous. The good news is that a little progress here goes a long way. Our statistical models show that even a 23 percent improvement in governance effectiveness, as evidenced by widespread understanding of how decisions are made and by whom, yields a 10 percent improvement in honesty behaviors. Here's how to get started.

The first step in designing effective governance is to identify what decisions are actually being made within the organization you lead. When I work with clients to define healthy governance, I start by sorting decision making into three categories:

- *Corporate decisions* include setting a vision and direction for the company, appointing top leaders, defining company values and culture, and managing the company's external reputation.

- *Strategic decisions* include decisions about investments the company will make, which customers it will serve, capital expenditures such as technology or new facilities, and setting corporate policies that all employees must comply with.

- *Operational decisions* include setting budgets, developing and launching products, talent management (hiring, firing, promoting and developing people), and measuring and monitoring performance.

You may choose different decision categories than the ones I've suggested depending on the size and maturity of your company, department, or team. The key is having some way to sort the types of decisions being made to ensure they are being made by the right people, which is the next step.

Next, it's important to know which voices need to be around the table when decisions are being made. We've all been in meetings that were over-crowded with too many spectators and nothing was accomplished. And we've also been in meetings where key players were missing when a decision was made, resulting in endless rework and doubling back to bring them up to speed. Decision rights must be distributed thoughtfully to ensure every-one involved in decision making is clear on the boundaries of their departments and roles.

There are two tasks that will help you decide where to locate decision rights. First, determine at what *level* of the organization decisions should be located. At the enterprise level, locate decisions that need to be made centrally, making them consistent across the organization. At the depart-ment or business unit level, put decisions that must be discretely made for functions or geographies. And finally, at the local or individual level, locate decisions that must be preserved for the uniqueness of individuals, teams, or special needs of employees or customers. If your company is serious about empowerment, this is what's required.

Second, clarify at which *seams* decisions are made. Many decisions require cross-functional participation. At the intersection of marketing, sales, R&D and manufacturing, for example, might be a need to coordinate innovation or product launch decisions. If the organization is in high-growth mode, there may be a need for a cross-functional talent council to ensure key talent is onboarded and retained. The key is to make cross-functional decision making as seamless and efficient as possible.

Once these two tasks are completed, the next thing you have to do is make sure each group that meets regularly is chartered with a specific purpose, clearly spelling out their degree of authority and resources. In one multinational company I worked with, the executive team, the business unit (BU) teams, the regional teams, and the country teams were painfully duplicating successive levels of work. Everything from P&L management to key hiring decisions to customer relationship management was being replicated in ways that caused angry confusion and turned meetings into war zones. Representatives from each group spent excessive time complaining about how one of the other groups was doing things that undermined what they believed was theirs to do. In a holistic redesign, each level was chartered to focus on the work *it* could uniquely execute. Strategy and priorities were set at the executive team level. Talent, customer segmentation, and marketing were given to the BU teams to focus on. Regional- and country-level teams focused on P&Ls, customer relationship management, and geography-specific priorities. Each of their respective meeting agendas was shaped exclusively by those focus areas, and all the requisite decision rights and resources were allocated accordingly. Agendas were published weeks in advance, and anything falling outside these areas was excluded.

When it comes to effective governance design, as you can see, the devil's in the details. But if you want to synchronize your organization, take the time to do the work. It's a pay-now or pay-later proposition. Put in the work upfront or live with the resulting frustrations and churn. Once you have clarity behind your governance, you can then make sure your decision systems are integrated across the organization.[29]

Agility: Synchronize and Flex

Once you've identified which groups have the authority and resources to make which decisions, the next step is to link them to ensure effective coordination. None of these groups is making decisions in a vacuum, and many rely on each other to execute decisions. There are two types of linkages that need to be created.

First, *meeting cadences* must be established to create a predictable rhythm for the business. Teams governing near-term priorities will need to meet more frequently for shorter durations of time, while those focused on longer-term priorities should meet less often for longer durations of time. Some companies choose to schedule standing meetings on the same day of the week to tighten synchronization. Creating an annual governance calendar on which meetings across the organization are published helps everyone understand which decisions are being made when and by whom. In the multinational company, the cadence of meetings was choreographed to keep each level appropriately linked and informed. Each group met monthly for two hours; the executive team on the first Monday of the month, the BU on the second Monday, regions on the third Monday, and countries on the fourth Monday. Any inputs or outputs from one to the other were immediately sent so that each group maintained their focus, and any decisions made by one with implications for others were quickly made known. This also allowed each team to keep their respective groups up to speed on progress, shifts in priorities, and the work of their counterparts.

Second, identify the needed *information linkages* that connect governing groups within an organization. Each group has a predictable set of information flowing into their meeting, and a defined set of decisions and conclusions coming out. Those inputs and outputs provide critical information to other decision-making groups. Defining how information moves between groups, by whom, and in what time frame ensures that the organization stays aligned, avoiding confusion and conflicts. Information linkages include things like group members acting as liaisons to other groups, succinct post-meeting updates sent to those who rely on that information, and online portals where real-time decisions and meeting minutes are posted. Keeping governing groups linked through shared calendars and technology that fosters transparency ensures the entire organization understands where decisions are made and the rationale behind them.[30]

Lastly, you need to build in a wide range of flexibility for what happens in the room when these groups meet. As I mentioned early in this chapter, if conversations are nothing more than orchestrated theater, you will perpetuate a culture in which people believe the only reliable source of honest information is *outside the room*, with the implicit belief that what happens *in the room* can't be trusted.

One CEO I worked with counteracted this risk by insisting his team bring "dueling fact bases" into the room when making complex decisions. He intentionally assigned people to build data-based counterarguments to any viewpoint being considered. Since he knows people are adept at making facts tell whatever story they want, he decided to make sure it happened in front of everyone rather than hidden behind closed doors in backroom deals made among team members. His gamble worked: the team grew more comfortable with passionately (and respectfully) debating conflicting viewpoints and reaching decisions they could all get behind. These exercises also helped diminish the risk and presence of chronic certainty, something many organizational cultures inadvertently encourage, especially among leaders advocating for or defending particular decisions or initiatives.

Does your culture prize assertive convictions? Is decision making perceived to be competitive? Do people feel as though appearing uncertain about their views will be perceived as weak? Processes like strategic planning, budgeting, and talent management can unintentionally create a false sense of prestige if people perceive others might gain something they won't. In such environments, the need to appear certain becomes a matter of survival. Research on competitive workplaces shows that when people feel anxious about competitive processes, they are more likely to behave unethically, and may embellish arguments to get their way.[31]

Empathy: Overcommunicate and Listen

Jacinda Ardern's story offers a masterclass in empathically communicating difficult information. She clearly considered her various audiences, tailored her messaging to each, and delivered consistent, repeatable messages that people could absorb. Her empathic and authentic style made her credible.

When it's your turn to be the bearer of difficult news, or even just an important decision, be sure that you consider every potential interpretation your audiences may have. What will people respond positively to? What will concern or anger them? Where is there potential for misinterpretation, and what can be done to avoid it? What messages are you most anxious about delivering, and how might they cause you to soft-pedal difficult information to avoid agitating others? Where are you using your own discomfort with the decisions you've made to justify stalling, lessen the brunt of the decision, or avoid conflict? Are you feeling guilty for making the decision too late or ignoring information that could have kept a problem from getting worse? If any of this happens, own it. If need be, apologize. Your honesty will buy you far more credibility than softening the blow will provide comfort. People will see right through your veneer.

Once you've communicated effectively, the most important thing to do next is *listen*. It's astounding how many leaders feel so much relief after communicating complex decisions that they assume their work is done. *It's just beginning.* Leaders mistakenly assume that conveying the message *is* the communication. But it's not "communication" until you are certain people have *understood it*. That requires you to listen to how they've interpreted it.

You need to engage in active conversations with your various audiences without getting defensive or dismissive, all the while listening to their frustrations, irrational interpretations, and unreasonable requests, so they can be confident you've *heard* them. You are not required to agree with what they say, grant what they ask for, or indulge their belligerence. But you are required to *understand and empathize* with it.

Seem like a lot to handle? Well, you're right. Designing organizational governance with clarity, agility, and empathy is no small task. Whether you lead a department of 20 or a company of 20,000, the spate of daily decisions and standing meetings you face can be exacting.

But there's no need to lose hope. By ensuring that those involved in making decisions are representing independent and honest viewpoints (vs. "groupthink" where everyone conforms to a common view), feel free to engage in spirited dissent, and have equal access to the same data sources and freely share that data, governance quality can significantly improve.[32]

In the next chapter, we'll dig deeper into creating a process that incorporates all of these actions. In particular, we'll look at the importance of psychological safety and how you can use it to foster a culture of "voice" in which people feel confident in bringing their full views and best ideas forward.

Get Busy: Make Your Decision Making Transparent

Ask for Feedback

If you host or participate in any standing meetings in which decision making occurs, you need a report card on how well you are doing. Using a simple, anonymous survey tool, ask regular participants to assess your process for:

Clarity – does everyone clearly understand your charter, decision rights, and authority?

Agility – are people freely sharing differing viewpoints and candidly disagreeing with one another, and is your group appropriately synchronized to other decision-making groups to ensure effective coordination?

Empathy – does your team effectively communicate decisions with empathy and then engage and listen to how those affected interpret your decisions?

Practice Dissent

Unless your team is of a rare breed, it's likely that there are times when people are withholding feedback, conforming with decisions they don't fully support, or avoiding conflict with vague doublespeak or passive-aggressive statements that feign agreement while inferring reluctance. Dialogical practices are difficult to master and need intentional practice. As an experiment, during your next meeting, take note of how often people speak in declarative sentences, and how often you drift from topic to topic, vs. how often people ask engaging questions to better understand another's views, or how often people offer conflicting ideas. If you want to foster dissent, set aside time to practice dissenting. Bring in fictitious but plausible scenarios with no clear answer and allow your team to "rehearse the future" by engaging in a debate. Bring in an outside facilitator to coach your team in improving their discussion skills.

Purge the Clutter

Deeply scrutinize your meeting agendas and composition to ensure the right content and voices are there. Has the meeting membership become bloated? Do people come with their own agendas? Are you just using the meeting for show-and-tell updates that could be accomplished another way? Do the topics on the agenda represent unique decisions and issues that *only this group* can address *while together*? If you have too many of the wrong people and too much of the wrong content, blow up the meeting and start over. Trust me, nobody is going to balk. Ask yourself, "If this group stopped meeting tomorrow, who besides us would care?" If you can't answer within 15 seconds, you know what you have to do.[33]

Be Honest About What Information You Share and Why

Take stock of your own transparency with respect to your team. Do you share some information more freely than others? Do you share it with some people more than others? If so, are you conscious of the biases or fears shaping your choice to withhold? What would happen if you were more evenly transparent with what and with whom you shared information? Is there some information for which the idea of sharing it makes you anxious? You need to uncover your own biases that limit your personal transparency if you want to improve it for your team and organization.

Dissect Your Decision Processes

Be intentional about what approaches you use for specific types of decisions with your team. What decisions require greater levels of inclusion? For which will you seek consensus? What types of decisions do you declare and expect your team to execute? For which do you ask for input before you decide? What decisions do you delegate and why? If your team doesn't have a clear sense of what decisions are treated with what approaches, you may inadvertently be confusing them and having them leave meetings uncertain about what decision was made, by whom, and what's expected of them. Make an inventory of all the decisions/decision types you and your team make, and for each, determine the best approach and stick to it.

Now that we've looked at how to improve decision-making processes in your organization and make them more transparent, let's zero in on how to foster an environment where you and those you lead feel safe enough to bring their full voice, heart, and mind to the table.

KEY TAKEAWAYS

- Dysfunction in decision processes poses a threat to organizational effectiveness. Research has found that if governance is seen as lacking healthy transparency, people are three and a half times more likely to have people lie or, without the truth, act unfairly toward others, and put their own needs above the organization's.

- Transparency can help organizations navigate the most disastrous of situations, the way Patagonia was able to navigate their shift to using only organic cotton in their clothing once they learned how toxic traditional milled cotton was.

- Transparent governance is more than just providing visibility into how decisions are made; it also includes clarity, agility, and empathy which, when combined, create the credibility behind decisions that can be executed with confidence across the organization.

- Designing decision-making systems should include: (1) clarity for people to know the boundaries of their authority; (2) the agility to invite multiple viewpoints to the table; and (3) sufficient empathy to ensure decisions can be communicated in ways that build ownership among those impacted.

- For step one, clarity, you must identify what decisions are actually being made within the organization they lead, followed by identifying which voices need to be present when making the decision. In addition, each group that meets regularly is charted with a specific purpose, clearly spelling out their degree of authority and resources.

- For step two, agility, you need to ensure effective coordination between the groups who have authority and the resources needed to make the decisions. Meeting cadences must be established to create a predictable rhythm for the business. Second, information linkages must be identified between governing groups. Lastly, you need to build in a wide range of flexibility for when these groups meet.

- For step three, empathy, you should consider every decision through the potential interpretations of all the audiences who will hear it. After communicating this effectively, your next job is to listen and then understand and empathize with others.

Endnotes

1 World Health Organization (2020) Archived: WHO timeline – COVID-19, 27 April, https://www.who.int/news-room/detail/27-04-2020-who-timeline—covid-19 (archived at https://perma.cc/U4EE-9LUH)

2 Holshue M L et al (2020) First case of 2019 novel coronavirus in the United States, *The New England Journal of Medicine*, https://www.nejm.org/doi/full/10.1056/NEJMoa2001191 (archived at https://perma.cc/9F4V-SR5D)

3 The Center for Systems Science and Engineering (2020) COVID-19 dashboard by the Center for Systems Science and Engineering (CSSE) at Johns Hopkins University (JHU), 25 August, https://coronavirus.jhu.edu/map.html (archived at https://perma.cc/4VWU-WEWE)

4 Nuclear Threat Initiative, Johns Hopkins Center for Health Security and The Economist Intelligence Unit (2019) Global Health Security Index, https://www.ghsindex.org/wp-content/uploads/2019/10/2019-Global-Health-Security-Index.pdf (archived at https://perma.cc/25JW-LBSM)

5 Palmer, S and Cropper, E (2020) New Zealand to ban travellers from China to protect against coronavirus. *Newshub*, 02 February, https://www.newshub.co.nz/home/new-zealand/2020/02/new-zealand-to-ban-travellers-from-china-to-protect-against-coronavirus.html (archived at https://perma.cc/C85W-2HH4)

6 The Editorial Board (2020) In a crisis, true leaders stand out, *The New York Times*, 30 April, https://www.nytimes.com/2020/04/30/opinion/coronavirus-leadership.html (archived at https://perma.cc/J54J-3TAL)

7 Baker, M G, Kvalsvig, A, Verrall, A J, Telfar-Barnard, L, and Wilson, N (2020) New Zealand's elimination strategy for the COVID-19 pandemic and what is required to make it work, *The New Zealand Medical Journal*, https://www. nzma.org.nz/journal-articles/new-zealands-elimination-strategy-for-the-covid-19-pandemic-and-what-is-required-to-make-it-work (archived at https:// perma.cc/29M5-VE79)

8 Roy, R A (2020) Jacinda Ardern holds special coronavirus press conference for children, *The Guardian*, 18 March, https://www.theguardian.com/world/2020/ mar/19/jacinda-ardern-holds-special-coronavirus-press-conference-for-children (archived at https://perma.cc/N2TF-AEWR)

9 Ibid

10 World Health Organization (2020) New Zealand takes early and hard action to tackle COVID-19, *World Health Organization News*, 15 July, https://www. who.int/westernpacific/news/feature-stories/detail/new-zealand-takes-early-and-hard-action-to-tackle-covid-19 (archived at https://perma.cc/53EH-DY46)

11 World Health Organization (2020) Archived: WHO timeline – COVID-19, 27 April, https://www.who.int/news-room/detail/27-04-2020-who-timeline—covid-19 (archived at https://perma.cc/U4EE-9LUH)

12 Manhire, T (2020) Almost 90% of New Zealanders back Ardern government on Covid-19 – poll, *The Spinoff*, 8 April, https://thespinoff.co.nz/politics/ 08-04-2020/almost-90-of-new-zealanders-back-ardern-government-on-covid-19-poll/ (archived at https://perma.cc/Y727-DCU6)

13 Friedman, U (2020) New Zealand's prime minister may be the most effective leader on the planet, *The Atlantic*, 19 April, https://www.theatlantic.com/ politics/archive/2020/04/jacinda-ardern-new-zealand-leadership-coronavirus/610237/ (archived at https://perma.cc/Y6MV-W4E4)

14 Ibid

15 Chouinard, Y, Stanley, V, Chouinard, M, Ridgeway, J, Gallagher, N, and Myers, L (n.d.) Company history, Patagonia, https://www.patagonia.com/company-history/ (archived at https://perma.cc/L5CJ-8QPK)

16 Fast Company (2020) Most innovative companies: Patagonia, https://www. fastcompany.com/company/patagonia (archived at https://perma.cc/NH52-PWQM)

17 Stanley, V (n.d.) About, Vincent Stanley, https://www.vincentstanley.com/ (archived at https://perma.cc/6C9Q-M5GR)

18 Chouinard, Y and Stanley, V (2012) *The Responsible Company: What we've learned from Patagonia's first 40 years*, Patagonia Books, Ventura

19 Ibid

20 Textile Exchange (2012) Patagonia: Going 100% organic cotton, http:// farmhub.textileexchange.org/upload/Future%20Shapers/Patagonia/Future%20 Shapers%20%20Patagonia%20Print.pdf (archived at https://perma.cc/ BA3H-ZQ8A)

21 Ibid

22 Bilott, R (2019) *Exposure: Poisoned water, corporate greed, and one lawyer's twenty-year battle against DuPont*, Atria Books, New York

23 Rich, N (2016) The lawyer who became DuPont's worst nightmare, *The New York Times Magazine*, 10 January, https://www.nytimes.com/2016/01/10/magazine/the-lawyer-who-became-duponts-worst-nightmare.html (archived at https://perma.cc/XKM2-42EE)

24 Ibid

25 Calafat, A M, Wong, L-Y, Kuklenyik, Z, Reidy, J A, and Needham, L L (2007) Polyfluoroalkyl chemicals in the U.S. population: Data from the National Health and Nutrition Examination Survey (NHANES) 2003–2004 and comparisons with NHANES 1999–2000, *Environmental Health Perspectives*, https://www.ncbi.nlm.nih.gov/pmc/articles/PMC2072821/# (archived at https://perma.cc/A3FY-GDCG)

26 United Steelworkers International Union (2005) Not walking the talk: DuPont's untold safety failures, http://assets.usw.org/resources/hse/resources/Walking-the-Talk-Duponts-Untold-Safety-Failures.pdf (archived at https://perma.cc/MQ5Z-MG97)

27 Lovallo, D and Sibony, O (2010) The case for behavioral strategy, *McKinsey Quarterly*, https://www.mckinsey.com/business-functions/strategy-and-corporate-finance/our-insights/the-case-for-behavioral-strategy (archived at https://perma.cc/PDQ5-3KS9)

28 Meeting King (2013) $37 billion per year in unnecessary meetings, what is your share? *MeetingKing*, 21 October, https://meetingking.com/37-billion-per-year-unnecessary-meetings-share/ (archived at https://perma.cc/AY2R-H3ZA)

29 Portions of this section originally appeared in *Harvard Business Review* and are reprinted with permission: Carucci, R (2020) How systems support (or undermine) good decision-making, *Harvard Business Review*, https://hbr.org/2020/02/how-systems-support-or-undermine-good-decision-making?ab=at_articlepage_relatedarticles_horizontal_slot2 (archived at https://perma.cc/HMT6-HECD)

30 Ibid

31 Steinhage, A, Cable, D and Wardley, D (2017) The pros and cons of competition among employees, *Harvard Business Review*, https://hbr.org/2017/03/the-pros-and-cons-of-competition-among-employees (archived at https://perma.cc/G8ET-FNU4)

32 Stangor, C (2011) *Principles of Social Psychology – 1st International Edition* [ebook] https://opentextbc.ca/socialpsychology/ (archived at https://perma.cc/NRV3-BBRA)

33 A portion of this content originally appeared in *Harvard Business Review* and is reprinted with permission: Carucci, R (2018) How to fix the most soul-crushing meetings, *Harvard Business Review*, 16 February, https://hbr.org/2018/02/how-to-fix-the-most-soul-crushing-meetings (archived at https://perma.cc/N47G-G77L)

07

Cultivate Spirited Voices
and Welcoming Minds

*Set your intention: How can I better welcome
disagreement, hard feedback, and unconventional ideas?*

Hope From a Bigger Story

Michael Abraham Shadid was born in 1882 in what is now known as Lebanon. He was the twelfth child born to his poverty-stricken parents; nine of his eleven siblings died of dysentery caused by contaminated food and poor hygiene. A few months after his birth, his father died, leaving his mother a one-room house, two mules, and the equivalent of about US $1,000, which lasted the family 10 years.[1] In 1893 his mother moved their family to Beirut, where he received a scholarship to the Syrian Protestant College (later the American University of Beirut). His dream of a better life for his family had begun to form.

Shadid knew of the college because Dr. George Post, a physician from the college, occasionally visited Shadid's village to treat the poor, sparking his desire to study medicine. In 1898, he and his sister moved to the United States and peddled jewelry for four years, earning enough money to pay his way through medical school. Within two years they sent for their mother and brother to join them.[2] Despite several family financial setbacks, Shadid entered Washington University medical school in St. Louis in 1903.

Shadid's early life experience of poverty and not having access to quality medical care shaped his values as he trained to become a doctor. In his autobiography, he reflects, "Among my earliest memories... are many that have to do with poverty. Why was I barefoot? Why were my clothes shabby and my lunch meager compared with that of other children? Why was my mother menial?"[3] These values, so strongly implanted, would stay with him as he began to build a practice of his own.

Shadid continued his medical training beyond Washington University, and eventually settled in rural Oklahoma to practice. For the next 20 years, Shadid became the veritable horse-and-buggy country doctor. He traveled from town to town, performing surgeries by candlelight. He trekked through dust storms and blizzards to reach ramshackle shanties occupied by poor farmers and their families. They were dying from preventable ailments like ruptured appendixes, and their wives and children were helpless against the havoc wrought by pneumonia, diabetes, and tuberculosis. By his own estimation, he delivered more than 3,000 babies. He was appalled to discover the lack of access to quality medical care, and even more disheartened by the frequency with which he saw farmers sell their entire group of livestock, sacrifice their crops, or even lose their homes just to pay for medical treatments. And he was deeply troubled by how frequently he saw fellow doctors exploiting these farmers' vulnerabilities by pushing for unnecessary surgeries and treatments just to bolster their fees. "While he was a physician's assistant, Shadid had watched an incompetent but greedy practitioner butcher an old man's extended bladder, improvise stomach surgery on a patient suffering from an ulcer and bungle a hysterectomy—all in one night. All three patients died."[4]

Around this time, Shadid had become fascinated by the farming community's natural ability to collaborate to form agricultural cooperatives. Several farming groups near him coalesced in 1906 as the Oklahoma Farmers' Union, which earned financial capital for farmers through group-owned entities such as cotton gins or wheat elevators, thereby sharing the burden of rising farm equipment costs. Shadid wondered if a similar cooperative model could be applied to healthcare.

In October 1929, as the country was on the brink of financial collapse, Shadid called together a group of farmers in the basement of the Carnegie Library in Elk City, Oklahoma. There he presented a plan for improving the quality of available healthcare by sharing the costs through a cooperative like the ones they'd created in their farming operations. Because he framed his proposal through a model they already understood, the farmers were predisposed to trust him. He told the farmers that if 2,000 people invested $50 per share as an annual fee, something they could afford, they would have enough money to build and furnish a community hospital in Elk City, staff it with specialists, and offer quality medical services at a significant discount. He offered payment plans to allow cash-strapped farmers to opt in. By May of 1930, Shadid had sold 700 memberships, and construction on the Elk City community hospital began.

The threatened reaction from the traditional medical community was predictably swift. They spread rumors that Shadid's plan was a scam and took out ads in newspapers claiming that the hospital would inevitably go bankrupt and that the quality of care would be inferior. They made viciously racist public comments about him, and there were even threats on his life. Some professional medical associations even tried to revoke his license to practice medicine.[5] But Shadid was undeterred, despite having to pause construction on the hospital due to the controversy it was stoking. Rather than focusing on refuting the naysayers, Shadid patiently but tenaciously focused on the farmers—the patients—he so deeply cared for. In August of 1931, the hospital opened its doors, and 3,000 members of the community attended the ribbon-cutting ceremony.[6] For the next 10 years, doctors and officials from all over the country came to witness the success of the hospital. Newspapers wrote stories about its impact on the farming community.

In the hospital's early years—which occurred during the Dust Bowl era and the Depression—Oklahomans suffered as drought and other weather conditions ruined crops and killed livestock. As always, patients struggled to pay their membership fees and medical bills. But Shadid persevered and continued to enroll new members. Between 1934 and 1949, the hospital was expanded seven times, and from 1932 to 1937 surgical procedures rose from 121 to more than 1,000. By 1949, there were more than 2,500 members. It was clear: Shadid's progressive model of cooperative health was succeeding, even in the face of enormous adversity. In 1943, Dr Paul de Kruif, a prominent physician, wrote about Shadid, "Courageously, resourcefully, Dr. Shadid and these Oklahomans have pioneered a way to beat our shortage of country doctors. They have proved that even a poor community can build its hospital, pay for it, and hire a staff of competent physicians and surgeons… made possible by prepaid group practice—the country medicine of tomorrow."[7]

In hopes of spreading the co-op model further, Shadid traveled to many states to educate interested communities on the basic principles and benefits of the model: 1) lowering medical costs for patients; 2) staffing hospitals with salaried physicians, incentivizing quality care without unnecessary medical procedures; and 3) prepayment, encouraging patients to seek care early and preventatively.

Shadid's pioneering work set the stage for future co-op organizations like the Group Health Association in Washington DC, the Kaiser Foundation Medical Care plan, and the Group Health Cooperative of Puget Sound. The Elk City Community hospital's legacy remains vibrant and continues to be carried out by its successor, the Great Plains Regional Medical Center in Elk City.[8]

While Shadid's efforts took place at a very particular time and within a specific field (medicine), his story offers universal lessons to anyone, and any organization, striving to make meaningful change. Every day, organizations face dilemmas they have attempted to resolve multiple times with conventional solutions that repeatedly fall short. We have to wonder, then, how many Michael Shadids are roaming the hallways of our organizations, attempting to have their novel ideas heard, or worse, have given up trying? Rather than acquiescing to the irritating squeaky wheels or dominating voices, what if we actively sought out the voices of our Shadids: voices with thoughtful and, yes, unorthodox ideas, measured approaches rooted in sound convictions, and the resilience to see their ideas through. Of the many exemplary ways Shadid used his voice and wisdom, one of the wisest was not wasting his time merely speaking *against* established medical practices. Instead, Shadid focused his passion and talents on speaking *for* patients, advocating for ways to improve the quality of their lives.

What if our organizations had more voices like that?

Cultivating a Culture of Spirited Voice

The concept of *employee voice*, the behavioral science term for the conditions under which people in organizations will readily speak their minds about problems like misconduct, someone's bad behavior, or impending problems, as well as freely offer ideas, has been the subject of research for decades. Most of the research has focused on dissecting horrific disasters that could have been averted had someone spoken up or, if someone did speak up, someone had actually listened. These include catastrophes like the Challenger Space Shuttle in 1986 and the Columbia in 2003, which were the result of known issues that had been raised and dismissed within NASA.[9] Or BP's Deepwater Horizon oil spill in the Gulf of Mexico in 2010, the result of "systemic and known failures" and to date one of the worst environmental disasters in history.[10] The recent groundings of 387 of Boeing's 737 Max airplanes due to mechanical issues, beginning in 2019, is another example.

Although qualified test pilots and the company's own engineers raised red flags about the new generation planes, their warnings were ignored by Boeing until two fatal crashes occurred.[11]

In each of the above cases, those in a position to act upon what they knew and prevent disaster chose not to. Was *the way* the information was brought forward ineffective? Or were leaders so driven to achieve their goal that they denied the potential consequences? These are the questions we'll probe in the rest of the chapter. Because as is too often the case within our organizations, somewhere between the offering and reception of employee voice, things broke down, with tragic consequences.

An alternative to silence is the concept of "speaking truth to power." A tried-and-true ideal of activist, political, and human rights groups, the idea describes courageous citizens delivering harsh and/or inconvenient truths to political leaders about things in need of change that they may be blind to, perhaps willfully. The term itself is attributed to the Quakers in their book *Speak Truth to Power: A Quaker search for an alternative to violence* published in the 1950s, though there are countless examples of this behavior throughout history. But sadly, the stories of those speaking truth to power often have horrendous endings—people sacrificing careers, reputations, and even their lives in an attempt to draw attention to injustice, misconduct, and even criminal misdeeds only to have those in power retaliate, dismissing or deflecting their newly spotlighted bad behavior.

When you see voices emerging en masse, however, safety in numbers can result, and things can sometimes improve. Consider the power of the recent #MeToo movement where women's voices revealing prolonged sexual abuse have brought down Hollywood, industrial, and political titans. In Czechoslovakia in 1989, the negotiations and protests of groups made up largely of students forced a peaceful transition of power from a single-party communist regime to Czechoslovakia's first non-communist government in four decades, and in just under six weeks, an event known as the Gentle Revolution. But under many circumstances mass activism, especially within organizations, is less effective, and frankly, shouldn't be necessary if we are designing governance systems that invite the spirited voices and views of those within our organizations.

As we discussed in the last chapter, our organization's governance systems gather countless employees every day into meetings on video screens or in conference rooms to solve problems, share ideas, learn new concepts, make critical decisions, and exchange important information. If you hope to create governance systems in which people show up to these conversations with their whole voice and bring you their best ideas, critiques, challenges, and warnings, then you have to start by creating an environment in which people freely have spirited exchanges up and down the hierarchy and across organizational boundaries. It's important to always remember, however, that at the other end of those spirited exchanges, welcoming minds and hearts must be waiting. *That doesn't mean agreement or acquiescence*—it means openness. Your job as a leader is to de-risk truth telling so that people don't fear the implications of doing it. Without those two foundations in place, even the best-designed decision-making governance will fail.

The most-cited reasons for employees not speaking up are a fear of retribution and a sense of futility. When weighing the cost of speaking up, employees consider the questions "*What are the risks to my career or well-being if I speak up?*" and "*Why should I bother if nobody's really going to care?*"[12] Sadly, the answers are usually not encouraging—for them or for you, their leader. Employees fear being labeled, retaliated against in some form, ostracized, or worse. All of these concerns are rooted in a loss of a strong sense of belonging. If a relationship or status within their community feels like it's at risk, people are far less likely to bring their true voice. Your job is to take away that risk.

Not surprisingly, if an organization with poor communication and relationships hits a major setback, the natural fragmentation will intensify, heightening the risk of ruptured community. In my interview with the social psychologist Jonathan Haidt, whom you met in the foreword, he offered this perspective on humans' ability to both cooperate and to pull apart:

> I take the view that in a way, we're all living way above our design constraints. That is, we're a species that evolved to live in groups of maybe 30 to 150 at most. We're tribal. We're really good at groupish stuff. That's why we will always have conflict and war, but it also means that we can cooperate with people that are not our kin. No other animal can cooperate in large groups that are not siblings. It's quite miraculous.
>
> Our tribalism has both its good and bad sides. When times are good, when we don't feel threatened, tribes are actually quite open. Real tribes are interested in trade, in exchange, in alliances and working together.
>
> At the first sign of threat, though, we retreat and form a defensive wall. When it feels like, "Hey, the future is great, there's plenty for everyone," then tribalism isn't much of a problem. But when you feel like, "The hammer's coming down, the market is crashing or the regulators are coming in on us,"

suddenly people get defensive in their tribes. Thucydides, in fifth-century BC, during a time of war when nobody could trust anyone, said something like, "The ability to see multiple perspectives on a problem rendered a man unfit for action." It's as if he says to his troops, "If you are thoughtful, get away from me because we need you to be committed. Just do what has to be done. Don't think. Don't complicate things with nuance." This is how our tribes become when they close ranks.

You have to see our minds as really operating on a dimension of open versus closed. There are certain things that make us open and then we're brilliant and cooperative, and there are certain things that make us closed. The more things feel threatening, the more closed we are.

Getting people to be open and cooperative and tell the truth is hard enough under routine conditions. But when things get rough, you can expect people to reflexively shut down. This is a big problem in a world defined by continuous change and technological disruption. Here's an inspiring story about a company facing major challenges that figured out how to beat the odds.

Guidant Corporation, now a division of Boston Scientific and Abbott Labs, offers an illuminating example of an organization that went from communicating poorly to one making employee voice an integral part of its culture. This story begins in 1993, when Ginger Graham was named President and CEO of Advanced Cardiovascular Systems (ACS), then a division of Eli Lilly, and spun out as Guidant Corporation in 1994. When she took over, performance was declining and divisional warfare among key groups was at an all-time high. R&D and manufacturing weren't even talking to each other. Management had broken many promises and morale couldn't have been lower. She was the company's fourth CEO in five years.

Shortly after Graham's hiring, she was tasked with addressing the US salesforce who, like so many others at the company, were deeply unhappy. She knew the people she was about to address didn't trust her, and by all accounts had no reason to. She decided that rather than trying to rally them, they needed to hear the truth from her: despite ACS's impressive history of innovation and reputation as one of the crown jewels in the medical device industry, this was not the same company. And everyone knew it. Her words shook the room. "I've always heard about what a wonderful company ACS is, but frankly, that's not what I see," she began. "What I see is deteriorating morale, disillusioned customers, and finger pointing. I see a place where R&D and manufacturing are practically at war. You folks in sales blame manufacturing. R&D blames marketing. We're all so busy blaming each other that nothing gets done. No wonder our customers are furious with us."[13] Believe it or not, the tough medicine worked. Once she realized her audience was relieved to know that she was willing to *admit the truth*, she realized she had earned their goodwill, at least for the time being. She took advantage of the moment, committing herself to "create a culture that would allow everyone in the company to feel free to tell the truth, from top managers to the people on the loading dock."[14]

Graham was aware of how information starved the company was, and how employees had almost no visibility into what was going on up and down the hierarchy. She notes in her *Harvard Business Review* article about such environments:

> People left in the dark fill the void with their own—mostly negative—
> interpretations of events. They point fingers at whoever they perceive is at
> fault—usually management. They fear they'll be blamed for whatever is wrong.
> Because no one feels free to talk about what's happening, the culture becomes
> poisoned with speculation, blame shifting, and self-protective behavior.[15]

Knowing how frustrated employees were with the poor communication they'd been receiving from management, and realizing the futility of an expensive study asking them for even *more feedback* about their frustrations (which nobody believed would be acted upon, anyway), she decided radical action was needed to reverse things quickly. Every executive at Guidant was assigned a coach… not a superior, but a rank-and-file employee. These coaches were trained to collect and offer candid feedback and expected to gather and deliver it to their assigned executive about the accessibility, clarity, and reliability of their communications, credibility of their decisions, and their ability to listen to and act upon the concerns of employees. The coaches gathered this information throughout the year, and then brought that feedback to their executive during their regularly scheduled meetings. Executives' behavior changed quickly as they received actional feedback on how employees in the organization experienced it.

At first the coaches delivered anonymous feedback. But as trust grew between management and employees, open conversations about financial performance, product development progress, and where things were succeeding and where they were falling short became more common. In town hall-style meetings of large groups of employees, progress against company goals was openly discussed. When a goal was missed, it was discussed until employees understood why it had been missed, what could be learned from the shortfall, and what needed to be done to course correct. All questions were welcomed at these meetings, any concern was fair game, and even feedback for management was invited. When problems were brought up outside of meetings, Graham directed managers to make a direct appeal: tell employees what the situation is, what needs to happen, and ask them to help.

That's not all Graham did to embed a culture of honesty among Guidant employees at every level. In her decade as CEO, storytelling became another key part of her approach. Like elders sitting around a fire, stories of great truth telling were passed along from executives to successive generations of employees, especially new employees, to propagate the culture they wanted to sustain.

To solidify her executives' comfort with feedback and vulnerability, she instituted a personal feedback process among her team that put each leader on the "hot seat." While they were on it, the rest of their team would offer the leader feedback on one area they could improve on and some suggestions for how. This kept executives humble, open, and constantly reminded of their need to own their shortcomings before they'd have the right to ask the organization to own theirs.

The results of Graham's unorthodox but powerful approach speak for themselves. During her tenure, Guidant grew exponentially, with market share and margins rising along with retention and morale. Innovation exploded, with dramatic breakthroughs in the cardiovascular device field. The company grew from $300 million in 1994 to $2.7 billion in 2001, and to more than 10,000 employees.

Since then, Guidant has certainly had its share of new setbacks. But the decade of transformation under Graham's leadership provides a blueprint for cultivating a culture of voice with leaders who welcome those voices: flip the hierarchy so that executives are being coached by employees, tell employees the whole truth (even the parts you think they can't "handle") and ask for their help solving problems, honor truth tellers in stories and rituals, and hold yourself accountable to honesty through truly open forums and ongoing feedback.

WALK IN THEIR SHOES

If you had been coaching Graham, how would you have advised her to handle the situation she inherited? If you had been on her team, how might you have responded to her radical approach? Is there anything from her story you would want to emulate?

Now that we've looked at what fostering spirited voices looks like in action, let's break down two of the key factors needed to make it happen: safety and skill.

Spirited Voices Are Nurtured in Safety

The concept of employee voice has a built-in paradox: the onus is on the *voice* to speak up, while those with the power to effect change are the listeners (and not always willing ones). The irony of hierarchy is that those with the least amount of authority are in the greatest position to spot opportunities or oncoming problems.

Amy Edmondson, whose thoughts on failure we initially discussed in Chapter 5, has been a pioneer in the field of psychological safety—creating the conditions under which people will feel free to speak their minds, raise concerns, share risky ideas, and offer candid feedback when things are off course or someone's behavior is unacceptable. An environment of psychological safety is a foundational ingredient to creating cultures of honesty. In each of the four findings I uncovered in my research for this book (clarity in identity, justice in accountability, transparency in governance, and unity across the organization), psychological safety was one of the factors we specifically studied to understand the role it played in each. It accounted for between 20 percent and 35 percent of each dimension's impact on truth telling, acting fairly, and serving a greater purpose. In other words, without psychological safety, you are amplifying your risk of lying, cheating, and self-interest by that much more. Edmondson's initial interest in the topic stemmed from her curiosity about how organizations learn things—or don't. "The whole idea was, in today's fast-paced, constantly changing world, organizations need to learn," she told me. "But they can't learn if they don't have access to their own data, experience and ideas. And so, if people aren't willing to speak up, especially around sensitive or subpar performance, then there is no way the organization can learn."

One issue, Edmondson notes, is that many people misunderstand what psychological safety actually is:

> One of the most common misperceptions is that psychological safety is about being "nice." But being nice, unfortunately, especially in the workplace, is often interpreted as, "Don't say anything that someone else might not like or not be able to save face." This is really the exact opposite of psychological safety, which is about permission to be candid. Another misconception is that

psychological safety is about a "safe space" in which nothing will happen that will trigger discomfort or be offensive. Real psychological safety requires being uncomfortable sometimes. And lastly, some people interpret psychological safety as permission to whine—to speak your mind about a concern with the expectation that someone else will do something about it. But real psychological safety has skin in the game for both the one being candid and the one hearing that candor. It's about performance—about innovation, about quality, about competitive insights. It's not at all touchy-feely. It's not easy to create this kind of environment.

Edmondson believes that psychological safety isn't a silver bullet. It's a factor in achieving high performance but requires that organizations maintain high standards along with it. Many people invert the relationship, falsely assuming that to have psychological safety, you need to lower the bar on performance expectations, but this couldn't be further from the truth. In her book *The Fearless Organization*, Edmondson writes:

> With routine, predictable, modular work on the decline, more and more of the tasks that people do require judgment, coping with uncertainty, suggesting new ideas, and coordinating and communicating with others. This means that voice is mission critical. And so, for anything but the most independent or routine work, psychological safety is intimately tied to freeing people up to pursue excellence.[16]

For leaders, fostering a workplace that's psychologically safe enough for people to feel free to speak up is an important step. When people choose silence over voice, it's usually because there are systemic factors in play encouraging that choice. But creating an environment that cultivates safe, spirited voices requires far more than just soliciting feedback or people's input. Ginger Graham's story shows the extent to which leaders must go to create systems in which people bring their whole voice. Setting an expectation that employees *do* speak up, and will not be punished for doing so, is just as important as extending the invitation to do so.

Here's a classic example of why setting that expectation is important.

Andrea is the CEO of a large real-estate development company I've consulted with. As my client, she complained to me about a frustrating executive team meeting she'd just finished. The main topic of discussion was the struggles of one of the company's historically high-performing businesses. Its leader had been in the job only six months and had made some changes to their marketing plan. She believed this was the problem behind the business's falling performance and knew everyone else on the team agreed, yet nobody raised this point during the meeting. Frustrated and perplexed, she vented to me, "It's not like we're shy about having hard debates. We are capable of being very blunt with one another. So why didn't anyone offer their insight to help out a struggling peer? If I'm the one that always has to do it, then what good is having a team?"

She was right. In general, people in her organization didn't shy away from disagreement, and they could comfortably spar with one another when their opinions differed. But when I asked them why they didn't bring up their concerns about their colleague's marketing shift, I got consistently bewildered answers. I heard things like, "Why would I have done that? It's not my business," "Gosh, that never would have occurred to me to say something, I figured the CMO would be the one to raise it in private," or "Are you serious? I'd look like a know-it-all if I'd done that!" Inherent in their responses are some of the most common justifications for choosing silence. Simply put, employees often believe someone else will raise an important issue.[17] Extensive research on the bystander effect, such as the 2018 study from researchers in Copenhagen, shows that people, even in dire circumstances, will remain silent, believing someone else will say something.[18] People also often second-guess their own conclusions, telling themselves they could be wrong about what they are seeing, or self-soothe by justifying their silence with minimization—"it's not really that bad." And, as I discussed earlier, the fear of breaking social bonds and shaking up important relationships is often heightened, especially on a team, when people consider raising difficult issues.

While Andrea's team was comfortable engaging in passionate debate and pushback, the notion of *initiating* such conversations *about each other* was foreign. In my experience working with hundreds of leadership teams, it's not uncommon for leaders to share unspoken agreements *not* to tread on one another's territories. And this is true even in environments where speaking up is safe and leaders make a point of welcoming feedback.

But if people only raise issues that matter to them, they are subtly reinforcing a type of individualism that undermines teamwork and cohesion. If you want people in your organization and leaders on your team routinely raising hot-button issues, regardless of who does or doesn't benefit, you have to do more than let them know "it's safe" to do so. You must make having difficult conversations an *expectation* and back this up with processes and behavior that reinforces it. To that end, here are some ways of doing just that.

Make It Clear Why Straight Talk Is Necessary

A shared sense of collective success helps unite organizations and reinforces the expectation that "issues that affect others are my concern." Let those you lead know that when they have insights about a colleague's challenges, you expect them to freely share them in a respectful, constructive way. When this doesn't happen, the default mode for many groups and teams is to operate on a "hub and spoke" model, whereby the leader becomes the primary source of keeping things synchronized, and everyone else is excused to worry only about their own "spoke." If leaders reinforce this belief too long, it conveys that the only issues employees must be concerned with are their own. Don't assume people will see the self-evident need to avoid this. The higher up in organizations leaders ascend, the more pronounced the individualism that distinguished them to get there will be. Help leaders shift from trying to stand apart to advance their career, to joining forces with peers to create collective success. This ensures they set the example for the rest of the organization, which is especially important when rooting out critical silences. If there are factors encouraging people *not to speak up*, like unfair reward systems, bullying managers, a history of deaf ears, or real examples of retaliation for speaking up, leaders should be on high alert to eliminate those factors.

Choreograph Round-Robin Conversations

In many of the teams I work with, we actually embed the practice of exchanging pointed perspectives and feedback. It's a bit like speed dating for executives: we spend a few hours in 20–30-minute one-on-one rounds, varying the questions we use to guide the conversations. Some teams do this on a quarterly basis. You could shape the conversation around leadership effectiveness, strategy execution, or the health of each respective relationship. In each round, both leaders exchange prepared views with each other, with commitments to follow up where necessary. This approach has been transformative for some teams, whose comfort with making each colleague's success their priority has then become the norm for the rest of their company.

Make Shared Problem Solving a Routine Part of Your Discussion

High-performance teams regularly include addressing their colleagues' challenges as part of normal work practices. This approach puts the recipient of the feedback in the driver's seat. I use this when new teams launch, especially with senior leaders. One member brings up a particular business challenge they are facing, framing the challenge at the outset of the conversation with about 15 minutes of context setting. Then, using a structured process, the rest of the team can ask questions to clarify their understanding. After the questions have been addressed, the team offers ideas, feedback, and even support to help resolve the challenge. I've seen leaders discover issues with their own leadership, view challenges from an entirely new perspective, and even resources shifted from one leader's department to another's. This approach helps minimize feeling defensive or dismissive as a result of others' challenging views because you are expressly asking for them.[19]

Candor in Action

Kim Scott is the author of the groundbreaking book *Radical Candor: Be a kick-ass boss without losing your humanity*. In it she offers a simple yet powerful view of what candor looks like when done effectively. In her model, radical candor is the combination of personally caring while challenging directly. Care without challenge is dubbed "ruinous empathy," and challenge without care is called "obnoxious aggression."[20] In my interview with Scott, she suggested that having systems in place where employees could easily raise concerns was very important. But she also acknowledged the importance of relational connections that make such conversations safe by informally inviting others to share their feedback and views:

> The place to start for self-awareness is to ask people what they think. Start by asking people, "What could I do, or stop doing, that would make it easier to work with me?" Make that a go-to question to ask people. Ask things like, "What is going on? Where am I screwing up here?" Of course, it really needs to sound like "you." One friend of mine likes to ask, "Tell me why I'm smoking crack?" Then after you ask, you've got to just shut up for at least six seconds. Amazing what people will tell you if you can keep your mouth shut for six seconds. That silence can feel like forever. But you really have to stay quiet. People will usually tell you something. They might not tell you everything, but if you can be quiet for six seconds, you'll get something useful.
>
> So now you've dragged somebody out on a conversational limb that they weren't sure they wanted to go out on, you've got to manage your inevitable tendency to feel defensive when you get criticized. Learn to respond with

empathy and listening. For example, "Just to make sure I understand, here's what I hear you saying." And then even if you disagree with it, repeat it back to make sure you've understood what they meant. Last but not least, you have to reward the candor with the feedback. If you only say, "Thank you for the feedback," you're never going to get any more feedback. If you agree with what was said, it's pretty easy. You fix the problem. It's harder when you disagree. If you disagree with the feedback, then your next step is to take a few minutes and focus on the part that you can agree with.

Almost nobody says something we 100 percent disagree with. So, find that 5 or 10 percent area of agreement and zero in on that. Sometimes the best reward for someone's candor is simply a fuller and respectful explanation of why you disagree. Being able to solicit feedback, and of course act upon it, is critical if you want people to voluntarily offer you the truth even when you *don't* ask. Because when you're a leader, flattery is going to come at you like a dangerous fog. And you've got to learn how to cut through that. Start by learning to ask for, and caringly listen to, truth you solicit.

Scott's insights point to one of the most important parts of inviting others' voices to the table: *receptivity*. Employees are well aware of all the management rhetoric about empowerment, inclusion, and feedback. They know you've been trained to believe in those concepts, and that you *should* employ them. But fulfilling your *obligation* to solicit others' voices is a far cry from actually *wanting to hear them*. They must *believe their voices are not just being requested but welcomed*. They must see you as hospitable.

Your work isn't done yet, however. Once you've created the psychological safety needed for people to bring you their voice, you must also ensure that they are competent to use it.

Skilled Voices > Loud, Angry Ones

Scroll through any social media feed from the last 10 minutes and you will find someone expressing outrage about something. It's practically become a law of nature, like gravity. *Get pissed off, throw ranting tantrum.* Lots of emojis combined with all-caps profanity has become the new standard of what it means to "use your voice." This in part because the lines between *voice* and *activism* have become alarmingly blurred. We have conflated speaking *your truth* with speaking *the truth*. We've become conditioned with trigger-happy instincts, desperate to adopt the posture of a giant middle finger the moment something infuriates us. We skip past curiosity and openness to the possibility that any view that differs might have merit, and give in to our reflexive impulse to refute those whose views we don't like, reject them as human beings, or convert them to our way of thinking. And we now feel free to do so without civility or decency.

Needless to say, this is *not* what it means to invite spirited voices.

But such vitriolic voices seem to be showing up in droves nonetheless.

In 2019, employee activism seemed to hit new heights. In Boston, Wayfair employees took to the streets in protest of their employer's deal with a federal government contractor to sell furniture to detention centers holding migrants near the US–Mexico border.[21] Later that year, 20,000 Google employees protested their company's treatment of sexual harassment cases, including paying out former executive Andy Rubin $90 million despite finding that harassment claims against him had merit.[22] In the past Amazon employees have protested doing business with oil and gas companies, and have also banded together to urge the company to stop selling facial recognition software to law enforcement.[23]

Progressive companies like Google have prided themselves on their open communication between workers and management. And Google has historically encouraged activism when it comes to causes employees believe in, like civil rights or environmental stewardship[24] (lest you forget, one of their original values was "Don't be evil"). But when the cause becomes the *company's* actions, do self-proclaimed "open" cultures like Google and other progressive companies remain, well, as open?

Curiously, most examples of employee activism against their *own* company haven't yielded much change. While minor concessions have resulted, more often than not management doesn't capitulate to employee protests, especially when it comes to fundamental business decisions like serving customers that employees find inappropriate (e.g., Google's contract with the US Department of Defense or building a censored search engine for China).[25]

All of this raises lots of questions. Perhaps most importantly, is employee activism a *form* of employee voice, or is it a *substitute* that has emerged to fill a void when employees see no other options for getting their voices heard? And in the spirit of empowering employees, have organizations created unrealistic expectations about what bringing your voice will yield? Are we perpetuating a sense of entitlement that confuses *having your voice heard* with *having your way*? Does having a digital forum for expressing anger really offer posters lasting relief or momentary catharsis? And is the anonymity of it just another way of avoiding employee voice or remaining silent? In today's environment, it is not always clear what the difference is between *voice* and *venting*.

A growing body of research on the effects of publicly expressing negative emotions suggests there are more harmful than positive consequences to doing so. In one study, researchers from the University of Indiana found that exposing people to differing views online can lead to increased anxiety and anger, and didn't lead to greater active participation in a cause (e.g., engaging in politics) but led to greater "cheap" participation—reposting, mocking, venting to friends with shared views.[26] Another study by researchers from the University of Oslo confirms that people who vent their anger online are more likely to only seek out information that confirms their views.[27] Tweetstorms and Twitter mobs have turned everyone's anger virtuous, legitimizing behaviors that border on abusive. UK-based psychotherapist and author Dr. Aaron Balik, author of *The Psychodynamics of Social Networking* and director of Stillpoint Spaces UK, believes anger as an emotional contagion is on the rise thanks to social media. Access to 24/7 news feeds and media means we can be perpetually triggered, our values and identities assaulted anytime we look at our phones. "Anger is quite a sensational emotion," he writes. "There can be a snowball effect where you become attached to the exciting sensation you get through your news feed, even if it's an unpleasant emotion like anger, and that's pretty much what an emotional contagion is."[28] He points to the important distinction between *expressing* anger and *processing* anger, warning that merely expressing anger the way many do on social media is not productive or helpful, and sometimes backfires. "If you are angry at someone who is always poking you, and you address it with them, the person can apologize and stop poking you. If you just run out into the streets shouting, 'I hate people who poke me,' and friends join you with subsequent statements like, 'People who poke suck!' nothing is actually being resolved."[29]

Psychologists confirm that postures of being *for* something vs. being *against* something are much more productive when seeking positive change. Being against something is more exhausting and taxing on our bodies and is very difficult to sustain. Our unconscious mind, where much of our behavior emanates from, works in images, and struggles to process what we *don't want*. *Against* language can be alienating, divisive, and judgmental; *for* language helps us find common ground and serves to sustain our motivation for change over longer periods of time, as it is rooted in our desire *for* something positive, not our outrage *against* something we hate.[30]

To learn more about outrage and its discontents, it's worth listening to Arthur Brooks, Harvard Kennedy School Professor of Public Leadership, and author of *Love Your Enemies: How decent people can save America from the culture of contempt*. In his bestselling book, he elaborates on the points made just above about our insatiable craving for anger:

> Many of us still compulsively consume the ideological equivalent of meth from elected officials, academics, entertainers, and some of the news media. Millions actively indulge their habit by participating in the cycle of contempt in the way they treat others, especially on social media. We wish our national debates were nutritious and substantive, but we have an insatiable craving for insults to the other side.[31]

So how do we balance inviting employees' voices without unleashing destructive tirades aimed at anything people feel entitled to complain about? Part of the answer lies with competence. Shouting in protest is easy. It doesn't require more than picket signs or online forums and rousing the wrath of others who share your ire. The premise is to voice what you are *against* with the presumption that someone else will do something about it. Bringing a *competent* voice to concerns, especially controversial issues, takes skillful work to effect meaningful change. It requires articulating a cogent argument with fact-based reasoning. It takes emotional intelligence to express frustrations in an authentic but measured way. It requires a level of empathy to approach opposing views with the notion that, no matter how outlandish they seem to you, they are legitimate in some way and have merit (more on this later, in Chapter 9). And it requires putting your own skin in the game, offering practical ways you will be part of the solution.

What Happens When Your Voice Isn't Skilled?

Vanessa is a Senior Vice President of Public Affairs at a global engineering firm that constructs major public projects like bridges, dams, and power plants. She reports to the company's chief operating officer, Dirk. For years Vanessa pushed Dirk and the firm to reconsider how they engaged with the local communities where they operated. Historically, the firm kept a low profile and, under the guise of humility, tried not to draw attention to themselves; they felt that their quiet but generous charitable giving was contribution enough. Growing increasingly frustrated, Vanessa would send numerous articles and news media to Dirk and the executive team showcasing other companies' contributions to their local communities, and how they enhanced the companies' reputations and local goodwill. After her requests for the firm to sponsor local events were consistently denied, she made her disappointment known. Dirk warned her that she was "spending political capital you haven't got, and it's getting harder for me to defend you to my peers." He told me that the executive team had grown immune to Vanessa's voice and resentful of the way "she tried to impose her values on the organization."

Vanessa came from a background of deep faith, and the executives assumed that her "agenda" to get the firm to change stemmed from that. But her real motivation was to get the firm to be more purpose-driven, to showcase more reasons to feel proud of the company *beyond* the projects they'd built. On the other hand, Dirk and the executive team felt harshly criticized by her and interpreted her advocacy for more civic engagement as "*You guys don't do enough.*" They saw the stream of articles as messages of their inadequacy. Vanessa took their rejection personally, as did other women in the firm, resigned to the belief that the "boys' club" was threatened by confident women.

I was called in by Dirk, who asked me to offer some coaching to Vanessa as a last effort before letting her go. When I interviewed several executives and spoke with Vanessa, I found their biases about one another deeply entrenched. She'd done a poor job of making her case for what was likely a very good strategic idea, and the executives had done a poor job of being open to her suggestions rather than reflexively dismissing her. Dirk had been an inept intermediary and advocate for Vanessa, failing to coach her on how to succeed, and, despite its many positive attributes, the firm indeed had a gender bias.

Not all was lost, however. Through a carefully constructed working session, we were able to help Vanessa present her ideas with sound reasoning. She apologized for her unintended harsh judgments of the executives, closely related how her ideas could help drive the firm's strategy, and made it clear she would take responsibility for spearheading the efforts she proposed. Additionally, we helped the executives suspend their harsh preconceptions about Vanessa so they could listen objectively.

This had a happy ending, but the story came dangerously close to a terrible one. Every day in organizations, ideas with great merit that challenge the status quo go unheard or expressed poorly, and the employees with those ideas feel disregarded. Had Vanessa been more skilled at influencing leaders more senior than her, she might have spared herself and the executives needless discord.

WALK IN THEIR SHOES

If you had been coaching Vanessa, how would you have advised her? If you were coaching her boss and his team, how would you have advised them? What would you have done differently?

The importance of bringing expertise to the table when having to say hard things is coming more sharply into focus as people grapple with trying to do it better and falling short. James Detert is the John L Colley Professor of Business Administration at the Darden School of Business at the University of Virginia and author of *Choosing Courage: The everyday guide to being brave at work*. He has spent a great deal of time studying workplace courage, and the conditions under which people successfully use their voice to speak truth to power. I interviewed Detert to learn more about his framework for *competent courage,* and how people can prepare themselves to effectively bring their voice to difficult issues. To start, he believes we must break down the mythology that attributes like courage are reserved only for a few, special heroes. "One of the things that has troubled me is the false notion that any virtue like courage or honesty is required only from some of us some of the time. I don't think there's any philosophy, religious system, or any system of thought that says virtuous behavior is only needed from some of us some of the time," he says.

In his research studying people demonstrating everyday courage, Detert found two important pre-existing conditions that set the stage for success.[32] Courageous people "were already thought of as capable, reliable, and trustworthy. They had reputations of being warm, emotionally intelligent, having good judgment and the best interests of the company at heart. They had built up what psychologists call 'idiosyncrasy credits,' like a bank of poker chips, so when they had to engage in moments of non-conformity, they had permission." The other precondition he observed was that competently courageous people chose their battles wisely. They didn't tilt at every windmill they came across but chose those issues for which they had the greatest convictions. These preconditions are important; if they aren't in place, Detert says, "It's unlikely that the organization is suddenly going to listen to you when you raise concerns."

Detert told me that one of the things that most surprised him in his research was the critical role of following up after you've raised an issue:

I think following up is the most neglected part in competent courage. And it's fairly obvious why. If we have steeled ourselves up for that difficult moment, you had that confrontation or difficult public presentation and your instinct is to retreat to your office either to lick your wounds or celebrate. The last thing your instinct tells you to do is get back out there right away. And yet it's often the most important thing to do. If you think it went well, it's usually the case that in the moment you didn't actually secure all the commitments you needed to put change in motion.

The other important aspect of follow-up is with those who didn't embrace your idea or views. It's likely that someone was potentially threatened or offended by what you've recommended, and you need to have the courage to follow up directly with that person and say, "Hey, I noticed on your face, or by your silence, that maybe you weren't on board with my ideas. Can we talk about that?" While it might be the last thing you want to do, it's vital to the success of what comes next. Most acts of courage that lead to important change may get set in motion by a moment of courage, but they stay in motion because courageous people know that they can't quit, especially if the first try didn't go well—which it often doesn't. Competently courageous people know that the process will be an iterative learning and ongoing learning experience, not a one-time event.

My own experience leads me to agree with this advice. Though, I'd even take it further. If we want to unleash the Michael Abraham Shadids in our organizations, the people with the most creative ideas and novel solutions to persistent problems within our organizations, then to Detert's guidance I would add:

Be an Ally

Don't speak as though the person in power is the enemy or an idiot. Assume positive intent when the need to say hard things to them arises, and make it clear you are on their side. Demonstrate empathy for the challenges of their role and situation without condoning the choice at hand. Be especially vigilant about any self-interest, spite, or anger that may be driving your motives.

Highlight the Greater Good at Stake

Don't make the issue exclusively about "them." Make it about the broader mission or values at risk. Point out the longer-term consequences of their choices and offer alternatives you feel are more aligned with values they and the organization hold. By helping them consider broader implications, you reduce the risk of them becoming overly defensive or resistant.

Don't Moralize

While your perspectives should be grounded in principles you should articulate, don't impose those values on those you are addressing. The moment others feel judged or hear a sense of moral superiority, they will shut down.

Let Go of the Outcome

You can't go into such conversations with a need to have your guidance prevail. See your role as creating options for the person you are confronting but make it clear the final decision is theirs, though you stand ready to participate in any way helpful. And go into the conversation knowing the risk you are taking. You must be willing to pay a price should things not go well. Every day I am faced with saying hard, often unsettling things to leaders. Sometimes they bristle defensively, and sometimes they are deeply hurt by discovering just how far their actions have drifted from their intentions. My job makes me a transference object that triggers deep-seated issues within leaders. I have to be ready for whatever those leaders bring, using it to help them become better without over-personalizing their testy reactions. Whenever I'm asked what enables me to be both bluntly forthright and compassionate at the same time, I respond with, "My biggest fear isn't a leader's reaction to what I say. My biggest fear is having them face a major but avoidable problem and saying to me, 'You knew, and you didn't say anything?'"

You should never stop cultivating other people's spirited voices. Invite and receive them with a welcoming heart and mind, just like you would hope for. A very simple standard I offer all my clients is this: if you don't have someone coming into your office a few times a week telling you something that's uncomfortable to hear, you can confidently conclude your leadership sucks.

Get Busy: Cultivate Spirited Voices and Welcoming Minds

Monitor Your Avoidance

Each of us has circumstances that tempt us to self-silence—conflicts we avoid, personality types we wither around, certain risks that make us especially afraid. And in these moments, we cower. But that forfeiture of our voice has a cost beyond our own missed opportunity: those we lead are watching. Our friends and children are watching. At the critical junctures where our voices are most needed, it looks like we condone silence. Inventory the places that bring you to silence, determine why, and put strategies in place that will bolster your courage to speak. Under what conditions do you avoid hard conversation? Where do you shrink back from moments requiring courage? As you think back on such moments, what has your avoidance cost you?

Learn to Confront with Skill

Giving others difficult feedback is a skill most of us don't relish using. We pull our punches. We ramble with long wind-ups to soothe our anxiety, only confusing the person we're trying to help. And commonly, under the ruse of being "nice," we just don't say anything at all. But as leaders, our responsibility is to help others become their best. Sometimes that means giving them compassionate but direct feedback about places they're falling short. I've said it before, and I'll gladly say it again: withholding feedback that could help someone improve is never nice or kind—it's cruel. So, if you struggle with doing it well, take a class, hire a coach, or rehearse in the mirror until you are effective. You may never be "comfortable" doing it. But that's not the goal. Just get good at it. When it comes to confronting others, what skills do you most need to cultivate? Do you pull your punches? Struggle with long wind-ups? Are you overly blunt and need to learn how to temper your message? Pick one area you can improve and double down on your focus to develop it.

Embolden Others' Voices

Throughout the chapter you read numerous examples of leaders who created conditions in which people felt free to offer out-of-the-box ideas, candid feedback, or concerns, or express personal vulnerability. Rituals that normalize this practice raise both the quality of voiced views and the range of people offering them. Use regular meeting openers where people write down ideas, feedback, or concerns on index cards and then randomly choose one or two to discuss. Or have a third party collect input and share it with the team on a quarterly basis. And if you want to move past anonymity, host informal lunches or virtual coffee hours that are expressly for raising concerns or feedback. Take heed, though, that you should never mistake collusion for openness—people should not raise concerns about a colleague who isn't present in the conversation. Where do those you lead need greater support to speak up? What practices could you employ to help them? Are there aspects of your meetings or team interactions, or how you lead them, that may be discouraging their candor?

Root Out Silencers

If there are norms or people that are discouraging the team from bringing their voices, find and eliminate them. People who are verbose, belligerent, or argumentative can intimidate quieter people. Your job is to give them feedback to help them self-regulate their behavior. In a similar way, meeting agendas crowded with too much content rush people past opportunities to speak freely. A culture that prizes confidence or certainty may discourage people from speculating about concerns that still feel hazy. The problem might even—gasp!—be *you*: your team may not yet believe you want to hear what they think. Ask your team if anything may be deterring them from bringing their voices and show your commitment by removing these obstacles. In what ways does your organizational culture silence people? How have you conveyed your desire for, and expectation of, candor? Do those you lead need more training? Have you failed to win their trust? Is there simply no time in your conversations for difficult issues to surface?

Demonstrate Having Your Mind Changed

This is especially important if you are particularly strong-willed or action-oriented. Your team needs to see that you can be influenced, and that no matter how unwavering you seem about a direction you've chosen, if they feel there is reason to raise concerns, you are willing to change your mind. Ask for pushback on your ideas—particularly the ones you feel strongest about. Insert "pauses" into your decision making by telling your team you'll hold off on implementing them for 24 or 48 hours while they consider, and bring to you, any risks. What issues or circumstances bring out your stubbornness? Where are you the most dogmatic about your viewpoints? Do people know you welcome being challenged on your ideas, even the ones you feel strongly about?

Be Vulnerable

Nothing accelerates trust among a team more than a leader's self-disclosure. Acknowledging your shortfalls and asking for help, disclosing aspects of your life where you are uncertain or struggling, and admitting when you don't know something reveals your humanity, which is your greatest source of credibility. It also signals to your team that it's safe for them to bring their whole selves—and their full voice—to work too. How confident are you that people really know *you* as a human being, not just as a boss? What parts of you have you actively hidden from others? What is your fear of being more vulnerable in those areas? How openly do you talk about your weaknesses or struggles?

Honor Courage When You See It

Any time someone you lead brings their voice to the table, especially if they're offering feedback about you, *no matter how defensive you feel inside*, celebrate their courage with gratitude and praise. When people offer unconventional ideas, challenge the views of colleagues during discussions, or raise concerns about behaviors that contradict what you've committed to, acknowledge their courage and hold them up as an example. Whose courage have you admired but failed to acknowledge? Who has offered out-of-the-box ideas or raised difficult issues within the past few weeks that you could go back and thank, apologizing for being remiss for not saying it sooner?

Now that we've concluded Part Three, transparency in governance and cultivating a culture of voice, let's dive into our fourth and final dimension of organizational honesty: creating unity across organizational groups.

KEY TAKEAWAYS

- To create governance systems in which people engage in conversation with their mind, soul, and voice, you have to create an environment in which people can freely and spiritedly exchange feedback and radical ideas, and share concerns up and down the hierarchy and across organizational boundaries.

- Because people's sense of belonging is tied to the degree to which they will use their voice, it is important for leaders to make sure there is no fear of retribution or sense of futility among employees with respect to speaking their minds.

- The two key factors to fostering spirited voices in action are safety and skill.

- Leaders must work hard to create systems in which people bring their whole voice. Organizations must maintain high standards alongside creating environments of psychological safety for employees.

- Having your team routinely raise difficult issues involves more than just making sure the environment is safe to do so. It also includes setting an expectation and backing it up with processes and behaviors that reinforce it. This is done through three steps: 1) make it clear why it's necessary to share and listen to all voices; 2) choreograph round-robin conversations in which leaders exchange pre-prepared views with each other with commitments to follow up where necessary; and 3) make shared problem solving a routine part of your discussion as it helps minimize feelings of defensiveness and ignorance.

- A leader must fulfill their obligation to solicit others' voices. This means not just inviting people to the table but also creating an environment in which people feel their voices are welcomed.

- Today, there is a blurred line between voice and activism. In order to invite spirited voices, advocacy for employee voices must be balanced with the needed skill to use those voices. Employee activism may signal that employees feel there is no channel for their voice.

- Psychologists have found that "against" language is alienating, divisive, and judgmental, while "for" language helps us find common ground and serves as a motivator for change.

- According to James Detert, the two capabilities that are vital to competent courage are how you self-regulate in the moment when you raise concerns to those in power and how you follow up afterwards. In addition, when speaking truth to power, it is important to be an ally to leaders, highlight the greater good at stake, don't moralize, and let go of your need to have the outcome go a particular way.

- You have the power to set the standard for bringing your spirited voice to the workplace while also inviting and welcoming others into the conversation with an open heart and mind.

Endnotes

1   Shadid, M A (1956) *Crusading Doctor: My fight for cooperative medicine*, Meador Publishing Company, Boston, as cited in Haddad, F S (2010) Michael Abraham Shadid: A Lebanese precursor of prepaid and cooperative medical care, *Lebanese Medical Journal*, https://pdfs.semanticscholar.org/c4a5/d0a93aa405225e3d7458fd4074661d2e4e21.pdf?_ga=2.151909689.1492129367.1599107244-457631569.1597336032 (archived at https://perma.cc/NG7U-SQE8)

2   Khater, D and Soleim, A (2016) Michael Shadid: A Syrian socialist [Blog] NC State University, 24 August, https://lebanesestudies.news.chass.ncsu.edu/2016/08/24/michael-shadid-a-syrian-socialist/ (archived at https://perma.cc/AFV7-F5BL)

3   Ibid

4   Shadid, M A (1956) *Crusading Doctor: My fight for cooperative medicine*, Meador Publishing Company, Boston

5   Haddad, F S (2010) Michael Abraham Shadid: A Lebanese precursor of prepaid and cooperative medical care, *Lebanese Medical Journal*, https://pdfs.semanticscholar.org/c4a5/d0a93aa405225e3d7458fd4074661d2e4e21.pdf?_ga=2.151909689.1492129367.1599107244-457631569.1597336032 (archived at https://perma.cc/NG7U-SQE8)

6   Ibid

7   Ibid

8   Great Plains Regional Medical Center, About GPRMC, Great Plains Regional Medical Center, http://www.gprmc-ok.com/about (archived at https://perma.cc/98KB-VD7M)

9   Park, C (2008) NASA remembers three space tragedies, *Space*, 27 January, https://www.space.com/4879-nasa-remembers-space-tragedies.html (archived at https://perma.cc/V5RV-XFBS)

10 United States Environmental Protection Agency (n.d.) Deepwater Horizon – BP Gulf of Mexico oil spill, *EPA*, https://www.epa.gov/enforcement/deepwater-horizon-bp-gulf-mexico-oil-spill (archived at https://perma.cc/7765-VE28)

11 Gates, D (2020) Boeing whistleblower alleges systemic problems with 737 MAX, *The Seattle Times*, 18 June, https://www.seattletimes.com/business/boeing-aerospace/boeing-whistleblower-alleges-systemic-problems-with-737-max/ (archived at https://perma.cc/JQM6-UAK4)

12 Wharton, J D (2016) Examining employee voice behavior: A systematic review of voice antecedents, University of Maryland University College, https://vanguard.idm.oclc.org/login?url=https://search-proquest-com.vanguard.idm.oclc.org/docview/1800548433?accountid=25359 (archived at https://perma.cc/9H9Z-7QW4)

13 Graham, G L (2002) If you want honesty, break some rules, *Harvard Business Review*, https://hbr.org/2002/04/if-you-want-honesty-break-some-rules (archived at https://perma.cc/333D-2GMP)

14 Ibid

15 Ibid

16 Edmondson, A C (2019) *The Fearless Organization: Creating psychological safety in the workplace for learning, innovation, and growth*, 1st ed, John Wiley & Sons, Inc. Hoboken

17 Milliken, F J, Morrison, E W, and Hewlin, P F (2003) An exploratory study of employee silence: Issues that employees don't communicate upward and why, *Journal of Management Studies*, https://onlinelibrary.wiley.com/doi/abs/10.1111/1467-6486.00387 (archived at https://perma.cc/K3V6-QADC)

18 Liebst, L S, Philpot, R, Bernasco, W, Dausel, K L, Ejbye-Ernst, P, Nicolaisen, M H, and Lindegaard, M R (2019) Social relations and presence of others predict bystander intervention: Evidence from violent incidents captured on CCTV, *Aggressive Behavior*, https://www.ncbi.nlm.nih.gov/pmc/articles/PMC6790599/# (archived at https://perma.cc/5RH7-8S8J)

19 A portion of this section originally appeared in *Harvard Business Review* and is reprinted with permission; Carucci, R (2017) How to make raising difficult issues everyone's job, *Harvard Business Review*, https://hbr.org/2017/05/how-to-make-raising-difficult-issues-everyones-job?_hsenc=p2AN qtz-8QlFHKXkj7qQiWdoGTHXTyYvH5KWqCXPkjR4kMDrBo SaVDF3V1pfSYBACSz93O10GXxUlp (archived at https://perma.cc/B4EQ-ZX9J)

20 Scott, K (2019) *Radical Candor: Be a kick-ass boss without losing your humanity*, Fully Revised & Updated Edition, Pan Books, London

21 Kelly, M B and Ruckstuhl, L (2019) Wayfair employees protest sale of furniture to migrant detention center, *NPR News National*, 26 June, https://www.npr.org/2019/06/26/736308620/wayfair-employees-protest-sale-of-furniture-to-migrant-detention-center (archived at https://perma.cc/BR9R-SZN6)

22 Bhuiyan, J (2019) How the Google walkout transformed tech workers into activists, *Los Angeles Times*, 06 November, https://www.latimes.com/business/technology/story/2019-11-06/google-employee-walkout-tech-industry-activism (archived at https://perma.cc/83HW-9TQC)

23 Lardieri, A (2018) Amazon employees protesting sale of facial recognition software, *US News & World Report*, 18 October, https://www.usnews.com/news/politics/articles/2018-10-18/amazon-employees-protesting-sale-of-facial-recognition-software (archived at https://perma.cc/GPV5-H4VR)

24 Bhuiyan, J (2019) Ibid

25 Ibid

26 Lu, Y and Myrick, J G (2016) Cross-cutting exposure on Facebook and political participation: Unraveling the effects of emotional responses and online incivility, *Journal of Media Psychology: Theories, Methods, and Applications*, https://doi.org/10.1027/1864-1105/a000203 (archived at https://perma.cc/327E-AFDR)

27 Wollebæk, D, Karlsen, R, Steen-Johnsen, K, and Enjolras, B (2019) Anger, fear, and echo chambers: The emotional basis for online behavior, *Social Media + Society*, https://doi.org/10.1177/2056305119829859 (archived at https://perma.cc/N27Z-JCAB)

28 Fleming, A (2020) Why social media makes us so angry, and what you can do about it, *BBC Science Focus Magazine*, 02 April, https://www.sciencefocus.com/the-human-body/why-social-media-makes-us-so-angry-and-what-you-can-do-about-it/ (archived at https://perma.cc/4VEX-Q3B5)

29 Ibid

30 James, M (2017) For, not against: Being for something is more powerful and healthy than simply being against, *Psychology Today*, 02 August, https://www.psychologytoday.com/us/blog/focus-forgiveness/201708/not-against (archived at https://perma.cc/WP6Q-ZW73)

31 Brooks, A C (2019) *Love Your Enemies: How decent people can save America from the culture of contempt*, Broadside Books, New York

32 Detert, J R (2018) Cultivating everyday courage, Harvard Business Review, https://hbr.org/2018/11/cultivating-everyday-courage (archived at https://perma.cc/7YYA-PVC5)

PART FOUR

Unity Between Groups

08

Stitching Organizational Seams

Set your intention: How can I build stronger relationships with my cross-functional partners?

Hope From a Bigger Story

On Saturday, June 23, 2018, Peerapat Sompiangjai turned 17. His parents had prepared a wonderful birthday party for him to celebrate the milestone. Peerapat, his soccer teammates, and one of their coaches on the Wild Boars local youth team had just finished their practice that afternoon, and before going home they made a visit to one of their favorite places: the Tham Luang caves, the fourth-largest cave system in Thailand, in the mountains near the rural village of Mae Sai. The boys had been in the caves before, but this time wanted to go in further and complete the teenage rite of passage of carving their names on the walls deep inside the cave. They rode their bikes through the rice paddies drenched from recent rains, hid their bikes and bags near the entrance of one of the caves, and ventured in. Their intent was just to be there for an hour or so, and then Peerapat would head home to his birthday celebration. But that never happened.[1]

Late June meant monsoon season was approaching. When heavy rains hit the caves, the water level can rise up to five meters, rendering them dangerous and potentially fatal. Everyone in Mae Sai knew—and knows—this.

Heavy rains fell abruptly that Saturday afternoon, trapping the 12 boys and their coach in the cave. Panicked parents discovered the boys' plans to visit Tham Luang on a messaging app and notified officials. When park officials found their bikes and belongings, a massive rescue mission was mounted.

The boys were trapped about two miles from the cave's entrance. They used rocks to dig out a five-meter shelf into the cave where they could huddle for warmth and safety. They were understandably terrified, but their coach Ekapol Chantawong, a former Buddhist monk, taught them to meditate so they could stay calm. They had to learn to breathe frugally to conserve oxygen. They had flashlights and though they had no food, there was drinkable water from condensation seeping from the cave walls. They just needed to keep up hope for a rescue.

Outside the cave, the Thai Navy SEALs were preparing for a massive rescue attempt. But cave diving rescues are notoriously dangerous, and most turn into body recoveries. Additionally, the SEALs had little experience with them. Within a few days, the best cave divers from around the world began to arrive and offer assistance. They were largely British citizens living in places like Australia and working in or retired from various professions like firefighting, anesthesiology, and IT. They dropped what they were doing and headed to Thailand to join hundreds of other rescue workers and divers and caving and mountaineering experts from the US, China, Israel, Europe, and Australia. The situation was dire.

The caves were flooding quickly. Muddy water was pouring in from the direction they needed to go. Engineers worked frantically to pump thousands of gallons of water out of the chambers of the cave to make access a bit easier. Ben Reymenants, a Belgian diver living in Phuket who volunteered to help the rescue effort, told a reporter it was like "dropping to the bottom of the Colorado River and hand-over-hand fighting your way upstream."[2] For more than four days, divers fought their way through the dark flooded caves, working 12 to 14 hours a day, moving about a meter at a time, chamber by chamber, looking for the boys.

Ten days after they had gone missing, the chances of their survival had been calculated to be less than 10 percent. But the divers remained determined to go as far as they could, using oxygen sparingly. They reached Pattaya Beach, a spot one mile into the cave where the boys' text messages suggested they might be holed up, but the boys weren't there. They pushed on. Finally, in the ninth cavern, two British divers were met with a rotting odor they feared was decomposing bodies. But to their delight, their flashlights revealed the 12 boys and their coach—hungry, tired, scared, smelly, but smiling. All 13 were still alive. But the joy and relief were short lived as the obvious question now had to be answered: how to get them all out?

The options for extraction were all perilous. One option was to stock the cave with food and supplies for six months until the waters receded, but oxygen levels were low enough that they would probably only survive a month. Another option involved drilling a tunnel down into the cave, but the risks were too severe. Rock climbers, engineers, even wildlife experts combed the mountain to uncover alternative routes to the boys but came up empty. They tried digging holes and sent in drones with thermal sensors to try and pinpoint the boys' location. But every "rational" option proved futile.

The only solution was to dive them out. But that posed two grave problems. First, the boys and their coach had no diving experience. Second, the route from where they were to the cave entrance was fraught with danger: several chambers were flooded to the ceiling and some of the chasms were more than 50 feet deep. The tightest choke point was less than two feet wide. The many twists and turns would have to be traversed in the dark with limited oxygen supplies to last the full trip. The option on the table seemed ludicrous: Sedate each boy into a coma-like state, cover their heads in full masks, bind their arms and bodies in canvases and zip ties so that if they did wake up, their panic wouldn't derail the mission, and swim each one out like a human duffel bag. The prediction of one of the British divers, who happened to be one of only two cave-diving anesthesiologists in the world, was bleak. "I didn't think it would work at all. I expected the first two kids to drown and then we'd have to do something different. I put their odds of survival at zero."[3]

Thankfully, he was wrong. First, the boys had to be given some basic training in swimming and diving to prepare for the trip (swim lessons are rare in Thailand and drowning is the leading cause of death for children under 15).[4] Each boy was put into a wetsuit, sedated heavily with ketamine (which offered the added benefit of scrambling memories), bound and transported by a diver. Some had to be re-sedated along the way. The most experienced divers transported the boys from cavern nine to three. At that point, US military medical experts checked each boy, and transitioned them to local divers and hundreds of volunteer rescuers from around the world to finish their transport on a rescue sled to the cave entrance. The operation was beset with numerous stories of near-tragic misses—getting tangled in telephone wires, losing the rescue cable, even one diver dropping one of the boys and another diver having to grab him and swim two out. The operation took about three days to complete. More than half a mile of the journey was entirely underwater. Tragically, one Thai Navy Seal, 38-year-old Saman Kunan, died from loss of oxygen trying to deliver oxygen to the boys and coach.[5] But 18 days after the boys disappeared, the riskiest plan worked— and all 13 were rescued.

It's estimated that around 7,000 volunteers contributed to the rescue, including over 100 divers. Twenty-thousand meals per day were cooked for the rescue teams. Some ran makeshift pumps at the top of the cave to divert streams of water, trying to buy rescuers time. Hydrologic drilling experts pumped out water, submerging the rice fields of hundreds of poor Thai rice farmers who, despite losing their entire crop, never asked for reimbursement. Local volunteers shuttled people back and forth to airports and trains, washed the rescue team's clothes, delivered supplies, and created makeshift places for them to rest. Teachers from the schools the boys attended gathered at the cave to welcome them out and created a meal brigade to feed the boys' families. Hundreds of local villagers gathered on the mountain to simply pray for the boys, their coach, and all the rescuers trying to bring them back safely.

How do you explain how that many people from drastically different cultures, technical disciplines, education levels, belief systems, and viewpoints on how to solve the problem, could blend their contributions into a unified, synchronized force against improbable odds, with such monumental success? You might be tempted to chalk this up to the empathy we all feel in the face of a universal crisis, assuming such astonishing collaboration is only possible in urgent situations but unlikely in day-to-day work. After all, when the cause is saving the lives of children, who *wouldn't* do whatever it takes to succeed?

If you did make that assumption, I'm delighted to say you'd be wrong.

Your Brain on Connection

That our brain is a social organ isn't a new revelation. Neuroscientists have been studying the effects of positive social interactions, and the lack of them, on our brains for years. Oddly, despite all we know about the human need for connection, we continue to design organizations in ways that deny that need. Psychologist Matthew Lieberman, author of the book *Social: Why our brains are wired to connect*, discovered in his extensive research of the brain that the neural networks that govern non-social reasoning are distinctly separate from the neural networks that govern social reasoning. He notes that when the non-social reasoning network is in use, the social reasoning network turns off, acting like what he describes as a "neural seesaw."

> Whenever we finish doing some kind of non-social thinking, the network for social thinking comes back on like a reflex—almost instantly. Why would the brain be set up to do this? We discovered that this reflex prepares us to walk into

the next moment of our lives focused on the minds behind the actions that we see from others. Evolution has placed a bet that the best thing for our brain to do in any spare moment is to get ready to see the world socially. I think that makes a major statement about the extent to which we are built to be social creatures.[6]

Lieberman also found that our natural fascination, sometimes obsession, with the thoughts and reflections of *others* suggests an innate need to be influenced by others. Sometimes this becomes an unhealthy desire for others' approval. But he suggests our identities are shaped by others far more than we may understand:

> We might think that our beliefs and values are core parts of our identity, but these beliefs and values are often smuggled into our minds without our realizing it. In my research, I found that the neural basis for our personal beliefs overlaps significantly with one of the regions of the brain primarily responsible for allowing other people's beliefs to influence our own.[7]

Our innate desire to connect is also seen in our acute efforts to *belong*. When we are new to groups, our amygdala is on high alert, sensing for threat or potential pain at the hands of those we don't know. We're working to decide, "Can I trust these people? Will they hurt me or have my best interests at heart?" The moment our brains detect belonging, via a simple cue like a smile, or a friendly question about who we are or what we think, or an affirmation of an idea, our brains instantly switch from feeling threatened to being protective. We conclude, "These people are important to me, so I want to protect the relationship."[8]

The most fascinating aspect of our brain's social conditioning, however, may be how it processes the *absence* of connection. When we feel isolated or lonely, the part of our brain that registers the negative feeling is the same part of our brain that registers *physical pain*. We literally *ache* for the pleasure of another's company.[9]

Given that our inborn social needs are hardwired, and given that we spend the vast majority of our waking hours at work, whether in person or remotely, our workplaces should offer some of the best opportunities for us to have our social needs met. For organizations, the results that come from satisfying workers' innate desire to connect and belong are not trivial. A BetterUp study of workplace belonging of more than 1,789 employees from a cross-section of industries, found that:

- workplace belonging can increase job performance by an estimated 56 percent, reduce turnover by 50 percent, and decrease the number of employee sick days by 75 percent;

- when employees feel like they belong, they are 167 percent more likely to recommend their organization as a great place to work;

- a single incident of "micro-exclusion" can immediately decrease an individual's performance on a team project by 25 percent;

- employees with a strong sense of belonging report a 56 percent higher level of overall job performance than employees who don't have that strong sense;

- for a 10,000-person company, if all workers felt a high degree of belonging, this would correlate with an annual gain of over $52 million from boosts in productivity;

- the presence of a single ally on a team, someone who demonstrates fair and inclusive behavior amidst exclusion from other team members, significantly prevents the negative consequences of social exclusion.[10]

Though our need to belong is reason enough to meet peoples' desire for connection, in an organizational context it has even greater significance. It signals our desire to be part of a bigger story than just our own, to contribute toward a purpose that satisfies our sense of significance. A unified organization is the vibrant context in which organizational and individual purpose comes to life. When we accomplish things through collaboration with others, things we could never accomplish on our own, our sense of purpose is amplified. Once a sense of belonging is established, people inherently repel at the notion of betraying that sacrosanct bond. Truth telling becomes an honor code, as the notion of lying to someone you are bonded to risks trading that sense of belonging for shunning isolation. And, as we discussed earlier, our brains will avoid that experience like the plague. To put it simply, any discomfort that comes from telling the truth and making sure things are fair becomes a reasonable price to pay for the privilege of belonging, and serving a shared purpose in a unified organization.

And that's why those 7,000 volunteers on the mountain above the Mae Sai Caves in Thailand accomplished what they did. They were driven by more than just the urgency of saving 13 lives. They were driven by the clear sense that *together*, no matter how big or small their contribution, they belonged to each other, and to the future of those boys. Whether you were diving through dangerous waters to ferry out a sedated teenager, making rice bowls for the medical workers, or washing clothes for the divers, you *mattered equally to each other* and to your shared endeavor. When many human spirits join forces into a larger, shared story, the bond is unassailable, no matter what the story.

Organizational Mitosis

In the context of our organizations, one of the things that breaks down our ability to connect is the way we organize our work. To understand the importance of creating, and sustaining a cohesive sense of belonging, we need to understand the forces that work against it.

Like cells within a growing baby inside the womb, as organizations scale, work divides, splitting into more specialized parts. This is most evident in the startup world, where hypergrowth fuels an accelerated division of labor. As more employees show up, work gets split up among them. But even when growth tapers off, organizations are consistently reconfiguring how work is organized to optimize results. Most organizations group work around functional disciplines like sales, marketing, information technology, finance, etc. But some also group work around geographies, like "Western Europe" or "the central region," or around customer segments, like "industrial users" or "home applications." Together, these grouping choices form a matrix organization in which people serve both a functional leader as well as a geographic leader. This is fairly standard practice in larger, complex enterprises. And if you've worked in one, you know just how difficult they are to work within.

Part of the reason matrix structures underperform is the nature of the work itself. Back in the days when the outputs of work—standardized products or routine services—were predictably similar, the rigidity of these structures created efficient economies of scale. Coordination across groups required consistent processes to accomplish, and repetition of output was the goal. But today, the nature of work is far more about ideas, analyses, customized insights, and the need to anticipate a competitor's action or a customer's unspoken need. The intellectual and creative nature of the work demands that people from different vantage points, with varied technical expertise, come together regularly, sometimes at a moment's notice, work collaboratively to meet whatever the need at hand happens to be, and then disband and move onto their next effort. To do this effectively, the boundaries around these grouping choices need to be porously easy to cross, and the coordination mechanisms that bring people together need to be agile and simple. Unfortunately, most organizations haven't learned to adapt their structures to meet the needs of today's work. The daily demand for high-performance collaboration is being clumsily facilitated by old structures and processes designed to discourage it.

To work around those inflexible structures, some have tried to adopt technologies like Slack, Microsoft Teams, and other "collaboration" tools as adhesives that bond people together from different parts of the organization. These platforms allow users to access information, share ideas and feedback, and keep projects moving 24/7 from anywhere in the world. And while these technologies have numerous benefits, as a primary means of creating cohesion they rarely work, because the predominant system of siloes prevails, and people—and their loyalties—gravitationally regress back into their assigned groups. In one mid-sized technology company I worked with, there were more than 240 Slack channels operating. Predictably, this was extremely confusing, and coordination actually got worse as nobody could keep up with which channels were being used for which purpose and people ended up arguing over whose was the "right" channel.

The tensions between traditional organizational designs that group work within boundaries that are difficult to cross and the intense, boundary-less, collaborative environment that characterizes work today wreak all kinds of havoc on organizations and the people within them. There are several reasons for this. For one, ingrained loyalty to a certain division makes cross-functional teaming exponentially harder as people will always put the needs of their own tribe above others. And most companies aren't prepared to close the gap. In one 2016 Deloitte study, only 21 percent of surveyed executives felt their company was prepared to build cross-functional teams, and only 12 percent understood how their people worked together in networks across the organization.[11] Another 2017 study on employee engagement showed that only 24 percent of employees feel effectively connected to their cross-functional peers.[12] The results are more than just employee frustrations. Customer experience suffers. A 2017 UK study by eConsultancy on customer experience found that 40 percent of employees observe that when departments have differing agendas, customer experience suffers.[13] Traditional hierarchy, or vertical relationships, have dominated organizational landscapes for so long despite the fact that most value gets created within horizontal relationships—that is, *across* organizational seams. Oddly, most leaders inherently know this, but struggle to break down the walls that separate the people who need to come together. European managers appear to at least value the notion of working across boundaries to help and cooperate with colleagues. A 2019 European Company Survey of more than 24,000 employees found that 93 percent of managers believe it is important or very important to evaluate employee performance based on their discretionary effort to help others across the organization.[14]

Still, when the organization fragments, so does the truth, especially when competing metrics or KPIs (key performance indicators) are involved. One division's devotion to efficiency and cost metrics becomes the object of resentment to a rival division that is focused on new product launch metrics, even though both divisions rely on each other to succeed. Embedded conflict in places like KPIs makes such clashes more than just relational. Now they are systemic. The ability of two functions to cooperate devolves to dueling truths that sound like, "I can't meet my commitments because *you people* can't do your job." This takes me to one of the most surprising findings in my research: when cross-functional collaboration is fostered, and relationships at the seams are free of rivalry, organizations are *six times* more likely to have people tell the truth, behave fairly toward one another, and serve their shared interests before their own team's. Even when employees or managers realize this, it may not matter, especially if an organization is set in its ways. One interviewee in my research told me:

> We are so command-and-control here that there isn't time to care about my cross-functional partners. The way we build our operating plans and set our KPIs encourages the border wars we have around here. My team gets measured on driving traffic to our website while another team gets measured on converting that traffic to customers. Since those are very different metrics, we end up cannibalizing each other's work to make sure our own team wins. We could share our data to help each other succeed, but we refuse to. We need each other but instead we treat them like the enemy. It's just nuts.

So, how can true collaboration thrive when competing with the gravitational pull of our individual tribes? And how can we expand the definition of our "tribe" to include a broader set of cross-functional collaborators?

Stitching the Seams

At a global consumer products company in the frozen food sector I worked with, there was contentious division between the Commercial Organization (the set of departments responsible for developing new products and bringing them to market) and R&D, leading to deep misunderstandings about what each side actually did. There were pointed differences in how each group defined a successfully commercialized product, and resentful misperceptions of how the other group seemed to make their work difficult. For instance, R&D viewed operations as "the people who only know how to say no to opportunities" while operations viewed R&D as "the time and money wasters of the organization."

To help bridge the gap of resentment and suspicion, I created a process grounded by a series of questions below for leaders in each group to work through in a facilitated conversation. I'm confident they may be just as useful to you if you need a fresh approach to bring people together (which, let's face it, you probably do).

What Value Do We Create Together?

Your company's greatest competitive differentiators are created by multiple functions coming together. Innovation happens when marketing, analytics, R&D, and manufacturing join forces to create new offerings the market wants. Great service happens when sales, customer service, and operations deliver seamlessly to customers. They create that value *together*. Oddly, many functions fail to realize the value they contribute to with other functions. They see the world entirely through what *they* are responsible for. Coming together with rivaling functions and asking what value you create together helps create a shared understanding of what's at stake for everyone. With my client, R&D and operations now see one another differently, and work more collaboratively, because they realize that only their combined expertise delivers products to market faster. Speed requires that R&D respect and apply a level of discipline to how they provide product specifications to manufacturing, and operations must be more agile to accommodate new products they've never had to make before. Between marketing and R&D, the value was defined as customer-prioritized innovations. By identifying which objectives in the organization's strategy they mutually contributed to, they reduced competing priorities. They are now better able to manage the healthy, natural tensions between things like containing cost and the necessary investments in opportunities that may not materialize.

What Must We Be Good at to Deliver the Value?

Having anchored your relationship in understanding value you create together, you can now focus on *how* best to achieve that value. You and your cross-functional partners should identify the four or five capabilities you mutually need to deliver the value you defined in question one. It could be translating market analytics into product opportunities. It could be technical problem solving or fast and accurate exchange of learning as projects move through the development process. This part of the conversation requires an honest assessment to identify any gaps in capability or missing processes required to integrate each of your respective efforts. Each of you must offer honest feedback on the other's performance level and acknowledge your own current level of ability—even if it's poor or non-existent. In the case of my client, we discovered there were no standing meetings that brought together all the divisions that provided key commercial inputs—regulatory, packaging, manufacturing, and marketing—to discuss problems with projects. As a result, information was slow to get to proper decision makers and was often distorted by the time it did. Creating a monthly forum in which these groups could come together to discuss challenges and solve problems allowed greater honesty. By acknowledging this missing piece, they became mutually committed to closing the gap.

How Will We Resolve Conflicts and Make Decisions While Maintaining Trust?

This is the hard conversation, about where coordination issues could incite conflicts. But it's also an opportunity to "rehearse" those conflicts in advance to determine how best to resolve them. You and your cross-functional partners should identify the critical decisions that you must make to create the value you identified earlier, and to determine where the final decision rights reside. You should also honestly acknowledge any historical baggage or unresolved distrust between you. This is especially critical for translating any "tribal protection" cues into "belonging cues"—where people let down their guard and suddenly feel a part of each other's shared success. You should air any concerns so any trust-limiting biases you have about one another can be addressed. You will feel greater empathy for one another as you learn about the demands and difficulties of one another's jobs that you hadn't understood before. During this conversation it's common to hear sentences like, "I had no idea you guys had to do that! No wonder our requests drive you crazy!" You will see each other's tone and expressions visibly change as you gain greater respect for each other and increase your commitment to mutual success.

What Do We Need From Each Other to Succeed?

To culminate the session, you must form detailed service-level agreements for one another. Negotiate things like timeliness of information sharing, quality standards, how far in advance notification is needed for decisions or modifications, and how routine work will be coordinated. It is also where any follow-up items are identified, like gaining access to technology platforms or needing to be included in certain meetings. These commitments are considered firm, and those of you in the conversation making them are empowered to do so on behalf of your respective departments.

You should build performance and relationship metrics into your agreements, and for the first six months, come together at least monthly and evaluate your progress. This process deepens your sense of belonging as you learn where you can improve, where you've done great work and have been helpful to each other, and how you can take your collaboration to new levels.[15]

Building bridges across organizational divides takes more than a reliable process of seam stitching. Creating a common story out of people's varied contributions takes more than shared effort, though both of those are vital. When organizations are badly broken, when the whole is less than the sum of the parts, leaders need courage and conviction to turn the pieces whole again. Interestingly, it's worth pointing out that the word integrity stems from the Latin derivative *integritas,* meaning "a state of being whole and undivided." Modern-day definitions of integrity refer to being honest and moral, but it's no coincidence that at its core, it means to restore wholeness. And few leaders have demonstrated the courage and conviction to restore wholeness between divided people more than Daniel Lubetzky, a Mexican Jewish lawyer known mostly for creating the successful snack food company, KIND. What is lesser known about Lubetzky's story is how it started.

Lubetzky's father was a prisoner at Dachau, the Nazi concentration camp in southern Germany, during World War II. As his father recounted the story of his capture to his son, he emphasized two pivotal moments that could have ended his life but didn't. The first was when the Nazis initially invaded his home in Lithuania. While soldiers were ordered to kill all the Jews in the building, the officer told Lubetzky, "I let you live because you were a person who always would offer me your hand, shake my hand... you would give me a little bottle of vodka, would talk to me like a decent person, and this is why I don't want you to die, because you are a good man."[16] The second moment was when his father was near death from starvation and a German soldier threw him a rotting potato, for which he could have been shot. To Lubetzky's father, showing kindness and treating others like human beings, no matter how malevolent and undeserving, was central to how one should live their life.

Passing on that life-changing lesson shaped the rest of Daniel Lubetzky's life.

His first venture was PeaceWorks, an economic venture between Israelis and Palestinians started in 1994 as a marketing, consulting, and distribution company. He began by making and distributing a sun-dried tomato spread he'd tasted when working in Tel Aviv. The manufacturer had gone out of business, but Lubetzky believed he could help revive the business with investment capital and his business knowledge. In his book, *Do the KIND Thing*, Lubetzky recounts the story of his initial partnership with Yoel, the original founder of that business:

> I introduced Yoel to a glass jar manufacturer in Egypt, who would charge a much lower price than his Portuguese supplier. Together, we worked to identify a supplier of sun-dried tomatoes in Turkey that would be far more competitive than the ones in Italy. And we sourced olives, olive oil, and basil from Palestinian farmers in Ouja and other small villages across the West Bank and from Palestinian citizens of Israel in the village of Baka El Garbiyah, near Umm el Fahem, including Abdullah Ganem, an eternally jovial grandfatherly figure. With geographically closer and more competitively priced ingredients and jars sorted out, we decided to give this business a shot.

Lubetzky had written a thesis in college, proposing that populations of people steeped in immovable conflict would be more committed to lasting peace when their economic interests were aligned. He writes:

> Setting up ventures owned and staffed by people from groups in conflict gives them a reason not to fight, and, eventually, a reason not to hate one another. When people work together or trade with one another, three distinct benefits emerge. At a personal level they discover their shared humanity and shatter cultural stereotypes. At a business level, they gain a vested interest in preserving and cementing their relationship because they are benefitting one another economically. And at a regional level, success gives people a stake in the system.[17]

Lubetzky was never naïve about what his efforts could or could not accomplish. He wasn't expecting small jars of sun-dried tomato spread to end decades of geopolitical conflict and generations of hatred. He simply believed it could be a start: "My little effort was always meant to build cooperation and collaboration, to give long-warring cultures peaceful and fruitful experiences with one another. I simply wanted to build small bridges that could perhaps serve as foundations for larger ones in the future."[18]

I'm guessing that any cross-divisional rivalries you face in your community or organization don't rise to the level of the Israeli-Palestinian conflict. But take note of Lubetzky's simple but profound theory that finding common ground and shared interest is where deep collaboration starts, and animosity begins to fade.

Here's what that might look like within your organization.

Collaboration by Design

Building bridges across an organization, both structurally and culturally, requires hard work and sustained effort. Flashes in the pan of teamwork campaigns or diversity and inclusion workshops may heighten consciousness, but rarely lead to lasting change. Here are two companies that provide exemplary models to follow.

Fewer industries are more homogenous than the construction industry, especially when it comes to gender diversity. Skanska, the Sweden-based global construction company, has set out to dramatically change its culture to be more inclusive and collaborative. To begin, they appointed Pia Hook as Vice-President of Culture for the global organization. Her mandate was to create a culture that, among other things, "cares for life" (valuing safety), and is "better together," which is partly defined as, "We foster an inclusive culture where we are open and fair, showing trust and respect for each other."[19] Hook sees these values as deeply interconnected, with diversity as a key driver of safety. She writes:

> We also see that diversity and inclusion impacts our safety performance by reinforcing a culture of care across demographic and professional differences as well as hierarchical levels. At Skanska safety is our number one priority: we can't and won't allow people to get hurt at our workplaces. Diversity and inclusion, not least a more gender-inclusive culture that challenges traditional macho behavior, will enable us to achieve our safety aspiration of zero accidents.[20]

Leaders across Skanska, starting from the top, participate in executive development programs that put theory into practice to drive home desired behaviors. Segments designed to "make it real" force leaders to bring what they've learned back to their jobs, collaborating across the organization on six-month projects aimed at real business challenges. Hook writes:

> Working in a cross-cultural-team with people from other Skanska business units, different time zones and with different professional backgrounds can be quite challenging. To facilitate the situation and promote learning, participants are supported in continuous reflection and dialogue on how the team is working, and how they collectively secure inclusion and high performance.[21]

One program even requires participants to undertake a year-long international assignment to create a visceral experience of what it means to feel different. Hook notes:

Apart from promoting learning from different business units, cross-cultural learning and networking, this gives the participants a first-hand experience of being different, being in a minority situation and being outside your comfort zone. It is our belief that this is an important experience that increases participants' cultural sensitivity and ability to pick up on exclusionary behavior moving forward. In addition, it increases their ability to relate to others who are different.[22]

Skanska's results are measurable. In their 2019 annual report,[23] they state that 43 percent of their board of directors are now women, 84 percent of employees feel that they treat each other fairly and care for each other, and 86 percent of employees feel that Skanska's workplace is free of harassment and bullying. Building bridges across differences, be they organizational or demographic, is vital to creating a cohesive organization, and Skanska has put teeth behind their commitments.

Back in Chapter 5 I introduced you to Ed Townley, the CEO of Cabot Creamery who led the Vermont dairy cooperative to become a thriving, admired company. You'll recall that when Townley started his run as CEO, the company was fairly fragmented: farmers had little understanding of the dairy business, and those on the business side were functionally focused on their respective tasks, with little need to understand the life of the farmer. Townley recognized that if he didn't narrow the schisms between so many key partners, he wouldn't be able to shift Cabot's culture and grow the company. When it came to accomplishing this, he wasn't afraid of making people uncomfortable in order to broaden their views of one another.

During our interview he shared numerous stories of how he created opportunities for lived experiences to build empathy and understanding across boundaries. Here are five examples he offered that vividly illustrate what stitching seams looks like in action. Like any great leader, Townley started from the top.

Connecting the Board with the Organization

To better understand the many intricacies of their business, the Cabot board decided to dedicate one afternoon of every monthly meeting to "learning something new." Rather than just asking board members to make presentations about various issues, Townley felt it was important for them to experience the reality of the business, so he often traveled with them to Cabot plants to get up close and personal with their company and employees. "I could have just presented pictures of our equipment or given them a report. But I needed them to *see* the business," said Townley. "So, I took them out to the plants. And not just the cursory plant tour you give dignitaries where everything is all cleaned up and polished. I'm talking about the plant tour where you go to see the boilers. The tour where you go to see rusty pipes. You go to see how many times things have been welded. That way, they really understand the capital needs of the company in full, whether we needed capital to replace equipment, or expand production capacity."

Connecting Farmers to Grocers

To build a bridge between the dairy farmers that produced the milk and the grocery retailers that sold the cheese, Townley sent farmers on a bus to New York City to spend the day at a grocery store where Cabot Cheese was offered. At first, grocery store owners were skeptical about the idea of having farmers in their stores. But when they saw customers' delighted reactions after speaking with the farmers, the initiative became a hit. The farmers stood outside the stores with signs that said, "Thank you for buying our cheese." "In one afternoon, those farmers sold a week's worth of cheese because they got a chance to tell their story, and once they tell their story, customers said things like, 'I'm never going to buy another cheese. Your farm is 200 miles from here. For a New Yorker, that's as local as I could ever hope for,'" said Townley.

Connecting Managers and Workers

As you may remember, Townley's time as CEO began with the unpleasant task of removing several executives who'd been convicted of stealing from the company. One of the unfortunate side effects of such behavior is fear and distrust, especially between leaders and employees. So Townley knew that the command-and-control, "This is how we do things" style of leadership needed to be replaced with a culture where leaders engaged supervisors and supervisors engaged shift workers, both up and down the hierarchy and across departments and shifts. "Supervisors now regularly ask shift managers about how to solve problems," said Townley. "They've discovered the power in asking the simple question, 'What do you think we should do?' and the long list of ideas that you get when you ask the people that know best. We also made sure that when Shift One had a great idea, they found a way to make sure Shift Two could implement it. My intent was to make sure everyone felt part of one empowered team. When a vice-president came to me asking for authorization for a decision clearly in his purview, I said, 'You're a Vice-President in this company. Whose authorization could you possibly be looking for?'" By pushing decision making downstream and engaging everyone in solving problems across the organization, Cabot found not only greater efficiencies, but more creative solutions and more engaged employees.

Connecting Cheese Masters and the Market

As the company grew, making more cheese than they ever had, their equipment capacity was taxed to an extreme. This caused some growing pains, and Townley and his team saw quality beginning to slip: Cabot wasn't winning competitions as frequently as they had in the past, and some of the cheese was starting to fail quality tests. To get a handle on this they brought their three cheese masters together, whose process in each of their three facilities showed "more variation than you would ever want," said Townley. Historically, plant management didn't want people from other plants "meddling" in their approaches, so the plants evolved using different equipment and methods. While perhaps well-meaning, this decentralized approach was clearly not sustainable. To decisively address the issue, Townley did something heretical in the cheese-making world: he brought in outside cheese experts to talk to the masters. "We knew they would be insulted but we had to do it," said Townley. He told the cheese masters, "You're going to be completely insulted that we'd bring somebody in from the University of Wisconsin, but we've got to come to grips with the fact that we've got three facilities making the same cheddar, and the quality of it is different. We're just not getting the consistency across the board that we need, and you three are going to have to work together to figure out why." When he recalled this incident to me, Townley grinned and added, "The reason it worked was because the three of them would rather work together than have somebody from the outside telling them what to do." As it turned out, the outside experts offered ideas the masters could each apply, and they began collaborating regularly. Moreover, the head of manufacturing started meeting regularly with all three cheese masters rather than visiting each plant separately. The following year, which turned out to be Cabot's 100th anniversary, they won more awards than they ever had.

Connecting Sales and Marketing

As Cabot's product portfolio grew, Marketing began collecting more sophisticated analytics on the market performance of each category, such as butter, cultured products, and cheese. With each new set of insights, they saw new opportunities for the sales team to optimize Cabot's customer base, product mix, and channels. The big question was what to do with this information. "The data group in Marketing was mining their data for all kinds of ideas, but when they threw it over the wall to sales, I'm not sure anybody seeing it lying on the ground knew what to do with it, much less cared what it said," said Townley. Around this time, the head of the analytics group came and pitched Ed the idea of forming a "strategic product group" that would organize the P&Ls around single categories and products, very similar to how most mature consumer goods companies organize large portfolios of products. Each group would have a general manager responsible for a designated line of business. This was a radical departure from Cabot's current way of operation. Wisely, Townley told him, "We'll be ready for that in about five years. If we try and introduce that much change now, it will fail." Introducing capabilities like data analytics to mature companies is fraught with risk for many reasons, mostly because it exposes the fact that you've fallen behind in something in which peer companies have advanced. The natural threat leads people to reflexively resist change. To avoid this outcome, Townley decided to start small, with a single product category—butter— and build from there. So, Cabot appointed one strategic leader to manage the company's butter business.

Early on, the people making the butter and the people selling the butter didn't want to listen to the newly appointed leader. Townley stepped in and told everyone that if there was a conflict between them all, he would get involved, which put them on notice that he expected them to work together. The new butter leader spent many days on the butter line working side by side with the people making it, getting to know them personally and sharing what he was learning. "Getting to know the people is key. That's how you earn their trust," said Townley.

"It took about 18 months, but that next year we increased our butter revenues by $2 million by using the data to manage supply and demand more effectively with accurate forecasting and insights about our customers. And that's when we decided to expand the approach to other product categories." Townley's leadership embodied Cabot's value of collaboration, and by staying true to it, Townley—and Cabot—significantly improved the company's performance. One of Cabot's core values says, "Success stems from focusing on the common good rather than enrichment of certain groups. Great things come when people work together."[24]

WALK IN THEIR SHOES

If you had been on Ed's team, where might you have resisted his approach? How would you have coached him? What would you have done differently?

For our 2014 book *Rising to Power: The journey of exceptional executives,*[25] which I co-authored with Eric Hansen, we reported on data from a 10-year longitudinal study we conducted on what made the most successful executives. We found that one key differentiator was a leader's capacity for *breadth,* the ability to coherently bring together otherwise disparate parts of the organization and unify them into competitive capabilities. Ed Townley's story is a masterclass in what breadth looks like in action.

If you want to be a leader like Ed Townley or Daniel Lubetzky, a leader who makes the whole of your organization greater than the sum of its parts, you need the courage of your convictions and a solid process to make it happen. Here again, progress over perfection still gains important ground. Our statistical models showed that a 25 percent improvement in cross-departmental collaboration, as evidenced by employees making effective efforts to coordinate across organizational boundaries, led to a 17 percent improvement in honesty behaviors.

I suspect that as you read through this chapter, multiple broken seams within your own organization came to mind; for most of us, they're certainly not hard to spot. Resolve that you will unify them into a greater story. Pick one and start stitching.

Get Busy: Connect People Across Seams

Honestly Identify Broken Connections

It's easy to dismiss organizational border wars or rivalries as routine aspects of the workplace. Given this, the first step to resolving them is admitting where they exist. Where are there disconnects between you, your team, and key stakeholders across the organization that you know need attention? What would happen if those relationships were repaired and strengthened? How would you go about repairing them? How have *you* justified your contribution to the conflict, rationalizing why you're "right" about whatever the challenges are? What would your cross-functional partners say about you and your team? Prioritize the fraying seams you identify and put a plan in place to address each one.

Create Lived Experiences

Using Ed Townley's example, where can you create the opportunity to "walk in another's shoes?" How can you shift the cognitive experience of *understanding* the needs of key cross-functional partners to an emotional experience of *empathizing* with their world and challenges? Start by having your team spend a day or two shadowing those in another department with whom you must better collaborate and invite members of their team to do the same in your group. Use the process described above to facilitate a "seam stitching" work session together. Bring your team together and brainstorm visceral experiences you could create to strengthen your empathy for and understanding of partners with whom you need a stronger relationship.

Cultivate Belonging

As leaders, we naturally assume our people are at ease and feel connected to the team. After all, why wouldn't they? But feeling *comfortable* is very different from having a sense of *belonging*. How well do your team members know each other? Do you sense some members holding back their ideas or participation? During your next few meetings, pay attention to whether everyone speaks, and the degree to which everyone listens. Do people respectfully challenge each other? Do you sense there is established trust on the team? What does everyone's body language tell you? Are they making eye contact? Are they leaning in and nodding as they listen—or sitting back and looking away with folded arms? Do your best to assess each member's sense of belonging. If you're not confident the level of belonging among them is where you'd like it to be, consider a simple, anonymous survey asking them about trust and belonging on the team. Reflect on your own sense of belonging in the group. Do you feel safe to share your thoughts? Have you been vulnerable with them? Have you included them in difficult decisions? Admittedly, cultivating a sense of belonging is difficult and sometimes feels nebulous. For less emotionally inclined leaders, it may feel touchy-feely and unnecessary. (If that's you, go back and reread the chapter, paying special attention to the data on belonging.) If you want the highest levels of performance from your team, a sense of belonging is table stakes.

Shift Organizational Boundaries

Many leaders put organizational boundaries in place around specific aspects of work (like functions, specialized tasks, or core processes) and leave them there in perpetuity. Step back and ask yourself, "If I were designing my organization from scratch today, is this how I would group the work?" To paraphrase Peter Drucker, if you weren't doing any parts of the work that you are doing today, would you start doing them now? If you answered no to either question, then you may have a more fundamental organization design issue beyond broken seams. Don't shy away from rethinking the optimal way to configure the work of your group. As part of the process, engage your team in an open conversation about the benefits and limitations of your current setup and see if there are ways to improve. Of course, don't engage in change just for the sake of it—be sure you are solving the right organizational problems, and not just symptoms. If your assessment of broken seams reveals deeper organizational problems, then tackle those.

Now that we've covered how creating unity contributes to greater organizational honesty, let's make things more personal. Who are the people you most avoid working with? What if you could turn these adversaries into allies?

For our final chapter, let's find out how you can.

KEY TAKEAWAYS

- People of different cultures, backgrounds, and belief systems are able to unify across organizational boundaries when both their work and their relationships are designed for unity.

- As organizations grow, work "divides," fragmenting the organization and creating silos; leaders must continuously re-evaluate where they place boundaries between working groups to ensure that coordination and collaboration can happen seamlessly.

- With today's work culture focusing on high-performance collaboration, it is vital for leaders to create flexible boundaries around grouping choices as well as using coordination mechanisms to bring people together to fit the organization's current needs.

- If cross-functional collaboration is strong, organizations are six times more likely to have people tell the truth, behave fairly toward one another, and serve their shared interests before those of their own team.

- Research has shown that as humans we desire belonging, and according to neuroscience, we are factor-wired for connection. In an organization context, the feeling of belonging to something bigger than ourselves drives us. In addition, allyship helps build fairness into the fabric of relationships.

- When we establish belonging, we are able to see that each individual matters equally to each other and the shared endeavor.

- To stitch the seam between your team and a cross-functional partner, answer these questions together: 1) What value do we create together? 2) What capabilities do we need to deliver the value? 3) How will we resolve conflicts and make decisions while maintaining trust? 4) What do we need from each other to succeed?

Endnotes

1   BBC News (2018) The full story of Thailand's extraordinary save rescue, *BBC News World*, 14 July, https://www.bbc.com/news/world-asia-44791998 (archived at https://perma.cc/8DJB-BSD3)

2   Bourne, J K (2019) The untold story of the daring divers who saved the Thai soccer team, *National Geographic*, 04 March, https://www.nationalgeographic. com/adventure/2019/02/national-geographic-2019-adventurers-of-the-year/ thai-rescue-cave-divers/ (archived at https://perma.cc/F2G3-FN9P)

3   Ibid

4   Ralph, P and Pasley, J (2019) This timeline shows exactly how the Thai cave rescue unfolded and what's happened since, *Business Insider*, 24 June, https://www.businessinsider.com/thai-cave-rescue-timeline-how-it-unfolded-2018-7#wednesday-july-4-the-team-begins-taking-swimming-and-diving-lessons-5 (archived at https://perma.cc/54BK-KZML)

5   Bourne, J K (2019) Ibid

6   Lieberman, M D (2013) *Social: Why our brains are wired to connect*, The Crown Publishing Group, New York City; Cook, G (2013) Why we are wired to connect, *Scientific American*, 22 October, https://www.scientificamerican.com/ article/why-we-are-wired-to-connect/ (archived at https://perma.cc/EQ88-FS76)

7   Lieberman, M D (2013) Ibid

8   Baumeister, R F and Leary, M R (1995) The need to belong: Desire for interpersonal attachments as a fundamental human motivation, *American Psychological Association Psychological Bulletin*, https://psycnet.apa.org/doiLan ding?doi=10.1037%2F0033-2909.117.3.497 (archived at https://perma. cc/3Q6J-QP5A)

9   Macdonald, G and Leary, M R (2005) Why does social exclusion hurt? The relationship between social and physical pain, *American Psychological Association Psychological Bulletin*, https://pubmed.ncbi.nlm.nih.gov/15740417/ (archived at https://perma.cc/8RNP-U5FK)

10 Carr, E, Cooney, G, Gray, C, Greenberg, S, Kellerman, G, Reece, A, and Robichaux, A (2019) The value of belonging at work: New frontiers for inclusion, BetterUp, https://get.betterup.co/rs/600-WTC-654/images/BetterUp_BelongingReport_091019.pdf (archived at https://perma.cc/Z9RW-6DBD)

11 Deloitte University Press (2016) Global human capital trends 2016, https://www2.deloitte.com/content/dam/Deloitte/global/Documents/HumanCapital/gx-dup-global-human-capital-trends-2016.pdf (archived at https://perma.cc/9WSX-HVY9)

12 Tiny Pulse (2017) The broken bridges of the workplace: 2017 employee engagement report, https://www.tinypulse.com/hubfs/whitepaper/TINYpulse-2017-Employee-Engagement-Report-Broken-Bridges-of-the-Workplace.pdf (archived at https://perma.cc/AXQ3-Y8FP)

13 Econsultancy (2017) Implementing a customer experience (CX) strategy best practice guide, https://econsultancy.com/reports/implementing-a-customer-experience-cx-strategy-best-practice-guide/ (archived at https://perma.cc/662V-PJUU)

14 Eurofound (2019) European Company Survey 2019: Workplace practices unlocking employee potential, https://www.eurofound.europa.eu/sites/default/files/ef_publication/field_ef_document/ef20001en.pdf (archived at https://perma.cc/S78J-P45Y)

15 A portion of this section originally appeared in *Harvard Business Review* and is reprinted with permission: Carucci, R (2018) How to permanently resolve cross-department rivalries, *Harvard Business Review*, https://hbr.org/2018/09/how-to-permanently-resolve-cross-department-rivalries?ab=at_articlepage_relatedarticles_horizontal_slot3 (archived at https://perma.cc/BW4Y-9JGW)

16 Lubetzky, D (2015) *Do the KIND Thing: Think boundlessly, work purposefully, live passionately*, Ballantine Books, New York

17 Ibid

18 Ibid

19 Skanska (n.d.) Our purpose and values, https://group.skanska.com/about-us/our-purpose-and-values/ (archived at https://perma.cc/7M27-7FB6)

20 Hook, P (2018) From "macho" to inclusion, LinkedIn, 17 December, https://www.linkedin.com/pulse/from-macho-inclusion-pia-h%C3%B6%C3%B6k-1f/ (archived at https://perma.cc/9ZTH-Z74R)

21 Ibid

22 Ibid

23 Skanska (2019) Annual and Sustainability Report 2019, https://group.skanska.com/496a54/siteassets/investors/reports-publications/annual-reports/2019/annual-and-sustainability-report-2019.pdf (archived at https://perma.cc/VHU2-PGYB)

24 Cabot (n.d) Cabot honors the Rochdale Co-operative Principles, https://www.cabotcheese.coop/co-operative-principles/ (archived at https://perma.cc/7CBH-UFQQ)

25 Carucci, R and Hansen, E (2014) *Rising to Power: The journey of exceptional executives*, Greenleaf Book Group Press, Texas

09

Turn "They's" Into "We's"

Set your intention: How can I more deeply connect with those whose differences I struggle with?

Hope From a Bigger Story

Los Angeles has a pronounced history of gang violence reaching back to the 1940s, where Black youth migrated from the South to California looking for employment opportunities in the booming war industries like building aircraft. Gangs proliferated through the 1950s and 1960s as racial unrest spread through the United States. By 1996, Los Angeles County had 274 gangs, 225 of which were located in just six predominantly Black communities—Los Angeles, Compton, Athens, Inglewood, Carson, and Long Beach.[1] In 2015, more than 60 percent of homicides in Los Angeles County were gang-related. Two of the most notorious rivaling LA gangs are the Crips (initially Cribs, but they carried canes and were nicknamed "crips," short for cripples) and the Bloods. It's estimated that among the two gangs, there are 50,000–60,000 members across the United States. Roberto "News" Smith was born in 1985 in Compton, California. By the time he was 11, he was well on his way to joining the Bloods. In the mid-1980s and 1990s, Compton was one of the city's hotbeds of gang activity, and News, like many other kids growing up in the depressed area, was not immune to its temptations. "When you're a kid, gangbanging looks fun," he says. "You see older kids you look up to and want to imitate. With the music, or getting into a little trouble, it makes you feel cool. My brothers were already in the gang, so it just made sense for me. But then when I was in tenth grade, two of my close friends were shot in gang fights. That's when things go from fun and games to just being bad. You think, 'Do I have to carry a gun now just to be safe? I know the cops won't keep me safe.'"[2]

Malachi Jenkins, born in 1986 also in Compton, had become involved with the Crips by the time he was nine. Jenkins, whose gang nickname is "Spank," says growing up in his "hood" was rough. "Even as a little kid, I always knew drugs, prostitution, and gangbangers were right outside my front door. Walking to school, you just learned to walk over dead bodies in the ally. You eventually just got numb to the pain. When I was in eighth grade, one of my best friends Leon was killed by some Bloods. That's when things felt serious to me. When you have to ditch school just to go to your friend's funeral, that's when you start to see how much things suck."

For many of their formative years, Spank and News were in and out of jail—for drug possession, joyriding, petty theft. Their lives were turbulent and full of danger. News says, "Being in jail, even just for a few months at a time, was the hardest part of all of it. You see hardcore life on the inside." Once Spank even got arrested because a rookie cop needed to get trained on how to book someone.

By all accounts, News and Spank should have hated each other. At the peak of their respective gangs' rivalry, you could get shot just for being seen wearing the color (blue for Crips, red for Bloods) of the "other" gang. And the street code for both gangs was clear: if you kill one of mine, I'll kill one of yours. During the height of gang war in the 1990s, the notion of befriending someone from a rival gang was unheard of. Beyond their differing gang affiliations, being born Black in poor, gang- and drug-infested neighborhoods meant a higher likelihood of early death, permanent incarceration, and chronic physical and mental health issues. Statistically, one if not both of them should be dead. By any measure, the odds of these two surviving their bleak worlds, much less becoming friends across gangs, were slim to none.

The two first crossed paths in 2004, at a Fourth of July party. They'd heard of each other through mutual friends, and connected after realizing they each liked the same girls. Spank says, "I hit on one of the girls News liked at that party without even knowing it." Because their respective neighborhoods didn't have any major conflicts between them, crossing that divide from rival gangs was slightly less risky. But, News said, "If our hoods had any serious beefing with each other or bad history, you couldn't really make friends with someone from the other hood." Spank said, "We could have just as easily wound up as enemies and hating each other. And maybe our different gangs could have made that worse. But we *chose* to be friends. We didn't see all the ways we were different. Instead, we saw all the things we had in common that may not have been as obvious at first." Their common taste in women would set these two members of rival gangs on a path of friendship that would change both their lives. Eventually.

When Spank was 18, he was in a car with several friends in a high-speed chase with police. His friends shot at the police. Spank was the last one caught, and the police brutally beat him. Since he wasn't the shooter, the charge of attempted murder of a police officer was dropped. When he got out of jail, he returned to Compton. One day, when he was 21, he saw a commercial on TV for a culinary school in Las Vegas. Tired of being harassed by the cops, cycling in and out of jail, and not making any money, he thought to himself, "That might be respectable." He called his mom and asked what she thought about the idea of him going to cooking school. She enrolled him the next day.

After cooking school, Spank moved to Portland, Oregon and started cooking for friends at parties, making a reputation for himself as an exceptional chef. Eventually, in 2011, he returned to Compton and reconnected with News, and the two tried their hand at several businesses. At the time they didn't have much money for eating out, but Spank would bring out his cooking skills and cook five-star meals for the two of them with whatever groceries they scraped together.

One day in 2013, while at News's grandmother's house, the two of them cooked up some chicken and rice enchiladas and beans, took tantalizing photographs of the food, and shared them on Instagram, letting Spank's many followers know it was available. Before long there were lines around the block to get that food. "We served it in those little cardboard trays with compartments, like in school, and we sold it with a one-dollar bottle of water," said News. The enthusiastic response told them they were onto something, and the two of them decided to open a food business together.

In the early days, just finding a consistent place to cook was a major obstacle. Between News's grandmother's house and Spank's mother's house, they would cook large volumes of what became their signature dishes, enchiladas and beans, and their specialty "pineapple bowls"—a half a pineapple hollowed out with rice, barbequed spiced chicken, topped with chunked pineapple, and a spiced sauce. Whenever they posted on Instagram, neighborhood residents came in droves, lining up to buy their culinary offerings. The neighborhood started calling them "Trap Kitchen" due to the volume of people coming and going at all hours from wherever they were cooking (a "trap house" being slang for a place where illegal drugs are sold). Once the cops, suspicious of what was going on, stopped to check in on the duo. When they heard "It's food, not drugs," they moved on.

Their differences made them a good team, with complementary talents: News was skilled at making money (the drug trade gave him financial skills and effective lessons in how to successfully market and distribute products) and Spank built a strong social media platform that attracted an increasing number of followers lured by the pictures of his cooking.

And like that, Trap Kitchen was officially launched. "We wanted to make good, healthy, affordable food available to people in our neighborhood who could never afford to get it in a restaurant," says News. In the early years, figuring out how to get food supplies and which meals sold and which didn't, dealing with their grandmother's and mother's complaining landlords, and just trying to stay afloat with cashflow were all obstacles they—like so many budding restauranteurs—had to overcome. By 2014, however, they hit a small but important milestone: they were able to purchase their first food truck.

In 2016, News and Spank took Trap Kitchen on a national tour to cities like San Francisco, Portland, Chicago, New York, and Atlanta. Along the way they received major media coverage, appearing at food festivals and concerts in those cities. People waited in line for two to three hours to get a taste of the food that had garnered a reputation for being gourmet quality and absolutely delicious.

Today, Trap Kitchen has seven food trucks, one brick-and-mortar restaurant in Portland, and more than 30 employees. It's even caught the attention of major celebrities; the likes of Snoop Dog, Martha Stewart, Kobe Bryant, Justin Bieber, Nicki Minaj, Ice Cube, Kevin Hart, and Kanye West and Kim Kardashian are just a few of the rich and famous who've had Trap Kitchen curate custom feasts for their private events.

Success hasn't gone to their heads. News and Spank are still grounded by their roots and continue to "keep it real." Both men readily admit they have their squabbles, but their differences now pale in comparison to what they've come to love and admire about one another over their 16-year friendship. Through the entire journey, the men have remained committed to their unlikely friendship across gang lines and recognize how special it is. "We are like family," says Spank. "We fight like brothers. But we love each other, and this is forever. We have been there for each other and had each other's backs and nothing is ever going to change that." News says about Spank, "I love his ambition. It inspires me to want more." And Spank says about News, "He is the most reliable person in my life. When I can't, or don't want to do something, I know he will be there for me."

News wants their friendship to stand as an example of perseverance and commitment to other Black men from their neighborhood, especially those who have been incarcerated. "We won't 'go Hollywood' because we created this for our people," he says. "Sure, we want to grow big and have Trap Kitchens in every city one day. We want to create jobs for people. Make them bosses. Make them feel part of something special. But we won't sell out our brand. We won't lose the quality of our food. We want to have a five-star restaurant one day. We want to be in resorts. We want people to see that if you want to pursue something, do it with all of your heart and never give up on it." For all these reasons, they've translated TRAP into an acronym as part of their brand: "Take Risks And Prosper."

Today, News is a father of five kids and Spank has one son. As committed dads, they are more aware of the example they now set. "I want young Black men to believe that there's more ways out of gang life besides becoming a famous rapper or sports star," says News. "You can do something meaningful in many ways with your life. We want to be mentors and coaches for our community. We want our story to inspire people to be kind to others, to reinvent yourself when you have to, and to believe that anything is possible." Their story presents a stunning example of what it means to *choose* to turn others who might have readily been an adversary into an ally, and when you do, what you can create together that you never could have apart.

The only way to stitch the seams of any organization, community or relationship is if those on each side of that seam reach across and join forces, despite their differences, as News and Spank so remarkably did.

But for many, especially in today's bitterly polarized environment, making that choice doesn't come easy.

Facing Our Tribal Instincts

The concept of tribalism has been discussed extensively by social psychologists and researchers in the wake of political schisms like the ones we are seeing in the United States with severe partisanship, and in Great Britain, with Brexit—the UK's decision to leave the European Union. The story goes that human beings, having evolved from hunter-gatherers, are predisposed to align closely with others in their tribe for safety and survival. This is seen as especially true in times of war and cross-tribal conflicts which, unfortunately, seem to be increasing with each new year.

But here's the rub: there is no neuroscientific or genetic evidence to actually suggest our tribalism is hardwired. What *is* hardwired, though—as we discussed in Chapters 7 and 8—is our innate hunger to belong and our fierce protection of that belonging once it's achieved. As we explored, there are many benefits to establishing an inviolate sense of belonging. But one of the unfortunate byproducts of strong tribal ties is the inherent expectation of conformity that comes with it. To protect our sense of well-being, and the allegiance we've pledged to our tribe, we stop questioning any facts or beliefs the tribe favors. Any views that contradict our tribe's, along with the evidence that supports those oppositional views, are dismissed as wrong and offensive, and often lead to outrage. For an example of this phenomenon in action, consider how easily made-up news stories spread. If someone your tribe admires, or a respected leader of your tribe, presents a viewpoint, there's no reason to question it—especially if it is meant to malign a perceived "enemy." In 2016, for example, an armed North Carolina man walked into a Washington, DC, pizza restaurant to investigate what he believed to be a criminal sex trafficking ring operating out of the establishment's non-existent basement. The supposed "PizzaGate" plot came to light in conspiracy-pushing right-wing corners of the internet, which linked the ring to high-ranking Democratic officials whose hacked emails allegedly revealed coded messages via pizza toppings that proved their involvement.[3]

Once debunked, such stories are dismissed as utterly ludicrous and with them, those who spread or entertained them as plausible. But consider that before any official debunking, millions may have privately wondered, "Is it possible . . . ?" That's how tribalism works: if you're already predisposed to "hate" Democratic elites, as the right-wing conspiracy theorists promoting PizzaGate were, you're not going to be inclined to question a story that your team promotes, regardless of how outlandish it seems. This is especially true if there are verifiable real-life incidents that have disturbing similarities to the promoted story—in this case, the saga of Jeffrey Epstein,[4] an alleged billionaire child sex trafficker who supplied underaged children to the rich and famous. If that's true, why *couldn't* a secretly coded message involving ordering pizzas with specific toppings be the way such depraved people got their evil jollies?

No one is immune to the impulse to *want* to believe, especially when the *need* to belong is threatened. At the center of our tribal need to belong and ready acceptance of the beliefs of the tribe we've embraced is the cognitive bias known as *confirmation bias*. A cognitive bias is a "shortcut" that our brain creates when making sense of the world. It's our brain's energy-conservation mechanism, a way to work less when processing the large amounts of information it takes in. There are many types of cognitive biases. One of the most pronounced, confirmation bias, occurs when our brains filter out any information that contradicts what we're already prone to believe and instead goes looking for supporting data that reinforces the conclusions we're predisposed to draw.[5]

Think about the times you have drawn erroneous conclusions that later proved false but which you felt convinced were true. For example, you're feeling uneasy around your boss when she gives a plum assignment to your peer, someone whose flagrant self-interest you resent. Your peer's gloating only fuels your insecurity. "Why wasn't I offered the assignment?" is the refrain looping in your mind. You convince yourself it's a signal your boss is losing confidence in your work, especially since he told you in your last review that you needed to take on harder projects. You spend days fretting over it, perhaps to the point of hunting on LinkedIn for another job. You later learn your boss had nothing to do with *offering* the assignment—your colleague went and asked for it. You could have done the same thing. Or maybe you're in a meeting where a member of another department whose past analyses you've questioned and found to be flawed is presenting. You immediately start hunting for the mistakes you've become conditioned to expect. When they don't appear, you assume he's just done a better job of *hiding* them. After the meeting, he pulls you aside and thanks you for all the helpful feedback you've offered him on past presentations, suggesting that it forced him to double down on his preparation and work that much harder on this one. Confirmation bias often operates in our subconscious, so we're not even aware of its presence. And that makes these kinds of cognitive blind spots that much more dangerous. Our judgments of those in other tribes, or "them," are so instinctive we don't realize who or what we're rejecting, or even *why*. But when we're on the receiving end of being "the other," and judged by another's bias, we are acutely aware of being the outsider.

And understandably, we don't like it.

Being Othered

Othering is the act of treating someone or some group as intrinsically alien. It's the process of exaggerating perceived differences, condemning those differences, and justifying the shunning of the person or group. Unfortunately, othering is all too easy, especially thanks to the technological wonders of the internet and social media platforms (more on that in just a bit). In my humble opinion, othering is one of the most cancerous issues of the 21st century— virtually every conflict between nations, regions, ethnicities, departments, and families has at its core one or more dimensions of group-based difference. From military conflicts between nations to rivalries between gangs, from resource conflicts between regions in a company to estrangement between siblings, the condemning finger of "othering" fractures our world. This is where our confirmation biases become so toxic, as they swiftly and eagerly collect mountains of "data" to support our othering of those perceived to be unlike us.

And nothing brings that into sharper focus than being on the receiving end of it.

Years ago, I was representing my consulting firm as one of three "finalists" vying for a major engagement with a global personal care products company. The woman leading the effort, Gabrielle, was French, but assigned to lead a large division of the company located in the United States. She was the prospective client who would select the final consulting firm. I had to wait in the same lobby area as the other two finalists, who, as it turns out, were women. I was presenting last. I watched as Gabrielle walked out the first presenter, signaled a warm farewell to her, reiterated the next steps in the process, and then proceeded to cordially welcome the next candidate. Each of us was told to prepare for a 45–60-minute meeting, which was to include a 20–25-minute presentation describing how we could respond to the company's challenge and request for help, followed by a conversation with Gabrielle and her team. More than 90 minutes passed by before Gabrielle and the second presenter emerged from the conference room laughing and amiably bidding each other goodbye, with Gabrielle again saying she'd be in touch.

Then, as if someone had abruptly turned the temperature arctic, Gabrielle turned to me, stern and curt, and gestured toward the conference room with a terse, "This way, please." There was no hospitable greeting, no apology for keeping me waiting. As it would with any consultant, my mind went ablaze with all kinds of angst and explanations for what was going on. Had she already made up her mind, making my presentation obligatory at best, but ultimately futile? Had I done or said something in the process up to this point that offended her? Had she just gotten some horrible news from her family or irritating email from her boss? I felt my mind simultaneously grasping for answers while letting go of any hope of landing the engagement.

I entered the conference room and did the compulsory introductions and handshakes with the other team members. I set up my laptop, pulled up my presentation, and signaled I was ready to begin when they were. Gabrielle nodded for me to start. Then she picked up her cell phone and started reading something. The longer she ignored me, the more frustrated I became. Did I pause and offer to wait, risking her embarrassment, or just keep going? I trudged on. Because my belief in forming high-quality consulting relationships begins with the premise of *help first, sell later*, I only had four slides to present, the last of which was a series of questions for the team to engage about their stated challenge. My hope is always to offer real value at the outset, whether I'm hired or not, to at least give prospective clients a taste of what working together might feel like. The other members of Gabrielle's team engaged with cautious enthusiasm, took copious notes, and said how helpful they found my presentation. But throughout, they kept glancing Gabrielle's way to watch for any signals of disapproval. She was silent.

When the conversation transitioned to asking me questions, the others had basic queries about my experience with similar organizational challenges and how our firm worked. Gabrielle then chimed in. In an almost irritated tone, she asked, "So tell me why you think you're the best qualified for this job. Why should we hire *you*?" This is a common question that prospective clients ask, so it didn't catch me off guard—it was *the way* she asked it that did. I knew how I answered the question would matter. I was feeling defensive, put off by what felt like inhospitable rudeness, and suspicious of the entire process. I was quickly drawing conclusions about her, and why she'd be a terrible client to work with. I was feeling othered by her, concocted into some alternative version of myself, and fast returning the favor toward her in my mind. I decided that, to be sure I could leave with my head held up, I needed to be honest. I responded, "Well honestly, Gabrielle, from the looks of things, it appears that you've already decided that you *shouldn't* hire me, so I'm not sure what I can say that would change your mind."

She looked indignant and caught. Her team was clearly taken aback, but not entirely surprised.

"Excuse me?" she responded.

"Forgive me for being forthright, but for any potential consulting relationship to get off on the right foot, candor has to be at the foundation," I responded, trying my hardest to keep my tone polite. "It's hard not to compare the warmth and friendliness with which you engaged the first two presenters with the sudden—what I can only characterize as *indifference*—that you've shown me. You've been on your cell phone most of my presentation, you haven't smiled or asked any questions, and while there could be any number of legitimate explanations for the sudden change, I'm certainly not inclined to conclude that I'm your top choice. If I've done or said something to offend you, you have my sincere apology. But before I can genuinely answer your question about why I'd be a good choice for you and your company, I'd love to hear if my observations have any merit."

She paused for what felt like the longest 15 seconds of my life. I was distracted by how tightly she was wringing her hands and the shade of red the side of her neck had turned. She asked her team members to excuse us and they left the room. I could only hope the sweat wasn't showing through my shirt.

"OK, fine. I'll be candid as well. The other two consultants were women from Europe. I'd hoped your firm would send one of your senior women to present. My experience with American consultants that are men has *always* been shyster salesmen who promise you the moon, and then bait and switch with junior people who actually do the work. They are only interested in saying whatever the prospect wants to hear to close the deal, not in adding any value. So, forgive my prejudice, but your gamesmanship of trying to come across as helpful during your presentation to *avoid looking like* that type of consultant only confirmed my misgivings. To be blunt, it felt manipulative and a little slimy."

There it was. I had been vilified and objectified by someone who didn't know me. I was a walking caricature in her mind and had been pigeonholed before I walked in the door. In some ways I was relieved to know the truth. But it hurt to be maligned as someone so different than who I really am. My Greatest Hits reel of past rejections and misjudgments played in the back of my mind. I wanted to lash back with a razor-sharp cutdown of her arrogance and hypocrisy that had already formed on the tip of my tongue. I was ready to burn the bridge and enjoy telling her off.

Even still, there was part of me that empathized with her. Her behavior signaled she was afraid of what this project entailed, and perhaps she felt out of her depth leading it. That she sent her team, who were obviously scared of her, out of the room clued me in that her sense of control was threatened in some way. Confessing her biases told me that at some point in her life, she'd likely had a painful experience with men in positions of authority. In essence, I suspected at least some of what was happening had nothing to do with me. The tug of war between my angrily bruised feelings and my professional empathy was at a dead heat. My response took us both by surprise.

I broke out into laughter. And I don't mean a little chuckle—a big belly laugh.

The vast contradiction between her honesty and her wildly misguided analysis struck me as funny. Her mouth opened and her eyebrows furrowed in disbelief as she watched me compose myself. When I did, feeling I had nothing more to lose anyway, I told her that of all of the legitimate things she *could have* accused me of, she'd be laughing too if she knew how far from who I actually am her characterization was. I said, "I may be a lot of things, but the *last* thing I would ever do is tell my clients what they want to hear." I went on to tell her how proud I and my firm are of the lasting client relationships we have built because we are dedicated to their success and telling them the truth when those around them won't. I also explained that we aren't the right fit for every client. I reminded her that the project she was embarking on was fraught with political risk (she'd told me that herself). I urged her to select a partner not based on feeling comfortable or whatever she thought "hard work-ing" meant, but to choose a consultant she would be confident would tell her the truth when things went sideways; someone she couldn't intimi-date the way she clearly intimidated her team. And lastly, I suggested she pick a partner she would say helped her stretch and grow as an executive, not just someone who seemed similar.

By the time I finished she had softened a bit, and she was more gracious as we parted ways. I genuinely wished her all the best with the project; since I didn't get the "I'll be in touch" sendoff, I expected it was the last time we would speak. I left hoping I had been true to my principle of *help first, sell later*, though the "helping" was far from what I would have expected. To be sure, she now knew what working with the real me was like, even if it wasn't what she was looking for.

To my astonishment, she decided it was. She called me two weeks later and offered me the engagement. In an early conversation at the project's outset, she said she'd shared my comments with her team, and they helped her see that while she might be uncomfortable working with us at times, my firm would be the best partner because our relationship would help her model the very change the project hoped to inspire among employees. The project's title? "Building a culture that welcomes disagreement."

WALK IN MY SHOES

If you had been in my situation, what would you have done? How do you tend to respond to people like Gabrielle? Anything you would have coached me to do differently?

Granted, most stories of othering don't go this way. Most, sadly, allow mutual misjudgments to prevail as truth and relationships drift into estrangements. We've all been "othered" at some point in our lives. From playground bullying and cruel teasing in childhood, to the horrific years of adolescence and our bodies and hormones wreaking havoc on us, to the early years of our career trying to find our path in the world—there is not a season of life in which our fragile sense of self does not meet the nasty reality of someone else's ostracizing cruelty.

These experiences can either harden or soften our hearts toward those different from us. Unfortunately, our brain's default choice is to harden. The cold fact about confirmation bias is that once we "other" someone, our brains go on scavenger hunts for data to justify our othering. Think about those in your organization, or life, with whom you have a strained relationship. What labels have you put on "them" to defend your othering? What data have you collected to bolster your case? How do you suspect they characterize their experiences of you?

Unless we are willing to re-examine our preponderance of evidence that has tried and convicted someone as the uncooperative colleague, the selfish friend, the demanding coworker, the meddling boss, the rude neighbor, the uncaring sister, the flaming liberal, the arrogant conservative, the lazy son, the corrupt leader—all evidence that has convinced us beyond certainty that we are *right*—we consign potential transformational relationships to a condemned "they." Even when our data has fragments of truth within it, if we never question it, or actively seek disconfirming data, we perpetuate the fragmentation of our organizations, communities, and families. Gabrielle was *certain* I was who she concluded I was. She collected limited data and added it to the impressive collection of evidence her confirmation bias had stored up over the years, and used all of it to peg me as the manipulative, self-serving consultant trying to close a deal no matter what.

We all do this. And while we are certain our data and conclusions are *right*, we indignantly protest when those fingers come pointing back at us. Being othered often fuels the confirmation biases that allow us to shun others. So goes the vicious cycle of othering.

Suspending disbelief and favoring empathy toward those we've deemed "they" is a choice. Granted, often a hard one when we've accumulated well-defended contempt toward them. But a choice, nonetheless.

And when we find the courage to make that choice, "they's" become "we's," and the outcome is remarkable.

The Courageous Act of De-Othering

Riaz Patel is a two-time Emmy-nominated TV executive producer at Axial Entertainment. He is a Pakistani immigrant. He is Muslim. And he is gay. Between 2016 and 2020 I've interviewed Patel multiple times for articles I've written and to follow his story and learn what reaching across dividing differences really looks like. Patel has lived a life of being othered, but despite this has emerged as one of the most compassionate, insightful authorities on the topic of bridging people across ideological, political, and racial divides, among other polarizing circumstances.

"I never had a group to fully belong to," Patel told me. "In the Muslim world, I was the gay one. In the American world, I was the Muslim or the immigrant. In the Pakistani world, I was the American. In the gay world, I am the minority one. There is nowhere I can go where I am the majority one. I have always been the 'other.' Growing up, there was no aspect of me that I was not conscious of trying to play down or hide or excuse or explain."[6]

Patel immigrated from Pakistan when he was a young child. During the '70s, immigration policies were particularly unfriendly, and his father, a British-trained surgeon, wasn't able to find work easily in the United States unless he was willing to repeat his residency, which he could not because he needed to work to provide for his family. The Patels settled in poor rural areas of West Virginia, then Maryland, as qualified doctors were in scant supply there. Speaking about formative childhood moments where his differences came into (harsh) view, he offered this difficult recollection:

> As my father started to earn a little extra money, to help my mom, who was raising three young kids, we hired a housekeeper. She had a son, Mikey, who was my age. She asked if she could bring him to play with me, and my mom said, "Of course, bring him!" So, Mikey became my first friend. At one point, one of my Dad's patients had given him a crucifix to thank him for saving his life, and as a remembrance of that, we had it hanging on our wall. For two years, our housekeeper naturally assumed we were Catholic. But after two years, she found out we were Muslim. She immediately gave notice and told my mom, "I can't come into your house anymore." And I never saw Mikey again.

Patel also told me about an incident that happened when he was nine and in the third grade. At the Catholic school he attended he had wanted to be the milk monitor—the person who went to the cafeteria, collected milk, and passed it out to their class. One day, as he was gathering the milk in the large, walk-in refrigerator, a second grader and a fifth grader came in, shoved him against the wall, and in a derogatory tone referred to him as an Iranian. Then they shut the door with him in the refrigerator. "I was shocked. I remember thinking, 'I'm not even who you think I am. I'm not from Iran. I'm from another side of the border.'" Patel's voice cracked as he recalled the story. "It's all still very fresh if I think about it."

Then he discussed the implications of being gay in a Muslim family. "Not only am I in an Eastern family and I'm gay, I'm the last male of my family with two sisters and nine female cousins. And so, my only responsibility is to get married and have children, which at the time was not possible. There was no place I could go and be myself."

Being "other" didn't end as an adult. Patel lived in New York City on 9/11. He recalls his experience in the aftermath of the attack:

> I lived downtown. I watched the Towers fall from the roof of my building. I remember the ash and the smoke and the smell. It was gruesome. Some friends of mine and I didn't know what to do and since my dad was a doctor, I thought, "If there are injuries, we should go stand in line and donate blood." St. Vincent's hospital was right down the street, and we went and stood in line. It was the morning of September 12th. I could feel the mood in the line shifting around me. At first, I thought maybe it was just in my head. Then, someone got in my face and said, "We should go and fucking kill your family." Others chimed in with similar comments. I'd never seen such blatant hate in the daylight of New York City, a block from my own home. My friends got me out of there and for the next few weeks, they took turns walking with me wherever I needed to go. We were hanging out in the local bar we always went to together. The bartender, who knew me, came up and said, "I hate to do this, but some people are uncomfortable. I'm afraid you'll have to go." I understood his predicament, so I left.

These are just some of Patel's life experiences that have shaped his profound understanding of what it's like being an "other." But while many would—not unreasonably—turn hardhearted and bitter, shutting the world out, Patel's response was determination to bridge divides:

> Sometimes people would take a swing at me and I couldn't tell what they were swinging at. Was it the gay thing? Was it the Muslim thing? Was it the immigrant thing? Was it the Pakistani thing? I started asking myself, "Who is really the other? What do they think of me? What is the difference between me and them? How does that wall between us and them change as news happens and culture happens?" And that has been the story of my life. I had to make the choice, "I can either be angry or I can try and navigate this gap and stitch up who you think I am to who I really am." And that's what I've spent my life doing.

Just before the 2016 presidential election, Patel realized that the only information he was getting already supported his political views. He never saw content in his news feeds that offered contradictory perspectives. Bothered by this echo chamber, he started listening to call-in news radio shows with very different political persuasions so he could hear firsthand the pain, concerns, and questions of those who saw the world differently. During one show, he heard about the plight of fishermen in rural Alaska and some of the economic challenges they faced. He thought to himself, "How are we ever going to hear anything different than our own views if we don't put ourselves in the face of those views?"

So, he decided to hear the "other" side out. Patel, his husband, and their seven-month-old daughter got on a plane and flew to Ketchikan, Alaska, to see if he could meet people he knew saw the world differently than he did. He was very deliberate about going before the election, and to get beyond the labels and rancorous name-calling that had so strongly intensified leading up to it. "I was shocked at all of the hatred at one another," said Patel. "At the time, I didn't know any political conservatives voting for Trump. The vile hatred from the progressives toward them was strange. I thought, 'They can't all be evil. They can't all be xenophobic, racist, homophobic people. That's just not how the world works in my experience. There just aren't entire towns of people who are evil. I want to know what I'm missing.'"

After Patel and his family arrived in Ketchikan, they went to a local diner and ordered breakfast. Patel struck up conversations with the waitress, a local fisherman, and then a candidate running for local office. He wanted to know about their lives, about their struggles in Alaska. He learned about the challenges of the fishing industry, the privatization of the lumber industry, how Alaskan citizens have "ownership" in their state through an annual oil dividend, and some of the difficulties imposed on them by the policies of the Clinton and Obama administrations. He also posed some hard questions to them, like, "I fear that you look at me as a Muslim and assume I'm a radical or a terrorist. Am I wrong?" To his delight, he found his interview subjects hospitable, engaging, and accepting. He flew home with an entirely different understanding and compassion for people he never knew. "If I were in their shoes, I would have voted for Trump too," he told me.

The experience changed Patel's life. Soon after his trip, he struck up a friendship with Glenn Beck, the host of the conservative TV network BlazeTV. They began hosting talk shows to showcase their relationship across their differences. They hosted live conversations about controversial issues like gun control, with guests from the NRA as well as non-profits started by mothers whose children had been killed by gun violence. Patel began to see a pattern among people with radically different views from one another. As they learned more about each other's views, they became more open. Their reflexive impulse to reject someone *and their views* softened. It wasn't that they necessarily *agreed*, but they *understood*—and therefore respected and accepted—those they'd previously vilified.

Patel flew to Saudi Arabia in 2018 to work directly with HRH Princess Reema, a member of the Saudi royal family and the current Saudi ambassador to the United States. While there he created TV programs, workshops, and personal development materials for the country's 10 million women. His work was focused on helping them develop their personal identity and sense of self as they begin pursuing new opportunities, careers, and dreams as equal citizens. As a gay Muslim man, going to a nation that outlaws homosexuality was no small risk.

Today, Patel hosts a regular program on YouTube called "Four Chairs." In each episode he gathers three people with radically different perspectives on controversial issues, and facilitates a discussion during which participants are exposed to conflicting views, often for the first time. The goal isn't to help them reach *agreement*, but to find common ground where they didn't expect to, and to discover common humanity amidst the areas where they fundamentally differed. So far he's dealt with the topics of racial inequality, police brutality, protesting, and monument removal, and his guests have included members of the Black community, police officers, activists, and both people who've been shot at and those who've fired shots. During the conversations Patel serves as the moderator, or "fourth chair." He says having an odd number of guests helps avoid a false binary that splits them into two non-negotiable camps. Three people forces the conversation to enter the territory of nuance, the "grey" area away from immovable, black-and-white thinking. It forces people to "shift chairs" and see the world through someone else's eyes. As the "fourth chair," Patel serves as neutral ground and an empathetic moderator. Each conversation begins by having all the guests find common ground—childhood memories, favorite movies and foods, etc.—to break the ice and establish a shared humanity. That sets the stage for the conversation to move safely into exploring differences.

In October 2020 I was privileged to be one of the guest panelists on the episode "How not to lose your mind during the election." The focus *wasn't* the politics of the election, but rather the polarization it was causing. My fellow panelists, a Black political communications consultant from Capitol Hill and a White female pediatrician, explored our differing (and discovered our common) perspectives about misinformation, political competence, and the motivations of candidates.

If there is a controversial subject that has polarized people, Patel has dropped himself into the middle of it. His early suffering caused by being othered has motivated his intense desire to bring people together across their differences, many of which are just perceived and informed by bad or incomplete information. People's unwitting ignorance about different perspectives is often fed to them by the content they consume, which they frequently fail to realize *isn't random*.

WALK IN THEIR SHOES

What experiences of being othered have you had like Patel? Have you (consciously or not) done things to "other" someone? What aspects of Patel's approach would you want to emulate?

Patel recalls flying from Texas to Washington D.C. He said he was watching the news at the airport in Texas and again when he landed in D.C. "I was shocked to see how different the narratives were," he says. "I realized these conversations among people who are different are so critical because otherwise, we will never know what we don't know. We will continue assuming that all we know is all there is *to know*. I had no idea how soundproof my echo chamber was until I took a sledgehammer and smashed it."

Patel's insight is sobering. We may not realize the extent to which our curated information systems intensify our divisions and stoke our othering, but, as we are about to see, it is an enormous problem.

Because when it comes to escalating our othering, we may not realize that we're getting help.

Technological Othering

The 2020 Netflix documentary *The Social Dilemma* offers a chilling look at what social media has become and the damaging consequences of it most of us have failed to see. It exposes how social media companies deploy sophisticated technological algorithms to monitor nearly everything we do online and then feed us information that will keep us engaged—information, that is, that largely supports views we have been proven to support and share, via tracking. This may seem benign when it comes to receiving ads that suggest shoes or exercise equipment we might like. But when entire nations can be politically destabilized using these platforms, when the mental health of our teenagers is put at risk,[7] and when people are readily lured to extremist groups, it's time to step back and reclaim our own agency in the information we consume, the opinions we choose to believe, and how we draw conclusions about those who differ from us. To offer one sobering statistic that reveals the power of social media engineering, a 2018 internal Facebook report found that 64 percent of those who joined extremist groups on Facebook did so because algorithms steered them there.[8]

One of the documentary's featured interview subjects is Tristan Harris, co-founder and executive director of the Center for Humane Technology and a former design ethicist at Google. Harris makes an appeal to all of us to step back and consider the consequences of what these algorithms can do if we don't rein them in with reasonable regulation and public policy. He made a similar point in a 2019 opinion piece for *The New York Times*, where he asserted that even if we could solve the most popularly discussed issue when it comes to online technology— privacy—deeper challenges would remain, not the least of which is our addiction to the approval and sense of importance gained from likes, heart emojis, and comments reaffirming our views. We'll become more satisfied by outrage and tirade exchanges than civil discourse. The social harm to vulnerable teenagers would become especially damaging, from cyberbullying to depression and anxiety. Harris asserts, "Content algorithms would continue to drive us down rabbit holes toward extremism and conspiracy theories, since automating recommendations is cheaper than paying human editors to decide what's worth our time... By influencing two billion brains in these ways, today's social media holds the pen of world history: the forces it has unleashed will affect future elections and even our ability to tell fact from fiction, increasing the divisions within society."[9]

Harris is sounding an alarm we all need to heed. For all of the good it can do, this technology—ironically, built to create greater connection in the world—has dark sides to which we've turned a blind eye. Nations, communities, friendships, and families are being divided by a steady, self-reinforcing diet of sensational, and often false, information that confirms what we already believe. It is igniting our rage against those who believe what we don't (or, worse, don't look like or worship like us), and is slowly unraveling the fabric of society by replacing civil discourse with ranting arguments. On top of all of this, this same technology rewards our antisocial behavior with notoriety—perhaps the most valuable currency in the internet of today. In a 2019 *Atlantic* article, Jonathan Haidt (author of this book's foreword and another interview subject of *The Social Dilemma*) and Tobias Rose-Stockwell, an expert on the ethics of technology, warn about the "incentives" of such a system: "If you constantly express anger in your private conversations, your friends will likely find you tiresome, but when there's an audience, the payoffs are different—outrage can boost your status."[10] The authors go on to cite a 2017 study by the Pew Research Center. That data showed that posts displaying angry disagreement got nearly twice as much engagement and reposting as other types of posts on Facebook.[11]

To put it plainly, our sense of belonging is being hijacked and fed by online strangers, leading us to abandon real relationships for counterfeit connections with people who appear to think like we do. Our tribalistic impulses are being amplified by making the boundaries of the tribe limitless—anyone who thinks like I do, gets enraged by what I do, and then likes, reposts, or comments on what I say, belongs; those who don't are enemies. With social media, any proclivities we have toward othering have a jetpack strapped to them. If we want to reclaim our agency over who we choose to build relationships with, and why, we need to be honest about these influences. And though it may seem counter-intuitive, being connected to people *who don't think like us all the time* is a much healthier and more civil way to live in relationships.

That's how they's become we's.

To make that courageous choice, there are some things we can do.

Get Busy: Make Your "They" Part of Your "We"

Distinguish Common Ground From Compromise

Too frequently, when it comes to navigating differences, people retrench under the belief that merely entertaining views different from their own is equivalent to compromising their principles. We fear that *hearing and understanding*, which is different from *agreeing with*, views that oppose ours means compromising our values or condoning beliefs and choices that contradict our moral principles. But learning to appreciate the convictions of others still allows you to hold onto your own. It allows you to respect why others hold their convictions, and opens them up to respecting yours. Who are the people whose views you most disagree with? Who do you readily dismiss as credible without question? Set up a time to interview them and simply learn about their views, *not* to debate them. See what you can discover. In late 2018 I interviewed Congressional staffer and former Assistant Secretary of the Treasury for Financial Institutions Chris Campbell for this book, and for an article I was writing. One of the few federal government officials to be unanimously appointed by both parties to such a significant role, he enjoyed a long, esteemed career in government and was named one of Congress's most influential staffers seven years in a row. He didn't earn these accolades by accident. "When working in situations where you were the political minority, you had to train your mind that there had to be a middle ground," he told me. "You had to put yourself in the shoes of those who thought differently. You had to ask yourself, 'How can we both win without compromising our principles and reach a decision that both sides consider a win?' I spent years having to do that in order to get anything done." Which of your "theys" have you pushed away in fear of compromising your beliefs? Which political, religious, business, or social beliefs do you struggle to condone, and therefore can't accept those who hold them?[12]

Assume That Opposing Views Are Legitimate

No matter how outlandish they seem, start by assuming that views you don't share are valid simply because the person with whom you differ holds them. Learn to be curious about even views you believe are wrong. Separate the views from the person who holds them to better understand what needs they serve. Remember, they perceive your views as just as preposterous, and you as an idiot for holding them. Get past your instinct to refute and reject and be willing to learn. What opposing views do you find most infuriating? Who are your organizational nemeses who proffer ideas or propose projects that you vehemently disagree with? What motives have you attributed to their views that may be inaccurate? What steps could you take to build a bridge to them to better understand where they are coming from? Start with inviting them to coffee or lunch and see where things go from there. Which opposing perspectives could you do a better job of seeing as legitimate even if you don't hold them? Which beliefs have you dismissed without considering *why* the person who holds them feels so strongly?[13]

Re-evaluate Your Echo Chamber

Who do you spend regular time with at work or outside work? Are there people with whom you are able to have heated disagreements and then amicably have coffee or a beer? Do people you lead regularly come to you with dissenting ideas or challenge your thinking? If you don't have people around you who comfortably and routinely offer differing views without fear of retribution or estrangement, you're in trouble—it means there is critical information you aren't getting about decisions you are making, relationships you are participating in, and priorities you are pursuing. Whether at work or on social media, pay attention to how you are participating, whose viewpoints you *aren't* seeing, and actively seek out contradicting information to broaden your worldview. Which information sources could you incorporate into your life that would bring disconfirming and alternative perspectives for you to consider? What is it about doing so that makes you anxious?

Socialize With Your "They"

When we disagree with people, we objectify them. We concoct "versions" of them that conform to and justify our disdain for them. On a piece of paper, jot down the names of people in your organization you regularly work with and with whom you have fundamental disagreements. How have those disagreements impaired trust or your ability to collaborate or lead? These are the people (and we all have them) to whom you nod politely in meetings but deep inside you're convinced are wrong. What if you actually spent time challenging your assumptions and talked directly with them about where your views differ? Might you share more common ground than you imagine? Here again, start with a simple invitation to coffee or lunch and let yourself be surprised by what you learn and what it feels like to have "them" see *you* in a new light.

Acknowledge Your Hypocrisy

Holding steadfast to convictions is a laudable thing to do. But doing so at the expense of other principles isn't. You can't staunchly advocate for more investments in employee development then never spend any time coaching your own direct reports. You can't march up and down public streets advocating for those you believe to be marginalized in some way then marginalize anyone who disagrees with you. You can't announce that you are passionate about empowering those you lead then only delegate the decisions and work you find unpleasant. And you can't invite others' feedback on your leadership then do nothing with it when you get it. The moment you declare something you

believe, you will get scrutinized for how well you live up to your own standards. You need to view your actions through the eyes of those who might not
see things as you do to be sure your actions and words match. Where have
your actions and words belied those ideals and beliefs you claim to hold
dearly? What standards do you hold others accountable for that, with an
honest assessment, you know you don't live up to as much as you'd like?

Face Your Fear of Differences

Our aversion to others who are different stems from deep-seated fears of
what those differences might mean. By default, we associate "difference"
with conflict, disagreement, winning vs. losing, and the loss of social status
or reputation. Though often irrational, our fears lead to self-protection and
resistance to expanding how we think. But the more exposure we have to
these others, the more that fear diminishes. Dig deep to understand what
troubles you about views that differ from yours. Does your resistance lie
with the idea itself? The person who holds the idea or their motives? The
intensity with which they are trying to persuade you? If you can isolate what
you fear, you can test the rationality of that fear against the value to be
gained by building common ground with a colleague.

Be Welcoming

Making sure others feel like they belong requires moving past *tolerance* or
acceptance. It means offering a warm, welcoming presence. It means being
vulnerable enough to help others feel not just that they belong but that they
belong *with you*. As a leader, have you (intentionally or not) created favorites
on your team? Is there anyone you've distanced yourself from with the
rationalization that "We just don't have the same chemistry"? Have you
found yourself doing little more than "showing them professional respect"?
Who are these outsiders you've made to feel less welcome in your life? What
is it about them you struggle with? Of course, I'm not suggesting that you
should create the same degree of intimacy with everyone, as if they're your
best friend. But as a leader, tiering your levels of acceptance means some
people will question their value in your eyes. If you want people to bring
you their best, you have to be a safe place for them to do so. They must feel
like they belong *with you*. To whom could you offer greater hospitality in
your life? Which "other" could you make feel more welcome?

***

That concludes our work together on what it takes to be honest within your organization and as a leader. I hope reading about so many exemplary leaders and organizations has inspired you to believe the effort is well worth it.

Before we go, there's one last thing to discuss. As I said at the outset of our time together, honesty is a muscle. It is a capability that must be built up. And like any muscle, it demands care and feeding and a commitment to remaining strong, especially when we fall short.

With your own journey now underway, let's finish with how you can keep it going.

KEY TAKEAWAYS

- While there is no neuroscientific or genetic evidence that says our tribalism is hardwired, there is proof that as humans, we crave belonging. Because of this, there is an inherent expectation of conformity that aligns with strong tribal ties.

- We tend to hold confirmation biases without even knowing it, making cognitive blind spots even more dangerous, especially with those we perceive as different.

- Othering is known as that act of treating someone or some group as intrinsically alien. We can all attest to having been "othered" at some point in our lives. Because of this, our brain defaults to being cautious.

- When feeling othered, first try to employ empathy to understand how you are being experienced before becoming defensive or dismissive.

- We need to find the courage to suspend disbeliefs and favor empathy toward those people we have deemed as "they."

- Riaz Patel's early suffering caused by being othered has motivated his intense desire to bring people together across their differences, many of which are just perceived and informed by bad or incomplete information.

- We are having help "othering" through technologies like social media platforms (Facebook, Instagram, Twitter) as national and regional divisions are inflamed through algorithmic feeds of information that reinforces biases and false beliefs.

- To build relationships of enduring strength, we must connect with those who are different from us; we discover the best versions of ourselves when we are reflected off of those most unlike us.

Endnotes

1   Law Library—American Law and Legal Information (n.d.) Organized crime – Crips and Bloods: Black American gangs in Los Angeles, https://law.jrank.org/pages/11947/Organized-Crime-Crips-Bloods-Black-American-gangs-in-Los-Angeles.html (archived at https://perma.cc/6DRH-TZKX)

2   I had the great pleasure of sitting down with Malachi "Spank" Jenkins and Roberto "News" Smith in September of 2020 for an in-depth interview about their lives and their work. These quotes are all from that interview.

3   Kang, C and Frenkel, S (2020) 'PizzaGate' conspiracy theory thrives anew in the TikTok era, *The New York Times*, 14 July, https://www.nytimes.com/2020/06/27/technology/pizzagate-justin-bieber-qanon-tiktok.html (archived at https://perma.cc/9FCJ-GH55)

4   Hallemann, C (2020) What we do and don't know about Jeffrey Epstein, *Town & Country*, 02 July, https://www.townandcountrymag.com/society/money-and-power/a28352055/jeffrey-epstein-criminal-case-facts/ (archived at https://perma.cc/5LWT-FYCA)

5   Heshmat, S (2015) What is confirmation bias? [Blog] *Psychology Today*, 23 April, https://www.psychologytoday.com/us/blog/science-choice/201504/what-is-confirmation-bias (archived at https://perma.cc/2HJW-VMLU)

6   This quote originally appeared in an interview in *Forbes*, and is reprinted with permission: Carucci, R (2019) How to build bridges between the most bitterly divided people, *Forbes*, 23 September, https://www.forbes.com/sites/roncarucci/2019/09/23/how-to-build-bridges-between-the-most-bitterly-divided-people/?sh=68ce0b395ecd (archived at https://perma.cc/3N42-8XUY)

7   Haidt, J and Rose-Stockwell, T (2019) The dark psychology of social networks, *The Atlantic*, December, https://www.theatlantic.com/magazine/archive/2019/12/social-media-democracy/600763/ (archived at https://perma.cc/AQ78-XMME)

8   The Social Dilemma (n.d.) The Dilemma, https://www.thesocialdilemma.com/the-dilemma/ (archived at https://perma.cc/3RG4-BRH9)

9   Harris, T (2019) Our brains are no match for our technology, *The New York Times*, 05 December, https://www.nytimes.com/2019/12/05/opinion/digital-technology-brain.html (archived at https://perma.cc/9URZ-UET6)

10 Haidt, J and Rose-Stockwell, T (2019) Ibid

11 Hughes, A and Van Kessel, P (2018) 'Anger' topped 'love' when Facebook users reacted to lawmakers' posts after 2016 election, Pew Research Center, 18 July, https://www.pewresearch.org/fact-tank/2018/07/18/anger-topped-love-facebook-after-2016-election/ (archived at https://perma.cc/E5F2-NVPH)

12 A portion of this content originally appeared in *Forbes* and is reprinted with
    permission: Carucci, R (2018) How to build bridges between the most bitterly
    divided people, *Forbes*, 23 September, https://www.forbes.com/sites/roncarucci/
    2019/09/23/how-to-build-bridges-between-the-most-bitterly-divided-
    people/?sh=5db4707a5ecd (archived at https://perma.cc/7DEG-MGH9)

13 This content originally appeared on the OpenMind platform blog and is
    reprinted with permission: Carucci, R (2020) The challenge of empathy in the
    wake of the election, *OpenMind*, 05 November, https://openmindplatform.org/
    blog/the-challenge-of-empathy-in-the-wake-of-the-election/ (archived at
    https://perma.cc/6HHP-9U99)

Epilogue

Learning How to Be Honest

Growing up Roman Catholic outside New York City certainly had its enduring benefits, not the least of which was learning the foundational values and
faith that shaped my life (memories of bakery-fresh bagels and coffee cake
after Sunday Mass are a close second). My faith remains the cornerstone of
my life, even though Catholicism is no longer the tradition through which I
practice it. I am grateful for the sense of community, service, and integrity it
grounded me in during my formative years. Of course, one of the side effects
of starting my faith journey in that tradition was having to work through a
few warped theological quirks as a child. For example, many of the fellow
Roman Catholic kids in my neighborhood used to debate whether you'd go
straight to hell for telling seven or more lies in a *day,* or in a *week*. Or which
"dirty words" counted as a "regular sin" and which counted as a "mortal" sin
and were thus unforgivable (which, ironically, contradicts the entire point of
going to confession and receiving a penance… but I digress). Those of us who
went to public school and only attended weekly catechism classes usually felt
outgunned by the kids who attended Catholic school. Over time, I tackled the
debates by working things out for myself, sorting out which lies, dirty words,
and bad deeds were worth worrying about and which ones God likely didn't
have time to care about, given all of the bigger problems he had on his plate.

Being charitable was one of the most pronounced tenets of my nascent
faith, but here again, some untangling was required. For example, was it
wrong to take money out of my mom's purse in the morning before school
if some of it was used to buy lunch for kids who needed it, or to buy candy
at the corner store to purchase protection from the bullies? Or, to avoid
being embarrassed at a friend's birthday party, how bad could it be to take
a $5 bill from my dad's wallet and add it to my friend's birthday gift, just to
ensure he knew how much I wanted his birthday celebration to be great?

I was naïve enough to think my parents didn't know, and that they actually believed my adamant denial when they confronted me.

It wasn't until later in life that I looked back and realized where some of my Robin Hood morality came from. The story begins, I believe, at a local bank where my mom was a manager for many years. This was during the days when banks would give you a gift for opening a new account; the more you deposited, the bigger the gift. Everything from electric can openers and blenders to complete luggage sets and large toaster ovens filled the windows of the bank to entice would-be account openers. Mysteriously, the storage closet in our basement began to fill with brand-new consumer products that looked eerily like the ones my mom's bank gave away. This strange phenomenon also seemed to be affecting the basements and garages of other bank employees, many of whom were my mom's close friends. When I asked her about it, she assured me that as employees they enjoyed the perk of "sampling" some of the gifts the bank gave away. At one point, inventory (which was my responsibility to meticulously document) had grown so large, I pondered opening a kitchen appliance store, but I didn't have access to a cash register. And when things ran low, I dutifully reported it: "Mom, we're down to one Mr. Coffee!"

The strangest thing was that we rarely made use of any of the merchandise ourselves. But when it came time for a bridal shower, birthday, wedding, anniversary, or "just because I love you" occasion, my mom pulled out all the stops. You didn't *just* get a blender, but along with it you got a coffee maker and a service for four set of Corelle dishes. If you happened to be visiting our house and mentioned that your hand mixer or electric shaver just broke, I was sent to instantly fetch your replacement! In our world, this ethical code just worked, as the ends seemed to justify the means, and I was sure God, at the very least, would honor our good intentions.

One day, however, this entire way of looking at life fell apart for me.

My grandmother lived with my family when I was a kid, and she loved houseplants. In our living room she had a "plant cart" that held the many different plants people gave her as gifts throughout the year. On occasions like Mother's Day, her birthday, and Easter, my aunts and all us grandkids would vie for giving her the most elaborate potted plant; at one point, our living room wall resembled a jungle in desperate need of deforestation. Back in those days, potted plants from florists came garnished with plastic ornaments on sticks—a little bear, or a sign saying "Happy Easter," or a monarch butterfly stuck out of the pot in between the greenery. One day, my mom and grandmother called me into my grandmother's room with very stern looks on their faces.

"Where are they?" they interrogated me. I had no idea what they were talking about. They went on to explain that all the plastic ornaments in the entire plant cart were missing, and they *knew* I'd taken them. I assured them I hadn't, but nothing I said convinced them. Every day after that, for months, my grandmother gave me her cold, hurt shoulder. My mother would implore me, "If you just admit you took them, she'll forgive you." I was flabbergasted. First of all, what on earth would I want with plastic plant ornaments? Second, why were they acting like an heirloom diamond brooch had vanished—these were plastic toys! What was the big deal? The irony wasn't lost on me. Here I was being accused of taking something that, for once, I hadn't—and being prosecuted as if I had. Was this payback for all the "sins" I had relegated to being inconsequential? I withstood my grandmother's shunning for more than three months. We didn't watch our regular TV shows together. She wouldn't ask me about my day the way she usually did. The sliced carrots floating in ice water that usually awaited me after school were withheld. I had been exiled by the woman who helped raise me over cheap plant ornaments whose disappearance I had nothing to do with. Was this really how justice worked in the world? Had my previous deceit finally caught up with me?

As it turns out, it had. About three and a half months after the ornaments vanished, my grandmother called me into the kitchen and quietly handed me the phone. It was my aunt Betty. Sheepishly, she confessed she was the one who'd pillaged all the ornaments, on her last visit. She claimed they were bad for the plant's drainage. She had simply thrown them away, not thinking much of it and without informing my grandmother. She apologized. I was relieved, and vindicated. I instantly wondered about all the things my grandmother would now do to make up for the emotional torture she'd inflicted. What could I get away with asking for if she inquired about what she could do to show her remorse? I even considered giving her a taste of her own cold shoulder by not accepting her apology but decided I really missed being close to her. Her explanation? "I just thought because you always like giving things to people that you'd gifted them to one of your friends. I was more upset that you wouldn't tell me than I was about the missing ornaments." There it was. My twisted sense of charity had come back to bite me. My notions of innocence and guilt had been reckoned with.

I learned my lesson: generosity at the expense of honesty isn't generous.

We all have defining moments in our life that form our sense of right and wrong. And as we mature, our moral compass becomes refined as we test and hone our expressions of integrity. In short, *we learn what it means to be honest.*

What were the early moments of your life that shaped your understanding of honesty? What examples were set for you? What seminal moments shaped your moral code? What ethical failures taught you hard lessons?

Unsurprisingly, this varies from person to person, and community to community. But what is universally true for us all is that to *stay honest* in our unrelentingly changing world, you have to keep learning—from your mistakes and your triumphs.

The great news is that because honesty is a muscle, it can be trained. But you have to work at it.

Teaching Honesty

Few places treat integrity as seriously as the US Military Academy at West Point. Integrity is a foundational element of West Point's training of new cadets, who are taught an honor code and are expected to live by it, without exception. The honor code simply and clearly states, "A cadet will not lie, cheat, steal, or tolerate those who do." To determine if they are embodying the code, cadets are told to ask themselves three questions as "rules of thumb":

- Does this action attempt to deceive anyone or allow anyone to be deceived?
- Does this action gain or allow the gain of privilege or advantage to which I or someone else would not otherwise be entitled?
- Would I be satisfied by the outcome if I were on the receiving end of this action?

These are sobering questions to be sure.

In early 2020, I spoke with Bernard Banks, a former General Manager of the Department of Behavioral Sciences and Leadership Development at the US Military Academy and at the time of writing the Associate Dean for Leadership Development and Inclusion at the Kellogg School of Management at Northwestern University. I wanted to hear what Banks had to say about the importance of teaching honesty, especially when it comes to future leaders.

To him, and West Point, everything flows from trust:

> West Point is in the business of developing leaders, and trust is the cornerstone of leadership. Once you've been proven untrustworthy, your ability to be influential is undermined. We know that even though we select some of the finest men and women to come to West Point, we cannot be so naïve as to think they've not engaged in cheating or some form of dishonesty before they arrived. A scholar from Rutgers did a study of more than 4,500 high school students: 74 percent admitted to cheating on a test, 58 percent admitted to

plagiarism, and 95 percent admitted to engaging in some form of cheating.[1] So, we know that if we want to train leaders of integrity, there's likely some prior life experiences we have to undo. We refer to this as "time under the code." The more time someone has living under the honor code, the more they see the positive benefits accruing, the more likely the behavior is to be sustained. We know that freshmen are likely to lapse more often than seniors. It's the same as building any muscle—the more reps you have in the gym, the stronger that muscle becomes.

Banks believes that like any lifelong learning endeavor, practicing honesty requires what he calls "learning trials." Rather than simply calling them failures, you have to see gaining new skills as an ongoing and iterative process. Eventually, you'll come to a place of equilibrium, where those around you come to trust who you say you are. "If you want your 'say-do' ratio to be 1:1, it takes work," he told me. "But that's when you will be seen as extraordinary. As soon as your say-do ratio is out of balance, and your actions and words are misaligned, you're now just like everyone else. And you've probably stopped learning."

Banks acknowledges the steep commitment it requires to examine the gap between what we say we're committed to pursuing and what we are *actually* doing. To close the gaps, he says, leaders must constantly scrutinize how they are measuring up to who they want to be relative to who they are. He suggests we ask ourselves, "Where in my life and my organization am I underwriting mediocrity? Where am I losing ground against my aspiration and justifying it with excuses? How important is it to me to close the gap? Am I being honest about what happens if I don't?"

These are the questions of consequence that must be asked if we want to keep learning how to be honest.

What Our Dishonesty Reveals

Note the obvious implication of what Banks says: learning to be honest starts by facing up to our *dishonesty*.

Why be dishonest? We all have our excuses. In fact, there's plenty of research on why people do the wrong thing—lie, cheat, or withhold the truth—and how often they do it. Most psychologists who've studied lying agree that people lie for several major reasons:

- to avoid hurting someone's feelings (You look great in that dress—really!);

- to be polite (I love this fish—you're such a good cook);

- to avoid embarrassment from something they did (Don't know what that smell is, but it wasn't ME); or

- to protect someone else from harm (She was with me the whole night).

From there, the reasons get a bit more self-serving:

- to cover up or deflect a mistake (I don't know how the report got so screwed up, but Bob had it last);

- to misrepresent yourself in some way (I'd love to take on that project— I've done that type of work many times);

- to maintain the respect of someone you don't want to disappoint (I've always admired your poetry—I'm a loyal fan);

- to conceal some reward you attained unfairly (Yeah, I had no idea I stood to inherit their house!).

Research from the University of Massachusetts on dishonesty has found that we all lie, on average, between one and two times per day.[2] Other studies have reported on the percentages of the different lies people tell, their differing motivations for lying, the conditions under which we lie, or the degree to which the truth gets stretched. But across numerous studies, there is broad agreement that we all lie sometimes. What I want us to consider, then, is *why?*

Most psychologists agree that the vast majority of dishonest or unjust behavior does *not begin* from a place of self-interest—it begins from a place of self-protection. In other words, most people are honest and fair most of the time. So, if they feel the need to lie or put their own needs ahead of others, it's because they believe there's some perceived threat or consequence they must avoid. If we can understand that, we can more thoughtfully investigate those threats, making more honest choices about them. If we do this as a community, we will create more honest organizations.

Think about the last time you lied, distorted, or withheld the truth, or acted unfairly or selfishly to your boss, a colleague, a direct report, a client, or a friend. Step back and ask yourself *why* you did it. Perhaps you felt overlooked or unfairly judged by your boss. Perhaps you feared your mistake would be more harshly criticized than warranted, and that your company's "we learn from mistakes" slogan only applied to "the favorites" and not you. Maybe you felt as though your colleague might take credit for your work, so you omitted key details in your presentation. Maybe you didn't want to hurt your friend's feelings, so you condoned a choice you might have otherwise discouraged. Or you were anxious about how negative feedback might threaten your client relationship (and your income), so you softened the blow.

Somewhere underneath your lie or unjust action was an unmet need you felt might be satisfied by acting that way. Perhaps a desire for greater respect, for protection from unsafe leaders, to avoid feeling estranged, or to feel a deeper sense of purpose. Your actions probably didn't offer you more than a fleeting moment of unearned regard in the eyes of those you mistreated or misled. And once that moment passed, you probably felt emptier, even shameful, for having behaved in that way to garner a reaction you hadn't truly earned. Then you had to quell those feelings with self-justification for doing so in the first place. "It's not fair," "If they deserve [x], so do I," "Why should I have to?" are all common defenses used to justify dishonesty. This entire process of self-justification can happen in a matter of seconds.

Here are the harder but equally important questions. What was it about the environment in which you chose this behavior that made your choice acceptable? Maybe even encouraged it? How is it that there was no deterrent or significant consequence for your choice? In the context of your organization, why was it okay? To create more honest people and organizations, we need to identify the conditions that bring us to dishonesty in the first place.

As I mentioned earlier in this chapter, I learned early in my life that generosity was a good thing. I also learned that it won me favor, even if the means for my generosity was acquired dishonestly. I've spent many years understanding the origins of that conditioning and unlearning a lot of it with the help of friends, loved ones, and some great therapists. Today, I better understand the need to balance generosity with a deeper examination of my motivations for any moment of giving. I've been enormously blessed in many aspects of life, so when my motivation to be generous is born of gratitude, I know I'm being true to that value. I've learned that true generosity is humbling, because you receive so much more than you could ever give. Most importantly, I've learned that the most generous gift I can offer isn't a present but my presence—to invest my time in helping others become the greatest version of themselves. And when I am drawn to give from a sense of guilt, obligation, pride, or reciprocity, I know I need to step back because I'm no longer expressing my value of generosity. I'm *compromising* it.

This lesson has taken a lifetime of effort to learn, and by no means have I mastered it. If the research for this book has taught me nothing else, it's that you can't be true *to* yourself until you are willing to learn the truth *about* yourself. Learning to be honest starts with a simple but deeply difficult task: lying to ourselves less.

Redeeming Our Honesty Failures

If Bernard Banks is right, that learning honesty inevitably includes many "learning trials," that means we've all accumulated breaches of honesty along the way—maybe even some big ones, and certainly many small ones. Perhaps some of them linger with inklings of guilt and shame, and a low-grade fear that actions we've kept tightly hidden will one day be exposed. Regardless of what your past honesty failures look like, the real danger comes when those learning "trials" are no longer isolated tests but regular occurrences, and the only lesson that sticks is that your dishonesty bears no consequence. That's when you've moved the line of acceptable behavior so often that each successive compromise creates a new normal.

Back in Chapter 1, we discussed how our brains are naturally hardwired for honesty. But unlike our electronic devices, there's no "restore factory settings" button. Still, that doesn't mean we can't unlearn things. If you've adopted some practice of dishonesty, no matter how benign you think it is—what you say on your résumé, what you tell your boss about your accomplishments, what you tell your spouse about your late-night meetings, how you ignore the person at work nobody likes, what you put on your expense report, how you treat neighbors who are "different"—and rationalized that practice in order to feel okay about it, I'd ask you to strongly reconsider those justifications. There are far more meaningful forms of redemption awaiting you if you'll pause and question the well-constructed excuses you've come to believe.

Here's a touching case in point.

Richard Bistrong was a sales executive for a large defense company selling military and security systems overseas. When he agreed to "pay a toll" to an intermediary during a sales transaction, he committed a felony. Bistrong was convicted of one count of conspiracy to commit bribery for violating the Federal Corruption Practices Act (FCPA), a charge that carries a maximum sentence of five years. But because of his cooperation with the FBI and the Department of Justice, he served 15 months.

Today, Bistrong travels the world working with governments, private companies, and ethics executives consulting and training on how to avoid corrupt behavior, how to spot the early signs of it, and how to take stands against it. His wealth of accumulated knowledge, and the pain of his failure, are now benefitting many less experienced professionals and sparing some of them the self-imposed hardship he had to endure. In 2017 I spoke with Bistrong about what he's learned along the way about honesty.

As he explained it, the defense industry is a particularly fertile ground for corruption. When selling defense products in international markets, major deals are often brokered by "intermediaries," people who bring together buyers and sellers. He told me:

> I knew early on that when the intermediaries used terms like "paying tolls," or "making people happy," or "taking care of people" what those wink and nod terms meant. I looked around region after region around the world, and it seemed to be standard practice. I thought I was committing a faceless crime. But I was wrong. I'd become ethically numb. I didn't think I was hurting anyone and didn't think about the unintended consequences of my actions. And I told myself that, in some ways, I was helping people—the poorly paid official who needed extra cash—and [I] was getting an important and high-quality defense product into a market for a great price, so the nation's security would benefit. But those were just the lies I told myself to feel better. The consequences are actually significant. For the nation you are selling to, you rob their people of governance, economic development, human rights, and freedom. The impact on society, my company, or my family was far greater than I was honestly considering. I lost my health, my liberty, and a piece of my soul.

Bistrong never imagined he would cross such lines. None of us ever does. Worse, we typically defend the lines we cross by comparing them to those who've behaved even more dishonestly. "At least I'm not as bad as…" are the words inscribed above the entrance to every slippery slope. And slippery slopes are the most dangerous when we conclude we're not at risk of sliding down one. Our rationalizations are much like the way we treat the speed limit. We know it's 55 mph, but if the guy in front of us is going 65 mph, we know we're good at 60. If they're going 75, we can push it to 65. Suddenly we get pulled over for doing 70 in a 55 and indignantly declare, "Why did you pull *me* over? Did you see *that* guy doing 80 right in front of me?" The obvious danger is deceiving ourselves into thinking we didn't do *anything* wrong because someone else did something worse.

"The problem is that the debates about dishonesty are often only playing out in our own head," says Bistrong. "That's when we're most vulnerable. Whenever you feel tempted to even consider crossing a line, call someone you love. Your spouse. Your parent. Bring your moment of truth into the light of day among those you trust. It changes everything."

While I'm not suggesting that you publicly confess all of your dishonest wrongdoings and then turn them into a platform to convert similar wrong-doers, I am asking you to consider the power of turning just one habitual choice that cuts corners on your values into a regular practice of honesty. Consider what might be redeemed not just in your life but in the lives of those you lead and those you love. Your habits may not rise to the level of a federal felony like Bistrong's, but his example of facing into bad choices and redeeming them is one we can all learn from.

Consider some of the extraordinary people whose stories we've explored throughout this book and the redemption those stories led to. Jaime Góngora and his work redeeming the FARC guerrillas. Marin Alsop and her creation of OrchKids for underserved communities in Baltimore. Bryan Stevenson's commitment to freeing wrongfully accused men and women on death row. Julita's fight to get her land back in the Congo. Hugh Thompson's coura-geous helicopter landing in Vietnam. Jacinda Ardern's leadership in New Zealand during the Covid-19 pandemic. Dr. Michael Abraham Shadid's championing of cooperative medicine for the rural poor of Oklahoma. The brave rescue of 13 boys from the flooding caves of New Zealand. Malachi Jenkins and Roberto Smith's emergence from LA gangs to start Trap Kitchen as friends and partners. Rob Bilott's epic crusade for justice for victims of DuPont's C-8 poisoning. Ed Townley's courageous turnaround of Cabot Creamery into a more cohesive, vibrant dairy cooperative. Hubert Joly's transformation of Best Buy into a purpose-driven organization. Ginger Graham's creation of a truth-telling organization at Guidant Corp. Patagonia's intrepid decision to address their toxic cotton challenge head on. Melony's leadership of her supply chain and logistics upgrades while sustaining hope for her organization. Or Riaz Patel's courageous reach across great divides to bring people together.

Of course, there were many others. Each one of these stories began with an ordinary human being, or community of human beings, bound together by a common need or opportunity, a desire for something more, and the determination to see change through—in themselves and those around them. The scale of that change doesn't matter. Big or small, each of these transformative stories was grounded in truth (saying the right thing), justice (doing the right thing), and purpose (saying and doing the right thing *for the right reason*, even when it's hard).

What if you chose to be just like one of those "ordinary" human beings? Whether for your family, your small team, your department, your enterprise, or even your nation… What if you actually believed you *could* lead and live with that kind of redemptive honesty?

In that case, the only thing left to decide is if you *should*.

Stories from the Future: Leading a Life of Honesty

It's been my great privilege to accompany you on what I hope has been an inspiring journey of learning what it means to be honest. I trust that the stories of the women and men I've introduced you to have roused you to consider your own story in a fresh light. I hope you've reflected on your leadership, your organization, and your life, and discovered ways to expand how you practice honesty. If you've chosen even one small practice to adopt or change, then I'll consider our time together worthwhile, and I trust you will too.

Our world today is desperate to know greater honesty. And the people in our organizations crave leaders they can trust to tell them the truth, act with justice, and lead with purpose. I hope *To Be Honest* has challenged and encouraged you to step into the breach and make the world a more honest place by becoming such a leader. Maybe you can't change the whole world— but you can certainly change *your* world. I shudder to think of my children inheriting a world that offers them honesty as the exception, not the norm. I'm realistic enough to know that stemming the tide won't be easy, but optimistic enough to believe that, together, we can. Don't sell yourself short with naïveté, or worse, willful blindness to the need for greater honesty—in yourself and the world.

Before we close, I'd like to stoke your imagination just a bit further.

When I work with leaders trying to envision their future, I engage them in an activity I created years ago called *Stories from the Future*. I begin by providing them with a series of short prompts that outline a story. From those prompts, I ask them to write a story that takes place three to five years in the future, in which they are a central character performing in new ways, employing new skills, and having significant impact. The story prompts range from delivering major addresses to prominent audiences, to inventing new technologies, to solving major problems, to overcoming personal obstacles. Through the stories my clients write, we uncover extraordinary patterns that reveal the conditions in which they are at their best. For example, one executive with whom I did this learned that he rose to his best when facing impossible odds—all of his stories revealed success during excruciatingly difficult challenges. Another discovered that she is happiest as a leader when she is convincing people to try unconventional ideas—her stories were all about breakthrough approaches. The stories excavate desires and ambitions that have often been buried, forgotten, or never articulated. And they provide a foundation for the leaders to embark on new chapters of their lives in bolder and more galvanized ways.

So, I'm going to end our time together by inviting *you* to write your story from the future, to envision your life of honesty reaching even greater heights. Ready? Here's the situation (insert your name where you see [you]).

Two people you know are sitting next to each other on a bus and strike up a conversation. While they both know you, they've never met each other. After a few minutes of talking, they realize that you're a mutual acquaintance. One of them, whom you haven't seen in some time, says with great affection to the other, "My goodness, I haven't seen [you] in quite a while, but they had such an impact on me. I've never seen someone set a greater example of honesty, and it has stuck with me ever since. I'm grateful for what I learned from [you] about what it means to be an honest human." The other person responds with eager anticipation, "Wow, I can see [you] really left quite a lasting impact on you. Please tell me the story of how they did it!"

Now write the story the person tells about the impact your honesty had on them. Let your imagination run wild—don't edit, don't wordsmith. Just write. And like any good story, include juicy details. Make the characters and settings vividly real. Add suspense and conflict. Make it a story worth telling.

Then, put the story someplace where you can re-read it every now and then. I promise you, if you let the story captivate you, it will be more than a story worth telling.

It will become a story worth living.

This is how we learn to be honest: we think deeply and dream about ways to do it better. We reflect on the places we fall short. We study those we want to emulate. We push the bar just a bit higher every day. And we envision ourselves reaching that bar with ever-expanding impact on those around us.

Do you believe yours is a life worthy of being emulated?

When those you most regard think about you, is honesty one of the first descriptors that comes to mind?

If you lived with greater degrees of truth, justice, and purpose, could dreams that have eluded you suddenly come into reach?

Is it possible that if you were more true *to* yourself by learning more truth *about* yourself, you could live a more joyful and gratifying life? That you would know, and give, more love, more hope, more faith?

If you more deeply examined your own honesty practices, is it possible you might discover untapped reservoirs of your own goodness and giftedness, and with them, your potential to help others discover theirs?

I believe the answer to all these questions is a resounding "yes."

Will you join me in that belief?

Because, above all, the privilege of answering "yes" to these questions *is the reason* to keep striving for, fighting for, and believing in the power of living lives of truth, justice, and purpose.

So, now you know what it really takes...

to be honest.

For one last time, because there's so much at stake, please,

Get busy.

Endnotes

1 McCabe, D, Treviño, L, and Butterfield, K (2001) Cheating in academic institutions: A decade of research, *Ethics & Behavior*, https://citeseerx.ist.psu.edu/viewdoc/download?doi=10.1.1.460.5320&rep=rep1&type=pdf (archived at https://perma.cc/QYE7-MAUD)

2 University of Massachusetts at Amherst (2002) UMass researcher finds most people lie in everyday conversation, *EurekAlert*, 10 June, https://www.eurekalert.org/pub_releases/2002-06/uoma-urf061002.php#:~:text=The%20study%2C%20published%20in%20the,was%20a%20very%20surprising%20result (archived at https://perma.cc/DY6A-YBM3)

APPENDIX

Statement of Research

Data Source

Data was collected from 210 multi-person assessments from more than 100 companies and industries. Total of ~3200 interviews conducted between 2003–2018.

Data Preparation

Preparing the data for analysis consists of several steps and represents a significant effort from a computational perspective.

The first step is to chunk the text into discrete chunks representing a single thought, concept, or sentiment. The most common approach is to break a larger document into paragraphs and sentences, but other more complex schemes are also possible that connect subjects to antecedents.

The second step is to tokenize the individual snippets into unigrams, bigrams, trigrams, and/or subject-verb-object triads for discrete matching against lexical terms. This usually includes some type of stemming in order to standardize across word endings.

Lastly, it is important to index the tokens in order to optimize the performance of the searching, matching, and classification against the lexica.

Lexical Ontology Development

Reasoning

In the past few years multiple approaches have been put forward in the psychological and sociological literature as rigorous and reproducible. We recognize the intent of these approaches and incorporated the strengths of closed and open vocabulary approaches along with an auditable human coding process. To accomplish the ontology development, we used SPSS Text Analytics.

Additionally, we have found the development of clear, understandable, and orthogonal features to be a very iterative process. Each of the steps in the development of a lexical ontology helps to clarify, elaborate, and elucidate the other steps.

Deep Reading

Where other methods start with an unsupervised topic model, we begin with a human coder doing a deep reading and building lexica. This was done using a grounded theory approach versus reproducing an existing instrument or scale.

Lexica Development

Each concept is modeled with its own lexicon with child concepts inheriting from parents. The lexica can include a set of terms and phrases for included as well as excluded documents. This allows for complex concept development and feature extraction which sometimes requires multiple features to capture a single complex concept.

Data Analysis

To analyze the variables that result from the lexica and understand their relationship both to each other and to the desired outcomes, it is necessary to model the sensitivity to changes among independent variables while controlling for effects between independent variables. This was done using log-linear regression modeling. The results of the model were verified through multiple other techniques in order to confirm the robustness and interpretation of the original model.

Each interview document was classified using this lexical ontology, and the resulting variables were analyzed using IBM SPSS Statistics. Additionally, we could then analyze and classify the variables that correlate most highly with both high performance and low performance. Several different techniques were used to make sure the classification was robust. Finally, to identify the variables that actually drive greater truth telling, we used several advanced analytics techniques, including log-linear regression, decision trees, and both parametric and non-parametric correlations.

Regression analyses were used to calculate the ultimate weights of the strengths and weaknesses as drivers of success. Log transformations were done on both the truth telling and various driver behaviors. Both stepwise and enter methods were evaluated, with stepwise being used for final weighting of the drivers. Adjusted R-squared values for driver of truth telling was 0.79.

INDEX